Creating Value

Concert & tour promotion
ventions focusing on the
brand of promotion company
"business it presents..."

Buildings

Creating Value

The Theory and Practice of Marketing Semiotics Research

Laura R. Oswald

OXFORD

UNIVERSITY PRESS

OXFORD
UNIVERSITY PRESS

Great Clarendon Street, Oxford, OX2 6DP,
United Kingdom

Oxford University Press is a department of the University of Oxford.
It furthers the University's objective of excellence in research, scholarship,
and education by publishing worldwide. Oxford is a registered trade mark of
Oxford University Press in the UK and in certain other countries

Published in the United States of America by Oxford University Press
198 Madison Avenue, New York, NY 10016, United States of America

British Library Cataloguing in Publication Data

Data available

Library of Congress Control Number: 2014942350

ISBN 978–0–19–965726–1 (Hbk.)
      978–0–19–965727–8 (Pbk.)

Printed and bound by
CPI Group (UK) Ltd, Croydon, CR0 4YY

For Mildred and Robert Oswald

■ ACKNOWLEDGMENTS

I was prompted to write this book by colleagues and readers who wanted to learn more about the theory and methods behind my previous book, *Marketing Semiotics: Signs, Strategies, and Brand Value*. It is hoped that the book satisfies both the demands of academics for a rigorous discussion of structural and post-structural semiotics as well as the needs of practitioners for a guide to the design and implementation of semiotic research for marketing.

I am grateful for the opportunity to have studied semiotics with some of the most creative minds in the field, including Roman Jakobson, Roland Barthes, Gerard Genette, Julia Kristeva, and Christian Metz, in seminars at New York University and at the École des hautes études en sciences sociales in Paris. They had the genius and courage to find connections between epistemologies, cultures, and ways of seeing that were heretofore siloed into discrete disciplines. I also benefitted from the work of Sidney Levy and John Sherry, who continued the interdisciplinary adventure at the Kellogg School, Northwestern University, by pushing boundaries between semiotics, marketing science, and the human sciences. While I was teaching in the humanities at Northwestern, they provided impetus to my own line of inquiry into marketing and semiotics by challenging the dominance of quantifiable and empirical methodologies in market research.

The Northwestern University library has formed a resource for all three of my books, and I wish to thank the librarians whose passion for research helped me track down obscure references over the years. Ellen Neuborne and Lynn Childress contributed to the readability of the manuscript and helped move the writing forward. I am grateful to Christina Hoppe for her support and her knowledge of British culture, and for the patience and support of family, friends, and clients who saw less of me in the past six months during the final press to complete the book.

Chicago, Illinois
April 2014

PERMISSION TO REPRODUCE IMAGERY

The author holds the copyright to graphs, tables, and figures. Any graphics that were used for these were purchased from Shutterstock.com. Since a book on semiotics necessarily demands reference to actual marketing images, the author made every effort to obtain permissions from copyright holders for ads and fashion images used to illustrate examples from the text. The author is grateful to the copyright holders of the following images for their specific permission to use their images. While every effort was made to contact the copyright holders of material in this book, in some cases we were unable to do so. If the copyright holders contact the author or publisher, we will be pleased to rectify any omission at the earliest opportunity.

Chapter 1: Author's copyright on all tables and figures.
Chapter 2: Author's copyright on all other tables and figures except the following:
  Figure 2.1: René Lezard copyright approved.
             Ralph Lauren copyright denied.
             Giorgio Armani neither confirmed nor denied permission.
  Figure 2.3: Green Street Studio, for Mike Campau, the artist, approved use of the artwork for the "Instant Gourmet" ad. Management asked the author to remove the trademark.
Chapter 3: Author's copyright on all tables and figures, except:
  Figure 3.1: The "Baby" ad for Nationwide Insurance. Copyright approved by Way Art Inc., New York, for the artist, Doron Ben-Ami.
  Figure 3.4: A cross-cutting sequence from the Geico "Pyramid" ad.

The author thanks the Martin Agency, New York, for permission to use these stills. The author thanks Douglas N. Graham from the Sutton Barth Vennari Agency, Michael P. Truesdale from the Reign Agency, and Murad B. Yunus from the Daily Talent Agency for agreeing to use their images in this book.

Chapter 4: Author's copyright on all tables and figures.
Chapter 5: Author's copyright on all tables and figures.
Chapter 6: Author's copyright on all tables and figures.

■ CONTENTS

■ LIST OF FIGURES

■ LIST OF TABLES

Introduction

In global consumer culture, brands structure an economy of symbolic exchange that gives value to the meanings consumers attach to the brand name, logo, and product category. Brand meaning is not just a *value added* to the financial value of goods, but has material impact on financial markets themselves. Strong brands leverage consumer investments in the cultural myths, social networks, and ineffable experiences they associate with marketing signs and rituals. *Creating Value: The Theory and Practice of Marketing Semiotics Research* is a guide to managing these investments by managing the cultural codes that define value in a market or consumer segment.

Creating Value extends the discussion begun in my previous book, *Marketing Semiotics: Signs, Strategies, and Brand Value* (Oswald 2012). In the first book, I cited numerous business cases that proved a direct connection between the financial value of brands and the clarity, relevance, and impact of brand meaning. I showed that managing brand equity was tantamount to managing the brand's semiotic equities. *Creating Value* focuses specifically on the methods used to leverage the semiotic value of goods through creative, strategic research across the marketing mix. The book also extends the theoretical discussion beyond the basics of semiotics and engages with debates in post-structural semiotics related to ethnographic performance, multicultural consumer identity, the digitalized consumer, and heterotopic experiences of consumer space. The book also challenges the current thinking on topics ranging from cultural branding and brand rhetoric to digital media management and service site design.

Creating Value emphasizes in greater detail than *Marketing Semiotics* the mutual influences of category codes and cultural trends on the perception of value. For example, value is codified in the colors, shapes, and fonts on packaging for a product category. Package design represents in shorthand the value proposition offered by a category such as healthy snacks and distinguishes it from other categories such as junk food. These codes enable shoppers to assess a product's quality on the basis of its packaging semiotics, without even reading the ingredient panel.

The book shows how to align brand positioning, communications, new products, and design strategy with the value systems that structure meaning in a product category, consumer segment, or global market. Cases and examples are drawn from the author's professional and academic research in North America, Europe, and Asia. Figures and grids clarify theoretical concepts and illustrate the strategic dimensions of research.

Marketing Semiotics: A Growing Research Paradigm

Since the publication of *Marketing Semiotics: Signs, Strategies and Brand Value* (2012), the term "marketing semiotics" has achieved common currency in market research, as evidenced in the new *International Journal of Marketing Semiotics*, the Semiotic Thinking Group on Linked-In, and in blogs and company websites devoted to marketing semiotics. The term appears with increasing frequency in the business press and marketing literature. There is even an annual conference called Semiofest, which draws semiotic research practitioners from around the globe to share insights and best practices to fellow semioticians. Throughout the book, the term "marketing semiotics" should not be confused with the Marketing Semiotics company, a research firm specializing in semiotics.

The field of semiotic studies in market research has come a long way since the Kellogg School's 1986 International Conference on Marketing and Semiotics (Umiker-Sebeok 1987) and the 1989 Copenhagen Conference on Marketing and Semiotics (Larsen, Mick, and Alsted 1991). In the past twenty years or so, the reach of marketing semiotics research has expanded beyond the analysis of advertising (Pinson 1998) to issues related to global marketing, cross-cultural consumer behavior, the use of public space, and social media management. *Creating Value* extends the semiotic research paradigm by delving deeper into the influence of consumer performance and creativity on meaning production.

DEFINING THE DISCIPLINE

The growing interest in semiotics for marketing is both a blessing and a curse, since more and more practitioners claim expertise in semiotics without specialized training or academic education in the theory and practice of semiotics. Non-experts often conflate semiotics with rhetorical analysis or linguistics, losing sight of the broader cultural implications of marketing signs for brand strategy. Marketers, in turn, may doubt the value and rigor of semiotics-based research if they have worked with amateur "semioticians" who lack rigor and strategic perspective. *Creating Value* aims to correct this problem by summarizing key theories and best practices in the field of semiotic research. The book combines a clear and comprehensive discussion of semiotic theory with guidelines for the design and practice of semiotic research for marketing.

Creating Value also sets out to move marketing semiotics into the mainstream of market research and to establish marketing semiotics as an academic discipline. To meet these goals, the book includes references and case studies that can be used to develop curricula and train practitioners in marketing semiotics. Like statistics or experimental research, semiotic research draws validity and reliability from a common set of skills, protocols, and resources related to semiotic theory, data collection, and analysis. They are very different from the tools used by empirical researchers and statisticians.

Unlike statistics and experiments, semiotics-based research accounts not only for the rational, observable meaning of things but also the essential ambiguity and instability of meaning and value in the marketplace. Consumers do not always say what they mean or mean what they say. What is valuable in one context may lose value in another. Furthermore, marketing signs change meaning as they move from one culture to the next in global marketing, or from one point to the next in a social media network. The researcher's knowledge in semiotics, poetics, and even design and philosophy may prove more adequate to the research task than statistics.

READERSHIP

Creating Value is targeted to academics, research practitioners, marketers, and advanced students of marketing, advertising, and culture studies. It was written in response to the many readers of *Marketing Semiotics* who requested more information about the actual practice of semiotic research. It also targets brand managers seeking to know more about the semiotic research process and its application to a business problem. The book is accessible to educators and students because it explains the theories drawn from semiotics and the social sciences by means of clear language, practical examples, and illustrations.

The book also targets readers interested in learning more about semiotics, using clear and concrete language to reach a broad readership. Since it applies semiotics to the very familiar world of the marketplace, *Creating Value* makes sense of the semiotics discipline, which is often convoluted by specialized jargon, hair-splitting debate, and even imprecision in the academic literature.

Semiotics in the Qualitative Research Paradigm

Semiotics-based marketing research builds upon traditional qualitative techniques, including focus groups, structured in-depth interviews, and ethnography.[1] It also represents a tradition in social science research that embeds data collection and analysis in theory development. In this sense, the marketing semiotic paradigm represents "the pragmatic embodiment of theory" (Herzfeld 1983a: 99), a hybrid of French structural theory and a field practice

---

[1] See, for instance, Bryman and Bell 2007; Daymon and Holloway 2002; Denzin and Lincoln 2005; Feldman, Bell, and Berger 2003; Fortini-Campbell 2001 [1991]; Manning 1987; McCracken 1988; Merriam 2009; Underhill 2009 [1999]; Van Maanen 2011 [1988].

that grew out of the American tradition in structural anthropology in the 1980s. Marketing semiotics extends this tradition to all areas of marketing research, including consumer ethnography as well as advertising, retail, and package design, and social media management.

Semiotic research is scientific inasmuch as it relies upon observable, recurring codes in a data set rather than personal interpretation. It is also an art because it requires a greater degree of spontaneity and creativity from the researcher than traditionally used in qualitative research. One of the advantages of semiotic research for marketing is that it exposes the inherent tensions and ambiguities structuring consumer creativity and cultural diversity in the marketplace. It relies on the power of metaphor, free association, and visual media to highlight these tensions in a set of data. Semioticians seek marketing solutions that leverage, rather than stifle, these tensions to keep brands on the leading edge of culture.

THE CONSUMER-CENTERED TRADITION IN MARKET RESEARCH

Marketing semiotics research is grounded in a management philosophy oriented to consumers and consumer culture rather than products and product benefits alone. Ries and Trout (2000 [1981]) describe how marketing changed focus in the 1980s to differentiate brands in an increasingly cluttered marketplace. Their book heralded the current, consumer-centric tradition in brand management that looks to consumers for the brand's "Big Idea," which David Ogilvy (2004 [1963]) sought around the conference table. Consumer-centered marketing outmoded Vance Packard's (1980 [1957]) famous persuasion model of marketing, by focusing on meeting consumer needs rather than manipulating consumers' minds through artful advertising.

The consumer-centric tradition has generated a wealth of research methodologies and approaches which challenge the time-honored assumption that rational forces and metrics drive markets. They include Levitt's (1986 [1983]) work on the "marketing imagination," Gobé's (2010 [2001]) work on "emotional branding," and Zaltman and Zaltman's (2008) writing on the metaphorical imagination. This tradition has recently morphed into the "culture-centric" focus of contemporary marketing and has spawned theoretically grounded scholarship in publications such as the *Journal of Consumer Research*. The marketing semiotic paradigm is an outgrowth of this evolving understanding of consumers, markets, and culture.

EMOTIONAL INTELLIGENCE

Semiotics-based research responds to an emerging need of marketers not only to understand the role of emotion and creativity in consumer decision-making but also to apply these insights to the strategic planning process. Advances in the social and medical sciences reflect a growing disenchantment with the conventional wisdom that humans are essentially rational beings. There is increasing evidence in medical scholarship that right-brain functions associated with human emotions and attitudes play an important role in assigning value to things, even in traditionally quantitative fields such as economics and engineering (see Simon 1984; Becker and Murphy 2001). For instance, Albert Einstein (2009 [1931]: 97) insisted on the importance of imagination in scientific research and claimed that the solution to relativity came to him in a dream state. Furthermore, deep, subconscious thought often communicates with the conscious mind through images, rhetorical figures, and slips of tongue rather than logical verbal discourse.

The popularity and success of Goleman's (2005 [1995]) book, *Emotional Intelligence*, is testimony to the currency of these ideas. Goleman argues for the importance of emotion and intuition in business success, and explains that the brain's structure essentially programs humans to integrate creativity and emotion into rational decision-making. He summarizes leading research on cognition that emphasizes the interplay between left-brain functions ruling reason and right-brain functions ruling emotional and social functions. These kinds of crossovers account for the ways right-brain functions moderate even the most rational decisions consumers make, such as keeping a diet, investing in a stock, or voting for a candidate.

The semiotician taps into the emotional intelligence of consumers by drawing out their creative potential. For example, consumers speak in metaphors, re-work social rituals, and adjust current fashion trends to their personal tastes. More often than not, the language, actions, and decisions of consumers have more in common with myth, drama, and poetry than with logical reasoning and scientific prose. Their behavior is prey to the vicissitudes of social change, stress, and denial. Furthermore, these kinds of influences, rather than rational decision-making alone, give rise to innovations in category trends, product uses, and the culture that have important implications for marketers and scholars alike.

BEYOND POSITIVISM

The complex and transitory nature of meaning and consumer identity elude the scrutiny of positivist research, whose claims to objectivity account for its privileged status in market research. Positivism relies on the underlying assumption that the truth about humans, like other natural phenomena, can be seized through direct observation and fact-finding (see Bryman and Bell 2007: 16–17). Positivism privileges logical meanings, rational behavior, and observable phenomena over indirect or unconscious dimensions of consumer behavior that fall beneath the radar of empirical observation. Empirical methods, such as direct questioning, experimentation, or hypothesis testing, assume a direct cause-and-effect relationship between observed phenomena and truth. Inconsistencies in the data are attributed to errors in the sampling or the execution of the research instrument, rather than to the intrinsic instability and ambiguity of meaning and consumer behavior.

The purported objectivity of the positivist approach may be only a "chimera" (Mariampolski 2006: 13). By masking the hidden truths that consumers communicate indirectly through nuance, metaphor, irony, gesture, and silence, logical positivism accounts for a rather narrow share of consumers' minds. Furthermore, direct questioning such as, "What do you feel about this brand?" or "What would make you switch to another brand?" stymies consumer spontaneity and creativity, and is often met with silence or stuttering. Direct questioning thus filters out a wide range of meanings and experiences from the data that hold the key to business innovation and compelling, relevant brand strategy.

In contrast, semiotic research succeeds in direct relation to the breadth and depth of the meanings it elicits from consumers. Rather than begin with the assumption of an empirical reality that transcends social behavior as such, semiotic research investigates how consumers construct their reality by means of discourse (Merriam 2009: 215). Semioticians are trained to draw inferences from consumer creativity and play, rather than their logical statements alone. Writing from the perspectives of cognitive psychology, sociology, anthropology, and linguistics, semiotic researchers[2] investigate questions about the nature of reality, identity, and social organization through the lens of the symbolic function.

DECONSTRUCTION AND THE PHILOSOPHY OF LANGUAGE

In *Creating Value*, I also extend the interpretive research paradigm by drawing attention to advances in post-modern philosophy that place in question the epistemological foundations of the interpretative process itself. Influenced by Derrida's (1973 [1967]) critique of the metaphysical foundations of phenomenology, post-structural semiotics challenges phenomenology's assumptions about the origins of meaning in the transcendental logic and unified consciousness of metaphysics. As Derrida puts it, "the whole of transcendental phenomenology is put forth in its supreme ambition: aiming to achieve both the constitution of an absolutely formal logic and ontology and a

---

[2] For example, see Belk 1988, 2006; Floch 2001 [1990]; McCracken 1988; Sherry 1990, 1998; Stern 1989; and Thompson, Locander, and Pollio 1989.

transcendental description of self-presence or primordial consciousness" (p. 127). Noise, ambiguity, fragmentation, and (cultural) difference are relegated to the margins of philosophical inquiry. By deconstructing phenomenology, Derrida proposes that disruption, difference, and non-sense are always and already at the origin of being and the production of meaning.

Though literary critics such as de Man (1973) equate deconstruction with a crisis of meaning and an absence of logic, post-structural semiotics takes a different perspective. For semiotics, Derrida's critique of phenomenology does not deny the importance of logic, meaning, and identity in meaning production; it simply negates the assumption that they transcend their inscription in symbolic representation. Post-structural semiotics defines logic and subjectivity as *constructions* formed by the intersection of codes and performance in symbolic activities, from speaking to serving a meal.

By means of case studies and examples, *Creating Value* illustrates how post-structuralism operates in the practice of everyday life in consumer rituals, media campaigns, and social networking.

Semiotics, Anthropology, and Consumer Research

The application of post-structural theory to consumer behavior has been greatly influenced by the semiotic tradition in ethnography. Semiotic ethnography grew out of the debates in the 1970s and 1980s of American anthropologists such as Geertz (1973), Sahlins (1976), and Herzfeld (1983b, 1989) with the structural theories of Claude Lévi-Strauss. Put briefly, they agreed that culture is codified like a language because of its shared, normative characteristics. However, their experiences in the field convinced them of the importance of consumer agency and the vicissitudes of everyday life on meaning production, leading them to emphasize the dynamic, performative aspects of consumer behavior that both rely upon and also deconstruct the codes organizing culture, language, and sociality.

CONSUMER CULTURE THEORY

Semiotic ethnography has influenced the theoretical orientation of interpretive consumer research and inspired seminal research on culture and consumption in the 1980s in work by authors such as McCracken (1986) and Belk, Wallendorf, and Sherry (1989). Semiotic ethnography has influenced, directly or indirectly, the consumer culture theory movement in consumer research (Arnould and Thompson 2005), which accounts for the role of culture on markets and consumers and also engages with important theoretical debates about the production of meaning, consumer identity, and culture in the marketing context.

Consumer culture theorists draw insights from the social sciences as well as the humanities in order to account for philosophical, ideological, and esthetic dimensions of marketplace communication. Like semiotic ethnographers, consumer culture theorists draw upon theory to identify emergent themes as the study unfolds and follow these insights to direct the course of research. Theoretically grounded analysis refines the insights into concepts and draws inferences from these insights for marketing science. Unlike empirical research, consumer culture researchers do not use findings to prove a theory, but employ theory to deepen understanding of consumer behavior and brand meaning.

THE SEMIOTIC DIFFERENCE

Marketing semiotics research forms a distinctive methodology within the interpretive research tradition in terms of its strategic focus, distinctive methodologies, and underlying logic.

- First, unlike consumer culture theorists, marketing semiotics research identifies the strategic implications of cultural insights for growing brand equity.
- Second, semiotics-based research applies not only to consumer behavior, but includes applications that do not involve direct research with consumers at all, such as retail and package design, advertising strategy, new product innovation, and social media management.
- Third, unlike textual exegesis or content analysis, semioticians decipher the meaning of individual texts or consumer interviews based upon the codes they share with a sampling of other texts or interviews in a research setting.

Code theory is central to the semiotic enterprise. Semiotics-based research exposes the codes structuring the normative, paradigmatic dimensions of a product category, consumer segment, or market, by tracking recurring patterns in the data. An example would be the relationship of gender difference to the organization of power in a cultural setting.

Semiotics also takes into account the tensions between the various sign systems at play in a data set. It accounts for contrasts between verbal and non-verbal messages such as the placement of goods in consumers' homes, the disposition of design elements in a service site, or the structure of the hypertext experience in a multimedia ad campaign. These tensions often suggest emergent consumer needs or cultural trends. To expose these emergent codes, the semiotician performs a binary analysis of findings using a research tool called the semiotic square (Greimas (1984 [1966]). The semiotic square consists of a double vector grid that exposes the dialectical logic structuring meaning in the data set. The semiotic square also deconstructs this dialectic, exposing new cultural spaces and potential opportunities for growing brand value.

The search for codes and meanings accounts for marketing semiotics' distinctive approach to research design, data collection, and interview techniques. The semiotic analysis first identifies the cultural codes in the patterns they form across a large group of data. The data set includes enough examples for the semiotician to infer an underlying logic at the basis of meaning production in a category or consumer segment. For this reason, regardless of the type of research, the object of semiotic analysis always includes multiple texts, whether advertisements, cultural texts, service sites, packaging, or consumer interviews.[3]

The quest for meaning also accounts for the specific techniques used in semiotic ethnography for mitigating consumer resistance and decoding indirect, ambivalent, and ironic uses of language. Semiotic ethnographers are also sensitive to the tensions between what consumers say and what they do, and they pay as much attention to the disposition of goods in the home and the organization of domestic space as to consumer speech. They are also trained to bring theory to bear on the analysis of cultural codes, rhetorical operations, and category trends which construct meaning, identity, and value in the marketplace.

Chapter Summaries

The cases and examples presented in *Creating Value* suggest the broad application of semiotic research for marketing. Semiotics is not confined to the analysis of advertising, popular culture, and consumer data, but encompasses all phases of the research design, data collection, and analysis of findings. Semiotics forms the basis for developing research methods and protocols that are designed to account for the rich complexity of meanings associated with the brand, category, or consumer segment. For semiotic ethnography, semiotics guides the design, recruitment process, and the moment-to-moment actions of researchers in the field. The researcher trained in semiotic theory and practice knows where to probe and how to assess relationships among the various sign systems at play in a data set, be it the consumers' home, a service site, or a multimedia ad campaign.

---

[3] See, for instance, Sherry and Camargo 1987; Zhao and Belk 2008; and Humphreys 2010.

Semiotics also plays an important role in managing the brand's symbolic equities over time. The semiotic audit evaluates the brand's equities across the marketing mix and aligns communication strategy with the brand's historical legacy and competitive positioning. Semiotic research plays an important role in developing design strategy for retailing and packaging, and provides direction for new product development, advertising, and social media management. Semiotic research identifies the codes structuring meaning and value in a product category and exposes opportunities for brand leadership and innovation.

Service site designers commission semiotic research to decode the spatial and social systems structuring meaning in the retail environment. Media strategists may use semiotic research to track the movement of meaning from one virtual space to another in mobile and Internet marketing, and gauge the effects of this movement on brand meaning and consumer engagement. Regardless of the type of research, the object of semiotic analysis goes well beyond the single text and includes enough data to illustrate the patterns structuring meaning in advertising, retailing, design, or consumer culture.

Semiotics research can also be used to identify current and emergent trends in popular culture by decoding samples from the mass media, including popular ads, movies, books, and Internet sites. Cultural codes transcend the individual text or consumer and account for the shared meanings and collective behaviors of groups such as consumer segments. The semiotic analysis reveals the broad ideological tensions, icons, and archetypes recurring in the data set and deconstructs the broad paradigmatic dimensions of the data on the semiotic square.

Semiotic research also forms the basis for developing design strategy that supports the brand legacy, engages consumers, and aligns design with contemporary codes associated with social and virtual spaces, rhetorical style, and the meaning of forms, color schemes, and spatial dimensions. Media strategists may use semiotic research to track the movement of meaning from one virtual space to another in digital marketing and the effects of this movement on brand meaning and consumer connections.

The chapter summaries suggest something of the scope and depth of semiotics for marketing research and its implications for creating brand value. Each chapter highlights a different marketing area, including advertising and social media management, brand strategy, design and consumer research. Except for the first chapter, which summarizes the theoretical foundations of the book, all the chapters present a research problem, review the relevant literature, and explain concepts by means of examples, graphics, and grids. They also present a case study that guides the reader through the design and execution of a research project. The chapters include the following topics.

CREATING VALUE THROUGH SEMIOTICS RESEARCH

Unlike the other chapters in the book, which can be read in any order, Chapter 1 should be read first, because it introduces the reader to the basic concepts and specialized vocabulary used in the book. The chapter reviews the theoretical foundations of the book in post-structural semiotics. It reviews the debates within semiotics over the past century which challenge the logic and closure of structural linguistics (Saussure 2011 [1916]) and account for the role of subjectivity, context, and play in meaning production. The chapter expands the theoretical scope of *Marketing Semiotics* (2012) and reviews the implications of discourse theory and structural semantics for brand strategy, multicultural research, social media, marketing, and retail heterotopia. Theories are illustrated with examples and figures based upon actual business cases.

ADVERTISING SEMIOTICS

Chapter 2 reviews the interpretive paradigm in advertising research and draws attention to the limitations of the current, text-focused research for brand strategy. Current approaches, including phenomenology, reader response, intertextuality theory, and formalism, isolate the individual ad from its contexts in historical and competitive advertising for the brand. The chapter presents a discourse theory of advertising research that moves the focus of analysis to the codes structuring brand meaning in multiple ads. The discussion both advances theory and proposes a methodology for aligning creative strategy to the brand's heritage and cultural environment.

The case study focuses on the application of semiotics to a problem related to creative strategy for a brand of coffee referred to as "**Instant Gourmet**" to protect the client's trademark. Semiotics identified the root of ambiguity in a new ad campaign by situating the analysis in a study of the codes structuring value in the coffee category as a whole.

BRAND METAPHOR

Chapter 3 explains that brands are metaphors inasmuch as they structure similarities between the brand name and logo and symbolic benefits such as status, identity, and even relationship. In this context, metaphor refers to the cognitive operations responsible for forming analogies in brand discourse. Metaphorical operations organize cultural systems into paradigms, assign meanings to goods in symbolic consumption, and move meaning between the brand, the culture system, and advertising signs in social media campaigns. Rhetorical operations also account for the cognitive ability to make connections between multiple users, spaces, and mediums in Coke's *hypertopic*,[4] social media campaign for the London Olympics, "Dance to the Beat of London."

The case study highlights the methods used to create a brand metaphor and positioning for the Ford Escape when the vehicle was still in the development phase. At the time of the study, the vehicle had no name or identity to work from. Researchers, developed a unique methodology that identified the symbolic dimensions of brands in the competitive set, mapped them on a binary grid, and exposed opportunities for positioning the new vehicle in the competitive environment. The study illustrates the role of metaphor at all stages of brand development, from eliciting consumer associations and stories and building the brand metaphor, to developing a creative strategy for advertising and media planning.

SERVICESCAPE SEMIOTICS

Chapter 4 positions servicescape semiotics in the broader contexts of service trends in the category and the culture at large. The chapter also brings to light an emergent dimension of contemporary servicescapes formed by the virtual spaces consumers visit via their mobile apps and Internet platforms while shopping and waiting in line. The chapter underscores the role of theory in semiotics-based research and its ability to generate innovative, culturally relevant concepts for both marketing practice and marketing science.

The case study for this chapter guides readers through the steps involved in developing a new servicescape strategy for pizza pick-up service. Findings led to a new paradigm in pick-up service based upon consumer pleasure and entertainment into a traditionally functional service model. Research also identified ways to expand the service experience beyond the store by adding concierge functions to the mobile apps used to order pick-up pizza.

CULTURAL BRANDING

Cultural branding is a form of brand management that aligns the brand with trends in the product category and popular culture. Chapter 5 advances

---

[4] The hypertopic media system is modeled after the semantic web that links users, documents, and spaces in an Internet community (Zaher et al. 2008).

current approaches to cultural branding by defining culture and brands as semiotic systems that intersect along the lines of symbolic pathways. The semiotics of cultural branding places the brand at the center of the research process. It orients the selection and implication of meanings between the culture system, the brand system, and marketing representation in all media, from advertising to retail design.

The case study presents the research methods used to find a cultural positioning and creative strategy for a brand of bottled tea that had disappeared from the radar for twenty-five years. In the absence of recent advertising and consumer data for the brand, researchers developed a cultural positioning and identity for the brand by mapping the broad cultural dimensions of the category and pinpointing a new cultural space for positioning the tea on a brandscape of the ready-to-drink beverage category.

SEMIOTIC ETHNOGRAPHY

Semiotic ethnography is a theoretically grounded practice of fieldwork that situates the depth interview in the informant's lived environment. Chapter 6 summarizes the theoretical basis of semiotic ethnography in post-structural semiotics and highlights the importance of semiotics for cross-cultural consumer research. The chapter reviews a variety of protocols employed in commercial ethnography to achieve deep, creative responses from consumers and also to meet the unavoidable demands of cost, timing, and client deliverables.

The case study examines the effects of culture on value creation in the French luxury market. A semiotic ethnography of affluent consumers in Paris gives rise to a model of ethnographic performance based upon the dynamic joining researcher, informant, and informant stories. It accounts for the ways consumers manage difference and change for personal gain, pleasure, and meaning.

Concluding Remarks

The chapter summaries point to the various contexts in which semiotics was used to solve marketing problems, produce deep insights, engage consumers, and create value for the company. As readers move through the book, they will discover an expanding paradigm in marketing research which draws inferences between the structure and meaning of marketing signs, consumer spaces, and ritual behavior and the creation of market value. The reader will find food for thought as well as guidelines for teaching and practicing marketing semiotics research.

1 Creating Value through Semiotics

This chapter reviews the theoretical foundations of the book in post-structural semiotics. It expands the scope of semiotics beyond Saussure's (2011 [1916]) emphasis on code theory to focus on the effects of context, subjectivity, and performance on meaning production and consumer behavior. Although post-structural semiotics acknowledges the importance of codes for the collective, normative function of discourse, it also accounts for the influence of cultural difference, personal choice, and the uncertainties of daily life on meaning. The chapter illustrates through examples the applications of semiotics to marketing research in areas such as brand management, creative strategy, retail design, and multicultural research.

The Structural Paradigm in Marketing Semiotics

Semiotics is a social science discipline that locates the study of semiosis—the active production of meaning—in cultural perspective (see Lévi-Strauss 1967 [1958]; Eco 1979). Semiotics also refers to the sign systems themselves. One might refer to the "semiotics" of a service site, for example, to refer to the meanings communicated in the general visual design, ambient sound, and color scheme. As a social science discipline, semiotics approaches culture and consumer behavior as systems of signs and symbolic rituals, regulated by codes and susceptible to objective analysis.

The present book builds upon the structural and post-structural traditions in semiotics. Structural semiotics applies the linguistic theories of Ferdinand de Saussure (2011 [1916]) to non-linguistic systems such as culture, visual media, public space, and consumer insights. It draws upon linguistic concepts such as the code, the system, and the binary condition of signs to make sense of the world (Barthes 1977a).

CODE THEORY

The theory of codes grants a measure of validity to semiotics-based market research that is often lacking in interpretive research, because codes organize

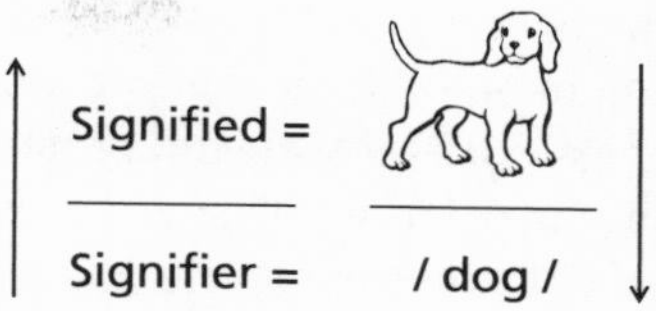

Figure 1.1. The Saussurian Sign

meanings in consistent, observable patterns throughout a data set. Like the anthropologist or etymologist, the semiotician infers the presence of these codes by tracing patterns of associations in a given set of data, including consumer interviews, advertising, popular culture, retail sites, or a product category.

The Sign

Saussure separated the materiality of signs, their "signifier," from their meaning, or "signified." The signified does not refer to the thing itself in reality, but evokes a concept in the speaker's mind. Saussure proposed that the signifier and signified form two sides of a dialectical sign structure, and that this relationship is codified. For example, the sign "dog" consists of the dialectical implication of the sounds /d/o/g/ and the concept of a dog (Figure 1.1). By articulating the sign into a signifier and signified, the Swiss linguist was able to demonstrate that the meaning of signs is entirely constructed by linguistic codes, rather than nature or personal choice.

Code and Performance

Furthermore, actual communication is characterized by a dialectical relationship between language code, which Saussure calls "la langue," and the individual manipulations of the code in semiotic performance, which Saussure calls "la parole." For example, syntactical codes regulate the alignment of subject and verb in sentences, and semantic codes regulate which words can be associated with others in the same sentence and still make sense. However, speakers can choose what they wish to talk about, such as dogs. For example, the statement "The dog barked" conforms to the syntactical and semantic codes of English, because, in fact, dogs bark. However, the statement would be meaningless if we replaced /bark/ with /chirp/, an action associated with birds. Speakers can nonetheless make metaphors, as in the statement, "The man barked orders (like a dog)."

Codes and the Social Semiotic

Saussure emphasized that language is a "social product" that binds social groups together in communication. The collective nature of codes explains, for example, why consumers in a given market agree on the meaning of the design codes on packaging mentioned in the Introduction.

Codes also account for the social dimension of non-linguistic sign systems because they regulate the association of specific meanings with symbolic representations in a given culture, such as the association of diamonds with status. Codes account for the collective interpretation of non-linguistic signs, such as shapes, gestures, and colors. Even branded signs, such as the Mercedes Benz logo, have entered the popular consciousness as symbols for social status and prestige.

Saussure identified the social function of signs long before social scientists identified the "social semiotic" at play in social organization (see Halliday 1978; Hodge and Kress 1988). Saussure's work reflects a debt to Durkheim (1997 [1883]), who proposed that social beings internalize the basic rules for ordering social life, contributing to a kind of collective consciousness of a society.

FROM LINGUISTICS TO SEMIOTICS: STRUCTURAL ANTHROPOLOGY

By bridging the gap between the structure of signs and their role in social organization, Saussure inspired Lévi-Strauss (1967 [1958]) to draw parallels between structural linguistics and cultural systems such as kinship. Lévi-Strauss adapted notions such as the sign, code theory, the paradigmatic analysis, and binarism to anthropology. In the process, he provided a model for the analysis of all sorts of cultural systems, including fashion, advertising, and design. In the same ways linguistic codes structure the collective interpretation of signs, cultural codes structure the collective norms that regulate social phenomena, from the role of men and women in society to the order of kinship in the distribution of wealth. Eco (1979: 76) in turn drew lessons from Lévi-Strauss (1967 [1958]) when he merged anthropology and linguistics, stating that signs are in fact "units of culture."

The parallels between semiotics and linguistics are both formal and cultural. By detaching the behaviors, interactions, and goods of informants from the meanings they assign to them, Lévi-Strauss modeled cultural meaning after the dialectical structure of the sign. As a result, he also found that cultural codes, not nature, structure the associations between non-verbal signs such as tokens and ritual behavior to specific meanings.

Lévi-Strauss also identified the symbolic function of social behaviors, kinship relations, and economic exchange and its role in ordering and perpetuating the cultural system. Lévi-Strauss also claimed that codes, not nature, determine the meanings and behaviors of people in social groups, from their dietary preferences to their family ties. In the theory of codes, Lévi-Strauss also explains how goods acquire meanings, a symbolic function that cannot be explained by the simple "meaning transfers" McCracken (1986) observes in advertising. I discuss McCracken's theory in depth in Chapter 5.

Lévi-Strauss (1967 [1958]) claimed that the anthropologist's main task is to decode cultural systems, from kinship to gastronomy, and to find in what ways these systems are, indeed, "systematic." His fieldwork methods laid the groundwork for accomplishing this task. He tracks the repeated association of cultural signifiers with signifieds throughout a data set, defines their binary characteristics, i.e. raw/cooked, and examines how codes have evolved over time.

Lévi-Strauss applied the principle of binarism to cultural phenomena, showing, for example, how the binary raw/cooked is paradigmatically related to binaries such as nature/culture in a society.

MARKETING SEMIOTICS

By identifying the structural dimensions of cultural systems, Lévi-Strauss laid the foundation for structural semiotics research in marketing. He provided a blueprint for decoding the meanings consumers associate with brands and product categories. Like structural anthropology, marketing semiotics does not consider the text, ritual, or design as a self-sufficient text, but a unit in a much broader system that includes a set of ads, packaging designs, service sites, or consumer interviews.

Barthes' (1977b, c [1964]) textual analysis of the Panzani advertisement notwithstanding, the textual analysis is but the preliminary stage in the strategic semiotic research process, which begins with a set of historical and competitive advertisements, or other sign systems, such as packaging. The analysis begins by tracking the recurrence of patterns in a data set composed of texts, rituals, and designs in a market or product sector. After identifying the codes structuring meaning in a data set, researchers identify ways a single text, ritual, or design both conforms to and breaks from the code in semiotic performance. These general methods of analysis enable researchers to apply semiotics to a wide range of marketing sign systems, from consumer interviews to social networks.

The Code and Performance in Market Research

The dialectical play between the code and performance structures consumer choices in ritual behaviors such as dining. Restaurant menus traditionally organize the meal in a specific temporal order, including appetizers, main course, and dessert. Although diners are given a choice of dishes within each category, and they can choose one or all three courses, it would go against code to order a complete meal in the opposite order.

As cultural productions, codes are culture-sensitive. In marketing, the cultural dimension includes both cultural values, such as formality versus informality, as well as category codes that communicate product quality and value at the point of purchase.

Cultural codes dictate how diners behave at a restaurant, for example. Given the formality of French culture, diners have very little choice in the order and presentation of the meal without suffering humiliation at the hands of waiters. In contrast, in China all of the dishes are placed before the diners at the same time, placing emphasis on the visual bounty of the table and the wealth and generosity of the host.

Category Codes

The product category forms a micro-culture defined by marketers that both draws upon and shapes trends in consumer culture, such as health-conscious food choices. Category codes enter the popular consciousness by means of advertising, packaging, and other marketing signs. In the packaged food sector, for instance, category codes define the cultural positioning of products in the store in relation to their ingredients and benefits. This marketing strategy responds to demands within consumer culture to clarify the benefits of foods for consumers, benefits that range from health concerns to social responsibility and ethical food production. Marketers and advertisers have clarified distinct lexicons and visual codes to differentiate the value proposition of processed, natural, and whole foods. They include distinct packaging and product designs, category narratives, ingredient strategies, and even pricing.

As a result of these semiotic strategies, consumers seeking a "natural" product need not spend hours reading up on the latest food science, nor even the product label. They will immediately recognize the semiotic codes associated with "natural food production" on the product packaging. Advertising that mixes and matches any of these codes in a single message fosters ambiguity and weakens brand equity.

At the grocery store, clearly defined semiotic codes signal to consumers the brand's place on the food quality spectrum, from Processed to Whole food categories (Table 1.1). Marketing semiotics research develops concepts and packaging designs for new product development by defining the semiotic distinctions between these food types at the levels of ingredients, package design, and brand messaging. Processed foods are traditionally associated with fun, flavor, hyperbole, and bright, primary colors, shiny aluminium packaging, and complex ingredient information. The ingredient label includes strange chemical ingredients, corn syrup, lots of sodium, and even Olean, which is a known carcinogen. Natural foods, on the other hand, are associated with health and goodness, make straightforward claims, and use earth tones, simple designs, natural paper, and transparent packaging with a prominent list of a few natural ingredients, such as the Häagen-Dazs 5 brand. Whole foods reference food sourcing, ethical production, and authenticity, using contemporary colors such as lime green to denote association with this cutting edge, New Age positioning.

Table 1.1. Category Codes: Snack Foods

Cultural Positioning	Rhetorical Style	Benefits	Semiotics
Processed	Hyperbole	Flavor, fun, unhealthy	Bright primary colors, exclamation points, fun over nutrition
Natural	Straightforward	Goodness, healthy	Earth tones, matte paper, straightforward, clear messaging
Whole	Metonymical-references food sourcing	Authentic, ethnical, local, personal	Contemporary colors such as lime green, or earth tones. Moralistic messages about food ethics, sourcing, and social responsibility

This research approach was used to develop new product concepts and package designs for the Nestlé Company, which led to development of the new Coffee Mate Natural Bliss brand, a line of all-natural coffee creamers.

Post-Structural Semiotics

Lévi-Strauss (1967 [1958]) was instrumental in adapting structural principles to non-linguistic sign systems and provided a model for the structural analysis of meaning in marketing. However, critics of structuralism in the mid-twentieth century rightly objected to the limits of code theory to account for the complexity of semiosis, because meaning production is subject to the effects of history, ideology, and consumer agency. Social critics such as Lefebvre (1991 [1974]: 64–65) claim that early structuralism reduced the creative potential of cultural systems to rational and static dimensions of linguistics. Although Lefebvre actually adopted Saussure's idea that sign systems, such as public space, are "social products" (1991 [1974]: 7), he found that the structuralists overemphasized the effects of structural codes on meaning at the expense of the equally important influences of context and social activism on semiosis in action.

DISCOURSE THEORY

The question of culture highlights the limitations of code theory on its own to account for the influence of context, subjectivity, and ambiguity on meaning production. In a little-known paper addressed to an international conference on the philosophy of language, Émile Benveniste (1967: 224) moves attention from the codes structuring signs to the dialectical relationship between codes and their implementation "in use and in action." The code and its implementation constitute respectively the structural and semantic dimensions of discourse.

Figure 1.2 illustrates how these two dimensions of discourse interact with each other in the active production of meaning in daily usage.

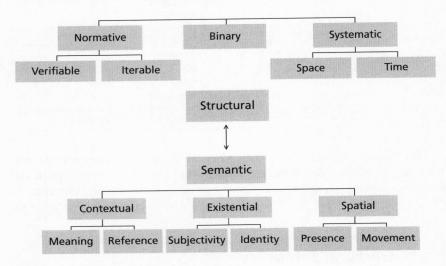

Figure 1.2. The Discourse System

Structural Dimensions of Discourse

The codes structuring discourse, in language or any other medium, share five basic structural characteristics. They are normative, iterable, verifiable, binary, and systematic.

Normative. Semiotic codes are cultural norms that structure the collective interpretation of signs and meaning in a culture. The normative function of codes contributes to the social dimension of marketing signs such as package and retail design. In everyday meaning production, consumers, and marketers manipulate these norms in unique ways.

Iterable and verifiable. Codes are iterable inasmuch as they can be used repeatedly in many contexts to communicate the same thing. The inverse principle is also true, i.e. that the meaning of codes can be verified from their recurring representations in a data set, such as a set of competitive advertisements for a brand or a set of interviews from a segment of consumers. The principle that the meaning of any single advertisement draws upon the codes structuring meaning across a data set is fundamental to the semiotic research methodology.

Binary. Benveniste (1967: 223) describes the binary nature of codes as an essential characteristic of semiology, because it implicates any given sign in the broader, paradigmatic structure of discourse. For example, a cultural concept such as /man/ is logically related to its opposite, /woman/. Cultural codes define how this biological difference is represented as the difference between masculinity and femininity in popular culture. Inasmuch as this paradigmatic system is a cultural construction, it forms the basis of gender archetypes in a given setting.

Semiotics-based research often draws upon popular culture to find the codes shaping consumer perceptions. For example, in the classic Hollywood cinema of the 1940s and 1950s, male characters drive the action of the story, seize women in their gaze, and communicate power through hard bodies and aggression (see Bordwell, Staiger, and Thompson 1985). In contrast, women are caught up in the action, are objects of the gaze, and communicate vulnerability in soft bodies and passivity. Although artists and consumers may subvert these archetypes in the interest of creativity and individuality, they nonetheless create and innovate in reaction to the dominant cultural codes (Figure 1.3).

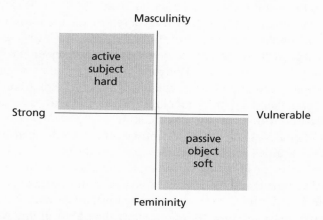

Figure 1.3. The Binary Structure of Gender in American Cinema

Understanding the relations between gender positions and their representation in visual representation is crucial to producing advertising that corresponds to the gender ideology of the target market. For instance, the Marketing Semiotics company conducted an audit of television advertising for a personal care brand targeted to women and found that the editing resembled the classic

Hollywood film style by positioning women in the ad as objects of the men's looks, giving the male characters authority over the narrative. This visual strategy contradicted the text of the ad, which spoke of women's independence and authority. These kinds of contradictions not only result in unsuccessful advertising, but ultimately erode the brand's integrity and trust.

Systematic. By exposing the dynamic interplay between the code and its implementation in semiotic practice, Saussure defined culture as a form of meaning *production*, rather than a natural given. Contrary to phenomenological interpretations of culture as an origin from which the symbolic function of goods derives (McCracken 1986), in the structural tradition, culture is a dialectical concept that influences and is influenced by the interactions of individuals and groups with the code system. Furthermore, as a form of cultural production, meaning occurs in time and space.

The binary relationship between the linear and vertical axes of discourse— their syntagmatic and paradigmatic dimensions—structures the spatial dimension of meaning production. The synchronic and diachronic axes of discourse structure the temporal dimension of discourse.

Space—The syntagmatic and paradigmatic axes. The syntagmatic axis forms the linear alignment of the actual terms in sign system; the paradigmatic axis forms the set of virtual associations that could be substituted for each of these terms and still make sense. This principle applies to cultural codes as well as language. For example, the custom of serving turkey on Thanksgiving in the United States is universal. However, based on many years of research, I discovered that ethnic consumers manipulate the obligatory turkey code in ways that reflect their cultural heritage, such as turkey with beans and rice, turkey moussaka, turkey casserole, and deep fried turkey. The paradigmatic flexibility of the cultural code, "Americans serve turkey on Thanksgiving," enables ethnic consumers to create a Thanksgiving meal that symbolizes both inclusion in American culture and identification with their own ethnic culture.

The paradigmatic structure of discourse also permits management to extend brand equities into new markets and products while retaining the fundamental brand positioning. For example, the Coca-Cola brand has stood for Fun, Refreshment, and the American Way for almost a century. Coke has retained its brand value over the years by sustaining these fundamental equities while managing how they are represented, both in line with global markets and in multiple media executions. The grid in Figure 1.4 is a research tool for generating a consistent set of brand signifiers across multiple media by aligning associations for Coke's equities on the vertical, paradigmatic axis.

Time—the synchronic and diachronic axes. The double axis structure of discourse also enables management to rework and revise a standard advertising

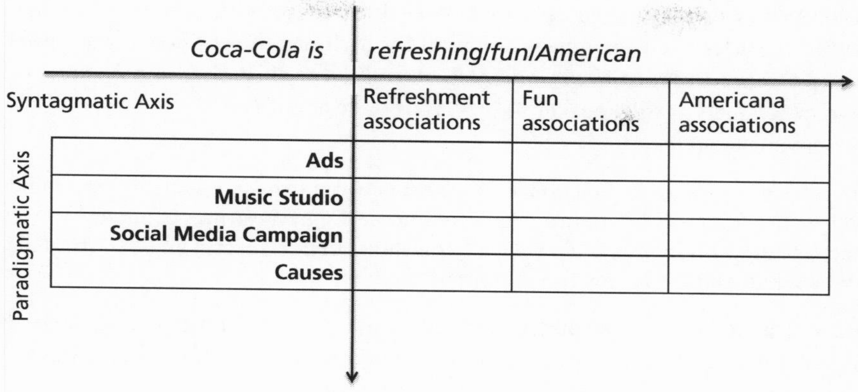

Coca-Cola is	refreshing/fun/American		
Syntagmatic Axis	Refreshment associations	Fun associations	Americana associations
Ads			
Music Studio			
Social Media Campaign			
Causes			

Paradigmatic Axis

Figure 1.4. The Coke Brand System

format in new campaigns by selecting and combining new elements into a standard format.

The dialectic joining the synchronic and diachronic dimensions of discourse accounts for changes in cultural codes over time. The temporal dimension influences the changes on the paradigmatic axis, such as the style, story, and setting associated with a brand archetype, such as the Kraft Singles kids. In a semiotic study of advertising for Kraft Singles, the Marketing Semiotics company identified a consistent narrative structure that included a scene with children eating a cheese sandwich, a statement about the benefits of Kraft for children, a cut away to the milk used in making Kraft Singles, and cut back to the children with a concluding statement. This unchanging structure forms the synchronic dimension of this campaign. Over time, the narrative positioning of children evolved in line with changes in consumer culture. In the 1980s, the children on screen were silent and a parental voice off screen told the Kraft Singles story. Later on, children began speaking about Kraft as endorsers of the brand, and eventually became storytellers themselves, adopting the role traditionally held by the parental voice off-screen. (For a more detailed analysis of the Kraft case, see Oswald 2012: 115–124.)

Semantic Dimensions of Discourse

By the mid-twentieth century it became clear that structuralism did not account for the creativity of semiosis in action. Speakers not only rely on codes to share meanings with others, but also modify the codes as needed to personalize their statements. Benveniste resolved this theoretical problem by introducing the semantic dimension of discourse into the structural paradigm. Structural semantics includes the various functions of the code that emerge when codes are used in communication. The semantic level of discourse is in play when speakers make propositions or statements *about something* addressed to *someone*. Semantics includes the speaker's intentions and reference to the context, and also accounts for existential dimensions of discourse, such as the speaker's subjectivity and identity.

Benveniste states:

[In semantics] we see its function as mediator between man and man, between mind and matter, transmitting information, communicating experience, enforcing a contract, eliciting a response, imploring, admonishing; in brief, organizing the whole life of mankind. (1967: 224, my translation)

Structural semantics accounts for the contextual, existential, and spatial dimensions of discourse that come into play when consumers use semiotic codes to meet practical communication functions.

Contextual. By drawing attention to the context of discourse, Benveniste identifies tensions between the static, dictionary meaning of isolated statements and the nuances formed by the reference to a specific context. These nuances may change the very intention of the discourse or modify its meaning with specific cultural associations. Austin (1955) cites the example of a promise to wed spoken as part of a dramatic performance. The fictional context of the discourse cancels any contractual obligations associated with wedding vows.

The referential function is not limited to linguistics but also operates in non-linguistic systems such as visual signs and ritual behavior. For example, if a teenager removes a Stop sign from the street to display it on his wall, he changes the intentionality and meaning of the sign by changing its context. On his wall, the Stop sign no longer directs traffic, but stands as a symbol for the teen's audacity.

As a semiotic concept, the "reference" does not raise metaphysical issues about language and phenomenal reality, but involves the semantic "world" in which a given discourse is embedded. The semantic context may include cultural references that are not clarified in the isolated statement. For example, gifting can mean different things in different cultures. In the "more is more" culture of North America, the value and importance of a relationship is measured in the size and cost of the gift. In France, where "less is more," the large size and high price may communicate vulgar materialism and disrespect.

Meaning and reference. The dialectic of meaning and reference to the context has importance for marketing research, because it underscores the importance of contextualizing any given text, be it an ad, a service site, or a consumer interview, to a larger set of texts that represent the brand, the competitive set, the product category, or a consumer segment.

For example, the meaning of a single print ad is formed by the dual influences of structural elements on the page, including rhetorical figures (see Scott 1994b), and reference to the broader contexts of the competitive and cultural environments. As I insist throughout the book, the semiotic analysis draws upon the codes structuring meaning in an entire product category and popular culture, rather than focusing on a single advertisement, design, or servicescape. The analysis identifies these codes by examining their recurrence across a large, representative sample of marketing and cultural texts.

In Chapter 2, I discuss an example of a new ad campaign for instant coffee that failed in consumer testing because it referenced three different value propositions for coffee quality in the instant coffee category, including gourmet, mass, and luxury. In order to clarify this ambiguity, it was necessary to study the codes for value in a wide range of advertisements for coffees in many formats at all levels of quality, including mass brands such as Maxwell House, gourmet brands such as Starbucks' Via, and luxury brands including flavored mixes such as Maxwell House's International Flavors. It was only by identifying the codes structuring the representation of coffees across the category that we found the source of the ad's ambiguity.

The semiotic square. The implication of meaning and reference in discourse exposes the tensions within meaning production that cannot be reduced to the simple binary analysis of signifier and signified. Greimas (1984 [1966]) developed a theory of structural semantics that breaks down the simple binary structure [A/B] by means of a process of negation that includes [not-A/not-B]. He mapped this dialectic on a double-axis semiotic square that exposes the nuances of meaning that fall between the binary dimensions of culture.

Although Greimas was a linguist, the semiotic square has important applications to the analysis of cultural binaries. For example, gender is a cultural category structured by the paradigmatic opposition of masculine and feminine characteristics derived from the biological differences between the sexes, i.e. men work/women care for families. However, since gender is, in fact, a cultural construction, not a reflection of nature, this simple binary does not account for variations in the representation of gender difference in a given data set. In the luxury category, for instance, the semiotic square accounts for gender as a cultural construction that cannot be reduced to a strict, stereotypical opposition between masculine and feminine types, but includes gray areas within the binary, not-masculine/not-feminine, that reflect emergent cultural alternatives to the dominant gender paradigm (Figure 1.5).

This rather simplistic example illustrates how reference to the context introduces complexity and nuance to cultural paradigms, exposing the spaces between binary opposites that are ripe for brand extensions and innovation. In the example below, the semiotic square exposed tensions within gender stereotypes, suggesting a more complex representation of gender identities,

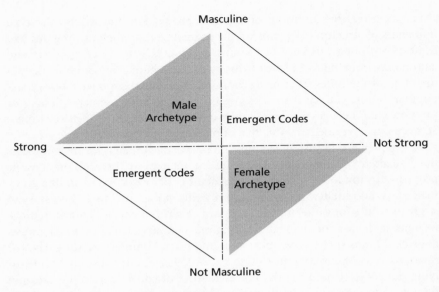

Figure 1.5. Mapping the Category on the Semiotic Square

including a brand positioning that embraces the power of women and the vulnerability of men.

[Female = Strong, Not Masculine. Male = Not Strong, Masculine.]

Structural semantics has important implications for brand strategy, because it exposes nuances and variations on a cultural binary such as gender, leading to greater choice and flexibility for positioning brands. For example, Dano, Roux, and Nyeck (2003) studied men's definitions of masculinity as represented by their perceptions of a wide range of brands for men's cosmetics. They found a wide range of interpretations and variations on the central paradigmatic opposition, masculine/feminine, including, at one extreme, the "macho male," and at the other, an androgynous male/female figure, and all the nuances in between. They then mapped the brands on a two-dimensional semiotic square that superimposed the binary masculine/feminine over the binary "care-for-self/care-for-others," and exposed a multitude of cultural brand positionings for masculinity in the men's cosmetic category. Their analysis illustrated the power of structural semantics to account for the great variety of nuances associated with gender identification and the variety of cultural positionings available to brands in a given category and market segment.

Existential. So far discussion has focused on elements of discourse that extend the structural paradigm from the theory of codes to the theory of how codes function within a given context or discursive event to make meaning. The existential dimension of discourse moves the discussion into the philosophical implications of discourse theory for consumer subjectivity and meaning production in the post-modern age of mobility, instability, and doubled identity.

In contrast with Greimas (1984 [1966]) and Eco (1979), who remain focused on the formal aspects of the discourse system, Benveniste (1971 [1966]) emphasized the implications of semantics for the existential and spatial dimensions of discourse. Furthermore, rather than simply theorizing about the metaphysical implications of the sign for the self and its relation to phenomena, Benveniste showed how specific semiotic codes, such as pronouns and rhetorical figures, mark relations of subjectivity, subject address, and space in discourse.

The personal and demonstrative pronouns, as well as adverbs for time and space, signify nothing on their own, but mark the movement of discourse point of view from the deictic center of the system, the [I, here, and now] of discourse, to relations of subject address—[I/you], and alienation—[I/Other]. Adverbs for time and space mark movements between [now/then] and [here/there]. Rhetorical figures also trace point of view in discourse, because they reflect the speaker's or narrator's judgments and opinions.

Rhetorical figures and markers for point of view inscribe the play of subject address and reference in visual representations such as advertisements. In a recent (2013) ad for Nationwide Insurance, the substitution of a car with a picture of a baby communicates the driver's affection for their vehicle. This metaphor marks the creative effects of the brand discourse on photographic representation and reflects the creativity of the marketer rather than an objective representation of reality.

In video ads, breaks in the continuity between shots, or gestures that draw attention to the organizing presence of an invisible narrator, reflect the effects of the brand discourse on the story. These kinds of markers also trace tensions in discourse between two sides of a doubled identity in role-play, ethnicity, and self-delusion. Benveniste gives the example of the divided self in Rimbaud's poetic statement, "I is an other," where it represents a figure of alienation.

Spatial. Benveniste (1971 [1966]) also accounts for the spatial dimensions of discourse by drawing attention to deixis, a performative aspect of discourse that inscribes relationships of subjectivity, subject address, and space-time in discourse. Figure 1.6 illustrates this concept.

Inter-subjective deixis structures movement between subject address and reference in discourse. The dynamic of subject address is traced by the first- and second-person positions in discourse. The dynamic of reference structures movement between the third-person positions in discourse. Spatial deixis structures the movement of meaning between the present and presence of the discourse, marked by the adverbs "here and now," and events taking place in a different time, a different space, the "there and then."

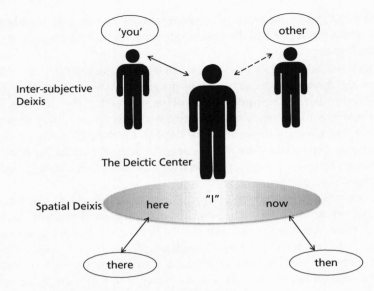

Figure 1.6. The Movement of Deixis in Time and Space

Derrida and the Deconstruction of Phenomenology

In summary, Benveniste moved structuralism beyond its fixation on signs by developing a theory of discourse that accounts for the movement of subject-address and reference in the construction of meaning and identity in meaning production. Inasmuch as Benveniste privileged the moment in which difference and ambiguity are resolved into the logic of the statement, he perpetuated the underlying metaphysical priorities of structuralism as to the fundamental rationality and coherence of semiotic systems and speakers.

Derrida (1973 [1967]) pushed semiotic theory even further by deconstructing the very foundations of structuralism in metaphysical philosophy. He claims that the tensions structuring the subjective, spatial, and referential dimensions of discourse are not digressions from the norm. On the contrary, the implication of I and not-I, here and not-here, and now and not-now captures something of the complex duality of personal identity and the essential ambiguity of meaning in any sign system. This duality prevails in speech as well as in other forms of discourse. Though this is not the place for a lengthy discussion of post-modern philosophy, Derrida's deconstructive turn strikes at the heart of the whole debate about the validity and "scientific" objectivity of empirical research, rooted as it is in phenomenology.

Derrida claims that phenomenology's assumption as to an original unity of the self to itself forms the basis of a cultural prejudice in the West that associates truth and reality with coherence and logic. The same cultural prejudice also defines those experiences associated with ambivalence or emotion as digressions from the norm. Derrida exposes fault lines in phenomenology by pointing out that the self is always and already divided from within, because thought, even in its most internalized and private musings, is structured by socially defined semiotic codes, such as language. Thought is inseparable from its articulation in linguistic structures.

Furthermore, the moment one externalizes thought in language or some other medium, they articulate a divide between thought and representation, between "being for oneself" and "being for others." Derrida thus places in question the assumptions of phenomenology as to an original unity of meaning and being that transcends language as such. These insights shed light on the complexity of the ethnographic encounter, where the primordial division of the self adds layers of subtext to the dialogue between ethnographer and informant. The case study for Chapter 6 illustrates this principle.

IMPLICATIONS OF POST-STRUCTURALISM FOR MARKETING RESEARCH

Post-structural semiotics has more than theoretical interest for marketing research, because it sheds light on some of the most compelling issues in contemporary consumer culture, including globalization, hypertextuality, and the social media. Marketers are only beginning to gauge the effects of these phenomena on consumer attention, brand perceptions, and shopping behavior, but one thing is clear: the non-linear, global, and digitalized environment of contemporary consumer culture invites an approach that applies theory to the practice of market research in order to tease out the tensions, ambiguities, and displacements in meaning in the market.

Practical Applications

The implications of post-structural semiotics for marketing are evidenced in specific research applications, including primary research with consumers, advertising research, and design research.

Semiotics-based consumer research accounts for the play of meaning between the statements consumers make and the meanings communicated by their behaviors, their lived environments, and other non-verbal contexts.

Semiotics-based advertising research focuses on the brand, rather than advertising texts. It accounts for the movement of brand meaning across multiple touch points in multimedia and social media campaigns.

Semiotics-based design research accounts for the importance of context for service site design, because the structure of experience in a given site draws upon the cultural codes structuring consumer space at home, at work, online, and in a variety of service categories including church and school.

In the following examples, I illustrate how post-structural semiotics sheds light on the dualities associated with multicultural consumption and the digitally mediated consumer.

Multicultural Identity

In consumer research, questions of context and subjectivity come to the fore in multicultural research settings, where consumers negotiate various subject-positions related to their ethnic and mainstream identities in their day-to-day consumer choices. In the example below, I illustrate how the theory of subjectivity helped shed light on the role of consumer goods in the complex identity projects of multicultural consumers.

Culture Swapping. In the late 1990s I conducted ethnographic research with a Haitian family to find out how their ethnicity influenced their choice and use of goods (Oswald 1999). I set up an initial meeting with my informant, a middle-aged housewife who lived in a home with her husband, children, and in-laws. I expected my informant to straddle two worlds, the Haiti of her childhood and the America of her adulthood. However, when I arrived at her home, I discovered a cacophony of languages and a multiplicity of cultural identities, including the French colonial experience of the father-in-law, the Americanized identities of the young children, and my informant's identification with Creole culture. My informant spoke Creole to her children, French to her father-in-law, and English to me in a single, polyglot conversation.

These shifts in the respondent's language in a single conversation brought Benveniste's theory to mind, because they reflected shifts in her identity position between three cultural contexts, French colonial Haiti, contemporary Creole Haiti, and mainstream America. Like Rimbaud's doubled identity, the ethnic consumer moves between multiple cultural frameworks in the course of a day or even a meal (Figure 1.7). Post-modern consumer researchers reflect Derrida's perspective on these cross-cultural encounters when they assume that difference and tension are not transgressions of the norm, but actually define the uneasy disposition of consumers as they navigate various contexts in daily life. Ethnographers such as Peñaloza (1994), Askegaard, Arnould, and Kjeldgaard (2005), and Üstuner and Holt (2007) investigate the ways ethnic consumers mitigate these tensions through symbolic consumption.

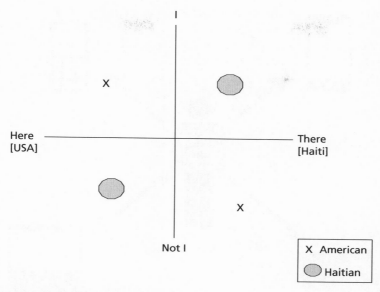

Figure 1.7. The Shifting Identifications of Ethnic Consumers

These linguistic shifts suggested that the respondent probably expressed her multicultural identity through other symbolic means as well, such as her choice and use of goods. This insight provided direction to the emergent design of the fieldwork, because it prompted me to focus research on the theme of culture swapping. As it turned out, the respondent shifted her use of goods the same way she shifted languages. She served ethnic Haitian foods at family dinners, and fast American foods at children's parties. She stored frozen goat meat in the freezer and kept Kraft macaroni and cheese in the cabinet. These observations put a new twist on Douglas and Isherwood's (2002 [1979]) theory of symbolic consumption, because they point to the inherent instability and duplicity of consumer identity and meaning production in consumer culture, as symbolized in their use of goods.

The example above not only suggests something of the complexity of ethnic identity but also illustrates the important role played by theory in the early stages of fieldwork. In this case, Benveniste's theory of subjectivity in language clarified the interpersonal dimensions of the field setting and provided direction for data gathering and analysis in the day-to-day conduct of ethnographic research.

Heterotopia: Semiosis in Non-Linear Space-Time

Benveniste's theory of deixis also accounts for the semiotic markers that implicate the subject or self in the space-time of the discourse. They include

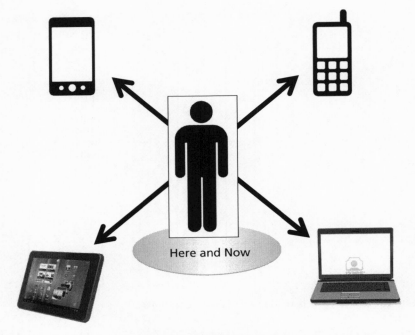

Figure 1.8. Heterotopia and the Digitally Mediated Consumer

demonstrative pronouns, such as /that/ and /this/, and adverbs of place, such as /here/ and /there/. From a pragmatic standpoint, one is either "here" or "there," in the present or the past. However, spatial deixis accounts for the movement of consciousness between the *presence* of the physical environment to the senses—the "here and now" of discourse—and the *representation* of absent realities to the imagination, "off-stage" and out of sight. In other words, it points to the inherent instability and even duplicity of meaning and subject-address in discourse.

Foucault (1986 [1967]) highlights the philosophical implications of spatial deixis for metaphysics. The capacity of human consciousness to move between multiple frames of reference in the mind challenges linear interpretations of space-time that are oriented to the "here and now" of empirical reality. Foucault uses the term *heterotopia* to describe the movement of thought between the deictic center—the here and now—of discourse (Figure 1.8), and the spaces split off from the center in time and space—the there and then—of discourse. Furthermore, this movement implies that consciousness, far from being a coherent, transcendent unity, is always and already divided between these poles. For example, the self is objectified in its reflection in a mirror, which theoretically divides the self from within into "self and other (self)."

Although he preceded the digital age, Foucault anticipated the growing impact of the digital media on the linear experience of space-time. Consumers may be shopping in a department store and use their smart phones to search other brands, Twitter their friends, or look for a restaurant. They may be lunching with one person while emailing or texting someone else. They may be drinking coffee in Starbucks while surfing the Internet or visiting their Cloud space on their laptops. This, the "digitally mediated" consumer, is drawn between the "here and now" of physical reality and the "there and then" of virtual spaces on computers, smart phones, and other digital devices.

Heterotopia and the Digitally Mediated Service Experience

In Chapter 4, I present a case study for Domino's Pizza that incorporates these principles into the design of pizza take-out sites. At Domino's, changes in consumer culture caused a decrease in consumer demand for home delivery and increased the number of visits customers made to the Domino's store to pick up their orders. Consumers now spend more time out of home than before, and often order take-out meals from their cars using the mobile apps on their phones.

A 30 percent increase in pick-up orders over several years placed in question Domino's core positioning as the brand with fast delivery service. Furthermore, increased traffic to Domino's service sites meant that consumers were increasingly shaping their brand perceptions on the basis of the service experience, not delivery. Pizza take-out franchises, including Domino's and Pizza Hut, tend to be small, drab, functional places focused on moving pizza from the kitchen to consumers over a counter. Domino's management commissioned a semiotic study for improving brand perceptions at their pick-up sites by redesigning the layout, décor, and service experience.

The Marketing Semiotics company recommended a consumer-centered service strategy that introduced elements of the traditional pizza kitchen into take-out service, including the sights and smells of hot pizza and friendly staff. We also expanded the scope of the service experience to include consumer visits to the Domino's app, where they place orders and can even see a video of pizza coming out of the oven. Recommendations included expanding the scope of the service experience on Domino's mobile app by including entertainment and concierge services to keep customers engaged with the brand while they waited for their orders.

Conclusion

Multiculturalism, digital technologies, mobility, and virtual sociality have deconstructed the traditional paradigms organizing personal and social identity, community, and the linear experience of space-time. In the various cases presented in this book, I demonstrate how semiotics-based research accounts for the effects of these dualities on marketing factors such as brand meaning, loyalty, and media planning.

The semiotician approaches the field setting as a multi-layered, multi-dimensional performance, whether the performance includes actual consumers or the play of meaning in a social media campaign. The researcher not only records what he or she observes, but tracks the movement of brand meaning, consumer attention, and identity across the field site or data set.

To make sense of this new environment and its implications for brand value, the following chapters present methods and theories for managing the effects of context, subjectivity, and spatial movement on brand meaning, consumer identity, and the service environment.

2 Advertising Semiotics

Communications experts define advertising in terms of its formal and cognitive properties as a medium of consumer persuasion. They focus on the textual strategies employed in advertisements to capture consumer attention, draw comparisons between a product and symbolic benefits, and form indelible impressions on consumer memory. From the marketing perspective presented in this book, however, advertising is defined as a vehicle for sustaining the brand positioning over time, maintaining its competitive distinction, and aligning the brand message with cultural change. Marketing semiotics research focuses not so much on the persuasive effects of a single ad as on the codes structuring meaning and the perception of value in the product category.

This chapter presents a semiotics-based methodology for growing brand equity by calibrating creative strategy in line with the brand legacy, category trends, and consumer culture. The methodology has important implications for brand equity management because it provides a quick and efficient way of assessing the brand's consistency, competitiveness, and relevance.

The discussion also advances marketing theory by challenging the dominant, interpretive paradigm in advertising research. Reviewing the current literature, one discovers a variety of approaches to the form and function of meaning in the advertising text isolated from the historical, competitive, and cultural contexts. However, as these approaches orient research to the advertising text rather than the brand, they fail to account for advertising's strategic function to sustain the brand heritage and differentiate it from competitors.

Before presenting a literature review of the advertising research scholarship, I present a preview of the business case for this chapter because it highlights the limitations of persuasion theory to account for the strategic function of advertising. I then review the literature and propose a new, semiotics-based approach to advertising research, followed by the full case study. The chapter concludes by showing how marketing semiotics research solved the business problem by embedding the textual analysis in the codes structuring meaning and value in the product category and consumer culture.

Case Preview: Finding a Cultural Positioning for *Instant Gourmet* Coffee

The case focuses on a 2009 print campaign for a global instant coffee brand which, for purposes of this case, will be called **Instant Gourmet** The image,

Gourmet in an Instant.

Coffee

Figure 2.1. The Instant Gourmet Ad

created by award-winning artist Mike Campau and Seventh Street Studio, grabs one's attention for its unique combination of photo retouching and computer-generated collage. In spite of the artistic merit of the ad, the campaign failed in testing because consumers could not agree on what it said about the **Instant Gourmet** brand. Some respondents associated the image with pop art, others with fine art, still others with French cinema. As a result of this ambiguity, the ad did not support the brand's positioning as a premium instant coffee for discriminating consumers. In other words, it was a beautiful ad that did not achieve strategic goals. The agency's creative strategy focused too much on the eye appeal of the image and not enough on its relevance for the brand's historical positioning in the coffee category (Figure 2.1). The question, "What does this ad mean?" became a riddle that undermined the ad's effectiveness.

To solve the riddle and account for the ad's ambiguity, the semiotic analysis began with an audit of historical advertising for **Instant Gourmet**, which clarified the brand's traditional positioning as a premium brand. The next step was to clarify how the brand distinguished itself in the category. By decoding advertising for major brands across the coffee category, the research exposed semiotic distinctions between the cultural categories of mass, gourmet, and luxury brands. In a very general sense, mass brands focus on the sociality of coffee, gourmet brands focus on consumer expertise, and luxury brands focus on personal indulgence. In spite of its striking esthetic features, the **Instant Gourmet** ad missed the mark because it mixed and matched codes from all three cultural categories indiscriminately, rather than communicating a single cultural positioning and identity for the brand.

The case illustrates the importance of building creative strategy upon a deep knowledge of the brand positioning and the codes structuring the meaning and value of goods in a product category. The semiotic analysis of historical and competitive advertising for the brand is a quick and efficient first step for framing creative strategy in the brand's cultural context.

The Interpretive Paradigm in Advertising Research

Interpretive advertising research focuses on the production and reception of meaning in individual advertisements, isolated from the complex social and cultural contexts of marketing discourse (Buhl 1991). It draws heavily from literary studies, including classical rhetoric,[1] formalism, textual analysis,[2] and critical theory,[3] to explain how consumers make meaning of advertising. Text-centered advertising research focuses on the analysis of word and image in the advertising texts.

TEXT-CENTERED ADVERTISING RESEARCH

For example, Scott and Vargas (2007) illustrate a formalist approach to advertising research that evaluates the influence of visual symbols on consumer perceptions of an image. The study illustrates the shortcomings of research that isolates textual elements from their context in the brand discourse. The authors not only isolate individual ads from their historical and competitive and contexts, they also isolate individual visual cues from their contexts in specific advertisements.

Consumers were asked to associate visual aspects of an icon with a list of product attributes, such as "softness" and "durability," for a brand of tissue

[1] See, for instance, McQuarrie and Mick 1996, 2003a, b; Phillips 1997, 2000; McQuarrie and Phillips 2002, 2004, 2007; Scott 1994a.
[2] See, for instance, Otnes and Scott 1996; Stern 1996b.
[3] See, for instance, Stern 1989, 1991, 1993a, b, 1996a.

paper. The icons were taken out of the context of advertisements per se. The authors found that a "fluffy cat" icon communicated "softness" more reliably than a flat, "graphic cat" icon. In other words, "fluffy" was soft, "flat" was not.

The analysis of visual effects falls short of accounting for ways ads make meaning in several regards. First, visual effects by themselves lack precision. As Eisenstein (1969 [1949]) makes clear in the theory of cinematic montage, visual signs derive their specific meaning by association with other images organized in a discourse.

Furthermore, the authors claim that visual cues taken in isolation communicate meaning without the aid of language. However, they employ verbal prompts to encourage consumers to assign specific meanings to each visual. They actually confirm Barthes' (1977b, c [1967]) observation that language anchors visual signs in a specific meaning. This explains why advertisements traditionally employ verbal taglines that anchor the image in the brand discourse. Without this anchor, images may show general functional attributes of the product, but do not communicate the brand's distinctive personality, mood state, or cultural positioning. For instance, is "soft" associated with gender difference, a story, or the perception of quality? A visual sign or a single ad will not provide this information.

In general, though interpretive researchers acknowledge that advertising is a "pathway" to the brand (Scott 1994a: 463), they tend to conflate brands with product attributes such as taste or texture. For example, Hirschman and colleagues (1998) propose a "model of product discourse." However, brands, not products, create discourse. Furthermore, brands, not advertising per se, create product rituals, such as the morning visit to Starbucks. Since the authors focus on a few examples of advertising for the coffee category, rather than comparing advertising for several brands, they disregard the role of advertising to support the brand's unique positioning, identity, or ritual and differentiate it from competitive brands.

Likewise, Otnes and Scott (1996) give an incomplete account of advertising's influence on cultural rituals when they omit the brand legacy and positioning from the equation. Brands transform culture by rewriting the codes associated with a product category. Advertising is simply a vehicle for this work. For example, Starbucks mainstreamed espresso coffee and the café experience in the United States by making innovations in products, service technologies, and retailing, and began using traditional advertising in the late 1990s when confronted by growing competition.

CONSUMER RESPONSE

Even when interpretive researchers propose alternatives to textual analysis per se, such as phenomenology,[4] reader response theory,[5] and intertextuality, they

---

[4] See Mick and Politi 1989; Buhl 1991; Stern 1993a.
[5] See Scott 1994b; McQuarrie and Mick 1999; Ritson and Elliott 1999.

highlight the role of literary conventions, cultural references, and personal narratives that consumers project into ads.

Intertextuality theory examines the influence of cultural texts on the meaning of a single ad, but does not account for differences in the way brands interpret these codes in distinctive ways that set them apart from other brands in the category.[6] For example, Hirschman, Scott, and Wells (1998) show how coffee ads take cues from the way coffee is represented in TV shows and movies. However, rather than contextualizing the ad in a generous sample of ads for the category, they emphasize how these interpretive frames "show how a text works." By contrast, Zhao and Belk (2008) identify a schematic analysis of multiple ads in a given culture, set against the backdrop of the culture's social and ideological history. Their semiotic approach not only identifies the broad myths structuring meaning in a culture but also exposes the impact of advertising on cultural production.

Another approach to the advertising text draws attention to consumer response. Mick and Buhl (1992) apply "life theme" theory to advertising response research. They interpret individual ads by means of the life-theme frames consumers bring to the interpretive task, emphasizing the individual-istic, rather than collective, nature of advertising meaning. The authors exposed three brothers, individually, to three advertisements, including one for Nielson beer, one for René Lezard men's suits, and another for Ballantine Scotch whisky. Based on prior interviews with each brother, the authors explain consumer perceptions of the product category represented in the ads, such as men's suits, in terms of their life experiences, expectations, and outlooks.

The authors naturally find that consumers who shun business and materi-alism also shunned suits in general as inconsistent with their lifestyles and values. However, they do not account for the influence of brand perceptions or advertising semiotics on advertising response. Later in the chapter, I illustrate an alternative approach to advertising response with a strategic semiotic analysis of the René Lezard brand in the context of competitive and historical advertising for the brand.

Another approach is reader-response theory. In contrast with life-themes research, reader response theory takes into account the shared formal con-ventions consumers bring to the interpretive process, such as genre and point of view. As Scott (1994b: 463) states, "A reader-response interpretation tries to show how a *text* works with the probable knowledge, expectations, or motives of the reader." This approach nonetheless focuses analysis on the isolated advertising text, rather than accounting for the cumulative effect of multiple

[6] See Sherry 1987; Sherry and Camargo 1987; Holt 2002; Kozinets et al. 2004; Thompson et al. 2006; Thompson and Tian 2008; Zhao and Belk 2008.

campaigns over time, the tensions between brands in competitive advertising, and the performance of brand meaning across texts and cultural contexts.

Although text-centered research may have interest for communication studies, it fails to account for advertising's strategic function in the marketing mix. By obscuring advertising's role in brand equity management, this trend has also deepened the divide between the disciplines of communication studies and marketing. Advertising departments at universities have become increasingly oriented to the humanities, focusing on theoretical issues in advertising communication and discouraging consideration of the practical application of theory to the business of branding. Likewise, marketing departments at business schools marginalize humanities research, limiting the potentially rich contribution of fields such as art history, film theory, and semiotics to marketing science.

The semiotic methodology presented below proposes an alternative to text-centered research that meets the requirements of validity and objectivity by anchoring the interpretation in the codes structuring meaning across a large set of ads.

SEMIOTICS-BASED ADVERTISING RESEARCH

Advertising is by nature a *public* discourse that draws upon the shared cultural codes of the target market, including the formal and cultural codes structuring the meaning and representation of goods in a given context. This, *the social semiotic* dimension of advertising, not only transcends the individual ad but also transcends the distinct life experiences, memories, and decoding ability of individual consumers.

In contrast with formalism or phenomenology, the strategic semiotic approach to advertising identifies the normative dimensions of advertising meaning, beginning with the esthetic codes' structuring the organization of texts, and extending to the codes' structuring meaning in the competitive set, the product category, and the cultural context. The semiotic analysis then assesses the way a specific ad or brand interprets these codes. Since the brand discourse can only be identified in terms of its legacy over time and its distinction from competitors, the semiotic analysis begins by identifying the codes that structure the meaning of suit brands in historical and competitive advertising. If the research involves testing advertising response with consumers, the respondent pool would only include users of the product and the brand.

Code theory not only focuses advertising research on the social semiotic structuring meaning in the marketplace, it also mitigates the effects of personal bias on the textual analysis. Since the codes and conventions structuring marketing signs are material, observable, and iterable, code theory grants semiotics-based advertising research a measure of objectivity and validity traditionally associated with empirical research.

A Semiotic Perspective on Advertising Response

In the following section, I compare and contrast strategic semiotic advertising research with Mick and Buhl's (1992) phenomenological approach to the meaning in individual ads. I then demonstrate the steps involved in auditing a brand's strategic identity in relation to historical and competitive advertising semiotics. I also show how this approach can be used to design qualitative research that segments respondents by their *shared* needs and wants relative to one brand or the other.

As discussed earlier, the authors propose a life-theme approach to advertising that explains consumer responses to a single ad by finding parallels between elements in the ad and elements drawn from the respondents' lifestyles. For example, brothers A and B responded differently to a René Lezard advertisement for men's suits. Brother A read the ad through the lens of the life theme, "being true versus being false." Brother A found that the suit "creates a dishonest image, especially for a teacher like himself" (p. 328). Brother B, who was insecure about his adult identity, read the René Lezard ad through the lens of a different life theme, that of "defining self versus not defining self." Brother B found that the suit "would demand certain behaviors he fears, related to a businessman's career" (p. 328).

The authors do not evaluate consumer perceptions of the brand name, or positioning, or the ad's distinction from other ads in each category. They do not ask how the ad's tagline, "René Lezard: Fashion for Fame and Fortune," influenced advertising response.

By focusing on the individual, rather than collective, response to advertising, the authors provide more information about the brothers individual personalities than about the ads in question, including their reactions to the brand message, the style of the ad, and the effect of the cultural context on their responses. Though life-themes research may have relevance for cognitive psychology, it divorces advertising from its marketing function, which is to broaden the shared "constellation of objectified meanings" (Thompson and Arsel 2004) that consumers associate with a given brand.

THE STRATEGIC SEMIOTIC AUDIT OF ADVERTISING

The semiotic analysis of competitive advertising for men's designer suits exposes the complex, strategic tensions at play in a product category that influence the meaning of any single ad. In contrast with Mick and Buhl's (1992) account of advertising meaning, the semiotic analysis underscores the collective orientation of advertising meaning structured by the cultural codes for concepts such as masculinity, intimacy, and style. It also accounts for the strategic function of advertising in the marketing mix, i.e. to support the brand positioning and clarify its distinctions from competitors.

The analysis begins by comparing and contrasting ten advertisements each for René Lezard and competitors. For the purposes of this case presentation, I limited the data set to two competitors, Ralph Lauren and Giorgio Armani, and limited the scope of the brand associations to three semantic categories, i.e. persona, lifestyle, and relationship. In contrast to Mick and Buhl's (1992) study, which privileges consumers' unique interpretations of a single René Lezard ad, the semiotic analysis focuses on the collective dimensions of advertising meaning for marketing.

The Competitive Perspective

The strategic semiotic analysis begins with an audit of the recurring patterns structuring brand meaning in a large number of advertisements. The advertising audit includes a *diachronic* analysis of historical advertising for the brand and a *synchronic* analysis of current advertising for the brand and competitors. The advertising audit exposes the distinct cultural positioning, including the values, tastes, and esthetic style associated with each brand by tracing their recurrence over multiple campaigns.

René Lezard. The ad in Figure 2.2 captures the persona, lifestyle, and relationship dimensions of the René Lezard brand that recur in the data set of ten ads. Cultural codes related to grooming and dressing reflect the brand's Bavarian origins and its emphasis on individuality and accessible luxury. The models sport beards and longish, natural hairstyles. They layer varied textures and colors and accessorize the suits with scarves and kerchiefs. The relaxed postures of the models complement the soft, textured tweeds and flannels they wear, suggesting comfort. The softened, even wrinkled condition of the clothes communicates the brand's cool insouciance. When women appear with men in the ads, the models look at the camera rather than each other, in poses that suggest warmth and symmetry rather than overt sexuality or distance (Figure 2.2).

Giorgio Armani. Armani advertising represents creative, successful men whose tight-fitting slacks, shirts, jackets, scarves, and leather accessories communicate the brand's modern Italian interpretation of masculinity. Armani's association with soccer star David Beckham reinforces the brand's reputation for bold sexuality, risk-taking, and personal achievement over social class. Sunglasses suggest a seductive play between seeing and not seeing in many of the ads. Visual contrasts between black and white and between shadows and clarity support this metaphor in the advertising. The day-old

	 RENÉ LEZARD	 GIORGIO ARMANI	 RALPH LAUREN Likeness (Stock Photo)
SEMIOTICS	Textured, relaxed, layered clothing, wrinkles, creative mix and match dressing. Beards, long hair, relaxed postures. Men and women are friends, urban or suburban.	Tight-fitting, pressed, shiny ensembles. Slick coiffed hair, urban landscape, steel and glass, dark glasses, men in motion, celebrities, women are seductively dressed and posed.	In the actual ads, RL uses stiff, fine fabrics, sharply cut tailoring, formal accessories, professionally coiffed, high class settings. Characters look into the camera rather than at each other.
PERSONA	European, comfortable textured, creative personal.	Italian, cutting edge, smooth, fashion-conscious, individualistic.	American, traditional, sophisticated, elite, wealthy, European luxury.
RELATIONSHIP	Spontaneous, friendly, warm, intimate.	Posed, seductive, intense, mysterious.	Formal, distant, cool, narcissistic.

Figure 2.2. A Brand Audit of the Competitive Set

stubble on the models, the black shirts, and the longish polished hair communicate the brand's trend-setting lifestyle. In ads showing men with women, the relationship is explicitly erotic and dynamic.

Ralph Lauren. Advertising for Ralph Lauren communicates the brand's association with elite American luxury in signs of traditional New England wealth, including mansions, polo matches, and Rolls Royce cars. The perfect features, frozen looks, and stiff poses of the models contribute a cool, almost painterly esthetic and elitism to the brand, suggesting a lack of human warmth, intimacy, and spontaneity. The stiffly coiffed hair, closely shaved skin, and colorful accessories suggest a kind of narcissistic sexuality. This interpretation is reinforced in the representation of men and women together in ads, where men focus their looks and attention on the camera, apparently oblivious to the women in the ads. (Management denied permission to reproduce an actual ad.)

The Binary Analysis

The semiotic analysis exposes the binary codes structuring the paradigmatic dimensions of the men's designer suit category, such as accessible/elite, and identifies the unique cultural positioning of the three brands in relation to these dimensions. The analysis also takes into account the way brands deconstruct these binaries in semiotic performance.

Table 2.1. Binary Dimensions of Men's Designer Suit Culture

Contradiction	Elite/Not Elite [S1/-S1]	Accessible/Not Accessible [S2/-S2]
	Trendy/Not Trendy [SS1/-SS1]	Traditional/Not Traditional [SS2/-SS2]
Implication	Elite/Not Accessible [S1/-S2]	Accessible/Not Elite [S2/-S1]
	Traditional/Not Trendy [SS2/-SS1]	Trendy/Not Traditional [SS1/-SS2]
Double Contradiction	Not Elite/Not Accessible [-S1/-S2]	Not Traditional/Not Trendy [-SS1/-SS2]

The binary analysis is a preliminary sorting exercise that maps the dominant cultural fields structuring meaning in a product category, such as Trendy/Traditional and Elite/Accessible. However, brands, like consumers, deconstruct these codes to carve a unique cultural space within the category. Therefore the competitive analysis demands a more complex account of the brand's semantic structure. Greimas (1984 [1966]) developed the semiotic square to account for the semantic dimensions of signs that cannot be reduced to simple binary forms. Greimas's semiotic square deconstructs the closed logic of Aristotle's square of opposition (Parsons 2012), because it exposes the semantic tensions beneath the formal semiotic structure of a category. These tensions are formed by secondary, tertiary, and quaternary binaries based on contrariness, contradiction, implication, and the double contradiction (Table 2.1).

The Semiotic Square

Plotting these binaries on the semiotic square makes visible the paradigmatic dimensions of the category and the complex movement of brand meaning within these dimensions (Figure 2.3). The double contradiction, such as Not Trendy/Not Traditional, forms a neutral semantic field that eludes the dominant cultural codes, exposing a space for cultural (and brand) creativity. Although the grid below does not account for the full complexity of each brand or the category's semiotic system, it illustrates how the semiotic square *spatializes* the cultural dimensions of a product category and *maps* the cultural positioning of brands in relation to these dimensions.

The semiotic square illustrates the dynamic and non-linear nature of brand meaning. It both draws upon the tensions between the binary poles of a cultural category such as Traditional and Elite, and interacts with other brands in the semantic field defined by the category. Ralph Lauren luxury is [Traditional] and [Elite] and fits squarely into the quadrant formed by these dimensions. Armani is an aspirational brand that prizes achievement over social class, so the Armani positioning moves between [Not Elite] and [Not

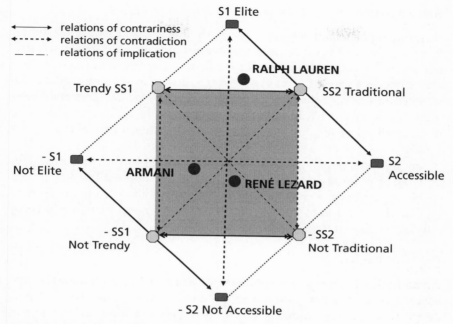

Figure 2.3. Semiotic Dimensions of the Men's Suit Category

Accessible]. Armani is trend setting but enduring, so it is neither [Trendy] nor [Not Trendy]. René Lezard luxury is [Accessible]. As a brand that prizes individuality, René Lezard eludes classification as [Traditional] or [Trendy].

The semiotic square also maps the intersections between the culture, brand, and advertising systems and their effects on advertising meaning. The example highlights the limitations of text-centered advertising research to account for these contexts and for their influence on consumer readings of any given advertisement.

IMPLICATIONS FOR QUALITATIVE RESEARCH DESIGN

Although the semiotic audit of advertising for the brand and the category often forms the basis of brand positioning and creative development, it can also be extended into a second phase of research that includes in-depth advertising research with consumers. Consumer research confirms findings from the advertising audit and also explores in more depth consumer fantasies and personal associations with brands in order to develop creative strategy.

Recruitment

Contrary to phenomenological research, which uses advertisements as stimuli to probe the depths of an individual consumer, semiotics-based research interviews consumers to find out how a brand performs in the marketplace. The strategic focus of semiotics research demands that respondents be screened in terms of their participation in a category, i.e. users and heavy users of a product such as suits. Non-users would be of interest only if the research aimed to identify ways to grow participation in the category as a whole.

Among users, respondents would also be screened by their relative awareness, use of, or loyalty to one brand or another. This approach to recruitment enables researchers to compare and contrast the brand perceptions of each type of user and also to identify unmet emotional needs that are not being satisfied by current brand offerings.

Protocol Design

For strategic advertising research, the semi-structured in-depth interview has advantages over focus groups and in-home ethnographies because it is designed to probe consumers about their personal lifestyles and unmet needs and also compare and contrast their responses to structured questions and projective tasks. The protocol is "laddered" (Reynolds and Gutman 1988), to move respondents from discussing their lifestyles and shopping behaviors to their social and emotional needs as they relate to a product category. For example, one segment of consumers may need a suit brand to fit into a clearly defined corporate image. Another segment may be seeking a suit brand that enables them to express their personal creativity and make a statement when they walk into a room.

The final stage of the interview moves respondents through a series of projective tasks, ranging from picture associations to storytelling, which invite them to free-associate between the brand and something unrelated to the category. A complete example of this methodology is illustrated in Chapter 3, devoted to brand metaphor. Respondents may be asked to select a picture of a flower or an animal that reminds them of the brand, and explain why. Respondents may be asked to complete a story that personifies the brands as characters in a scenario. For instance, by imagining how each brand would behave if it was stranded on an island with other brands, respondents communicate how well the brands communicate their respective positionings in the category. Is it friendly, aloof, or seductive, for example? These kinds of exercises can also be used to expand the range of brand associations beyond those in current advertising, and identify unmet emotional needs in the category that none of the brands currently satisfies.

The Binary Analysis of Qualitative Data

An important aspect of semiotics-based consumer research is the segmentation of respondents in terms of their lifestyles, values, and emotional responses to brands in a competitive set (Yankelovich 1964). The semiotic analysis involves comparing and contrasting findings from each stage of the in-depth interview. The binary analysis then clarifies distinct consumer types that identify—as a group—with the persona, lifestyle preferences, relationship style, and even esthetic style, of their preferred brand. The semiotician maps these distinct lifestyle segments on the semiotic square in order to represent strategic relationships among consumer types and between consumer types, brands, and cultural dichotomies such as conforming/rebellious. The semiotic square also reveals "white" spaces in the category, such as "not conforming/not rebellious," that may define a new cultural space for the brand that is not currently occupied by competitors.

The segmentation analysis begins at the recruitment level. Respondents in this kind of study are not recruited randomly, but meet the narrow specifications of category usage and loyalty determined in advance of the study. The in-depth interview fills in the how and why of consumer preferences for one brand over the other. It explains emotional, lifestyle, and aspirational motivations for their brand preferences, including the role advertising played in their decision and how they could be persuaded to switch brands.

Case and Discussion: Positioning Instant Gourmet Coffee

The **Instant Gourmet** case illustrates how to conduct a semiotic audit of communication for a brand of coffee that for the purposes of this analysis has been given a pseudonym, **Instant Gourmet** (Figure 2.4). The study does not include qualitative consumer research. Ideally, planners commission an advertising audit of historical and competitive advertising in the early stages of creative development to align creative strategy with the brand's historical legacy and emergent trends in popular culture, and to evaluate the brand's competitive difference from competitors. The audit can also be used during the creative process to evaluate the coherence, strategic clarity, and cultural positioning of new advertising concepts for the brand.

The case highlights the limitations of text-centered research for evaluating the strategic and cultural dimensions of an advertising campaign—dimensions that contribute to a campaign's relevance for consumers and sustain the brand's presence in the category. It also demonstrates how the brand audit, conducted early in the planning process, can forestall costly advertising mishaps by aligning the creative process with the overall brand strategy.

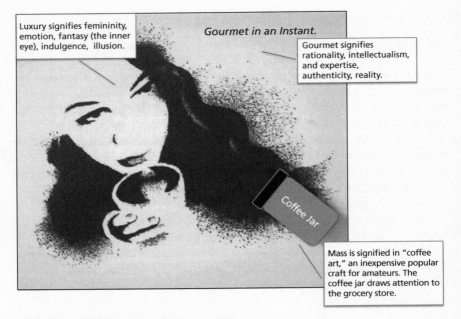

Luxury signifies femininity, emotion, fantasy (the inner eye), indulgence, illusion.

Gourmet in an Instant.

Gourmet signifies rationality, intellectualism, and expertise, authenticity, reality.

Coffee Jar

Mass is signified in "coffee art," an inexpensive popular craft for amateurs. The coffee jar draws attention to the grocery store.

Figure 2.4. The Instant Gourmet: Code Mixing

BACKGROUND

A 2009 print campaign for **Instant Gourmet** instant coffee failed to gain traction in the marketplace in spite of the attention-grabbing creativity of its visual composition and its ubiquitous placement in print and outdoor media. Mike Campau, a photographer renowned for his expressionistic representations of celebrities and brands, produced the visuals for McCann-Erikson, Los Angeles. The campaign, which can be viewed on the Seventh Street Studio website, consists of collages in digital photography, paper, instant coffee grains, an **Instant Gourmet** package, and the tagline about **Instant Gourmet** coffee. Campau created portraits, mainly of women, out of coffee grains by converting some stock photos to true black and white, filling in the contours with real instant coffee grains, and digitalized the composition in a sepia tone. The process deconstructed the illusion of reality in the photograph, drawing the eye between the outline of the woman and the real materiality of the coffee grains.

Although the imagery stands out for its distinct artistic merit, the campaign fell short of meeting strategic goals because it references at least three different positionings and three categories of value for the brand, including the popular culture of mass brands, the pleasure-driven culture of luxury brands, and the connoisseurship of gourmet brands (see Table 2.3). Furthermore, this problem is not merely a matter of creative execution. It originated in long-standing inconsistencies in management's long-range strategy, inconsistencies that ultimately undermined the brand's identity and perceived value for consumers. I will provide evidence of this claim as the case unfolds.

THE **INSTANT GOURMET** BRAND LEGACY

Instant Gourmet is a pseudonym for a premium brand that elevated the perception of instant coffee from a bland convenience to a flavorful indulgence. An ad from 1984 superimposes a jar of "**Instant Gourmet**" over a photograph of a coffee wholesaler inspecting bins of coffee beans, with the tagline, "Is there a coffee made with those incredible tasting gourmet store beans? Yes. [**Instant Gourmet**]." The 1984 ad references a specific cultural positioning related to the authenticity, expertise, and integrity of gourmet foods and beverages. The authenticity of photographic realism supports these claims.

In contrast, the 2009 campaign makes the **Instant Gourmet** claim in advertising that communicates ambiguity between category codes for luxury, gourmet, and mass brands of coffee. The image is constructed from coffee granules, a kind of "coffee art" that resembles sand art, a popular craft and a cheap art form. A real coffee jar is superimposed over the granules, drawing attention to the reality of the product and referencing the grocery store. The granules fill in the lines of a photographic imprint of a woman's face framed by luxurious wavy hair. She looks inward, as if dreaming. The female figure references luxury's association with leisure, fantasy, and femininity. The tagline, "**The Instant Gourmet**," references the expertise, masculinity and intellectualism associated with gourmet culture. The gourmet theme is supported by the subdued brown and red tones of the coffee and the coffee jar. The mixture of codes in the representation creates a tension between illusion and reality, amateurism and expertise, which creates ambiguity about the actual positioning and value proposition proposed by the brand (Figure 2.5).

These kinds of inconsistencies account for the contradictory responses of consumers to the ad. In consumer testing, respondents delivered a wide range of interpretations based upon their visual culture and tastes, from avant-garde French cinema to Ukrainian sand drawings. Since advertising testing focuses on consumer responses to a single ad, it cannot evaluate the ad's consistency with the brand's historical positioning or its relevance in terms of current trends in the product category. Like the life-projects study mentioned above (Mick and Buhl 1992), ad testing evaluates only the respondent's reaction to the formal structure of the ad.

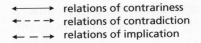

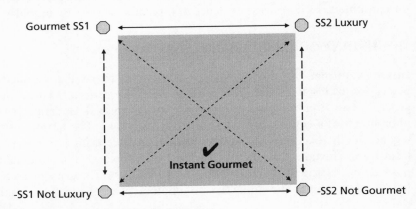

Figure 2.5. The Perils of Ambiguity for Brand Value

The Research Process

The research process begins by decoding the meaning of coffee in the product category and popular culture, and ends with applying these codes to the analysis of the ad. The process not only identified the source of ambiguity in the ad but also clarified a direction for future campaigns that aligned creative strategy with the brand heritage, category trends, and consumer culture.

RESEARCH DESIGN

The **Instant Gourmet** ad summarizes two key dimensions of premium brands, gourmet and luxury, by associating the coffee with an image of a fashionable woman in sunglasses drinking coffee. To clarify semiotic distinctions between gourmet and luxury, research began with an audit of advertising for related premium products such as gastronomy and fashion. The analysis resulted in a clear classification of premium coffee brands based upon their identification with either luxury or gourmet, and their distinction from economy mass brands.

After establishing distinct codes for gourmet, luxury, and mass product categories, we brought these codes to bear on the analysis of the coffee category and the "Instant Gourmet" campaign. We collected historical advertising in print, out-of-home media, such as posters at bus stops, and television media for **Instant Gourmet** going back to 1984.

The competitive data set included ads for all forms of coffee, including café service, beans, ground, and instant, in premium and mass categories. We included store brands such as Maxwell House, Folgers, Lavazza, and Café Bustello, café brands such as Seattle's Best, Starbucks, and Dunkin' Donuts, and instant brands, including Nescafé, General Foods International Flavors, Medaglio D'Oro, Café D'Vita, **Instant Gourmet**, Maxwell House, and Starbucks' Via. This process clarified the source of ambiguity in the "Instant Gourmet" campaign and provided management with a semiotic solution to the brand's uncertain identity.

THE MEANING OF PREMIUM

Within the premium market there exist two dominant cultural discourses, gourmet and luxury. Gourmet and luxury represent distinct cultural discourses that contribute to distinct semiotic systems within the premium sector. The gourmet category is the dominant paradigm for premium food and beverage; luxury is the dominant paradigm for premium fashion and design. They also structure very distinct semiotic systems at the levels of visual style, ideology, and value proposition. In data taken from advertising and magazine articles for food and fashion, we identified a paradigmatic set of binary oppositions structuring the value proposition, mood state, gender, and perception of quality of gourmet and luxury consumption (Table 2.2). These distinctions proved to be consistent across the food and beverage category generally.

Gourmet Culture

Gourmet consumer culture emphasizes connoisseurship, expertise, and food quality. Gourmet culture is steeped in European gastronomy. It is a masculine domain, as illustrated in the dominance of men tasting, sniffing, and measuring ingredients in the cultural data. The value proposition is based upon the

Table 2.2. The Premium Goods Sector

	Gourmet	Luxury
Sector	Gastronomy, wine, spirits	Fashion, design
Experience	Work, achievement	Leisure, esthetics
Value Proposition	Connoisseurship, expertise, awards	Creativity, originality, celebrity
Quality Perception	Authenticity, integrity	"Taste," appearance
Mood State	Intellectual, serious, hard	Sensual, pleasurable, soft
Gender	Masculine	Feminine
Esthetics	Dark, understated; hard edges, symmetry	Whites, pastels, and shiny; soft edges, flow

connoisseurship and ranking of the producer, as measured by diplomas, rankings, badges of quality, and taste tests. These ranks are codified in chefs' dress, from the white chefs hat and apron, to the sommelier's apron. The perception of quality is measured by the authenticity, quality, and source of ingredients. The gourmet mood is serious, intellectual, and hard-edged. Gourmet esthetics, from restaurant décor to packaging, includes dark, understated colors such as black, dark brown, reds, and greens, hard edges and symmetry, emphasizing the authenticity and integrity of the product, which is targeted to people who seek expertise rather than ostentatious display.

Luxury Culture

Although luxury brands build upon high-quality materials and expert craftsmen, the value proposition of luxury for consumers relates to self-presentation, pleasure, leisure, and *savoir-faire*, a form of cultural capital related to social appearance rather than expertise. Luxury is a feminine domain, as reflected in the predominance of women relaxing, sipping, and pampering themselves in the data. In contrast with gourmet, which is grounded in authenticity and reality, luxury relates to fantasy and aspiration. In fashion advertising, fantasy is communicated in soft backlighting, the dream-like gazes of models, and the inaccessible lifestyles referenced in the image.

The association of luxury with the feminine originated with the rise of the bourgeois class in Victorian society, where wives were expected to withdraw from productive work in order to enhance their husbands' social standing (Veblen 2009 [1899]). Women became full-time consumers of expensive goods, from fashion to home goods. The woman-centered focus of luxury gave shape to the fashion industry, where the evolution in styles, products, and luxury culture continues to be played out on representations of women's bodies (Castarède 1992).

The luxury value proposition is defined by the brand's creativity, individuality, originality, and ostentatious display, and communicates a mood of sexuality, pleasure, and soft edges. The perception of quality is reflected in the high price, celebrity, and exclusivity of the product, in artful packaging and presentation, and in creature comforts such as sweetness and pampering. Luxury esthetics feature flowing fabrics, rounded edges, whites, pastels, and black colors, and gold or silver accents.

Brands may incorporate signifiers for both gourmet and luxury discourses, as long as they clarify how these elements support their value proposition. For example, gourmet is the dominant paradigm for premium food and beverage; luxury is the dominant paradigm for fashion and design. This means that a "luxury" food brand will emphasize unusual design, display, and packaging elements, while a "gourmet" food brand will emphasize the inherent quality, integrity, and rarity of the product itself. More often than not, gourmet brands incorporate luxury design elements on packaging, such as gold trim, without losing their authenticity and integrity. However, if management dresses up gourmet brands in lavish packaging, alters them with exotic flavorings, or in any way associates gourmet with the frivolity and superficiality associated with luxury, they tarnish their gourmet equities in connoisseurship and authenticity and communicate an ambiguous brand positioning. The **Instant Gourmet** case, as we shall see, illustrates this point.

THE PREMIUM COFFEE CATEGORY

The premium coffee category is characterized by higher perceived quality than mass brands, based on higher price and social status cues, unique technologies such as "freeze dried," and superior ingredient claims. Judging from advertising, Premium brands also target couples and individuals rather than families and groups, emphasizing personal taste over sociality. The coffee category includes three main cultural positionings, including mass, gourmet, and luxury (Table 2.3).

"Gourmet" Coffee

American gourmet coffee culture originated in the 1960s with small roasting companies such as Peet's on the West Coast that targeted a niche segment of sophisticated consumers with special knowledge of fine coffee. When

Table 2.3. The Semiotic Dimensions of the Coffee Category

	Gourmet Brands	Mass Brands	Luxury Brands
Brands	Peet's, Intelligentsia, Gevalia	Folgers, Maxwell House	Starbucks, Seattle's Best
Value Proposition	"The Beans"	"Every Day Low Price"	"Creativity"
	Product authenticity, integrity. Expertise, coffee for coffee's sake	Good flavor, reliable Warmth and energy	Pleasure, creativity in preparation and presentation
Culture	Masculine, realistic, understated, intellectual	Social, domestic, comfortable, not gender specific	Fantasy. Pleasure, relaxation, pampering, fun, feminine
Signifiers	Dark earth tones, unadorned, serious, the art of coffee	Coffee as metaphor for emotional benefits Coffee as art, *bricolage*	Feminine. White, pastels, fantasy, the art of presentation
Target Segment	Coffee aficionados, connoisseurs, sophisticated shoppers	The mass market	The premium coffee-lover seeking a sweet hot beverage with an espresso boost

Starbucks' Schultz opened espresso cafés across the country in the 1980s, he popularized gourmet attributes such as the authenticity and quality of the beans themselves, the expert roasting process, and also the special art of espresso making. When Starbucks introduced single-serve Via instant coffee, they competed head-to-head with **Instant Gourmet**'s market share of the gourmet instant coffee market.

Signifiers for gourmet. Coffee brands communicate "gourmet" in signifiers drawn from gastronomy, including packaging in dark earth tones such as brown, green, and red, simple designs, narratives about product sourcing and roasting, and an emphasis on intellectualism. Espresso cafés such as Peet's and Starbucks employ soft, accent lighting rather than fluorescents, and furnishings reminiscent of a library, such as old leather and wood. Starbucks even created a proprietary lexicon for the cafés to emphasize the unique properties of the brand.

"Luxury" Coffee

When Schultz decided to move specialty coffee into the espresso café business in the 1970s, he challenged the beliefs of coffee *aficionados* in Seattle that gourmet quality is in the beans, not the preparation. By moving from the warehouse to the café, Starbucks introduced European café culture into the coffee market, moving emphasis from gourmet to luxury culture over the years.

Starbucks has shifted emphasis from coffee sourcing and roasting to coffee consumption, and from intellectual pursuits to consumer pleasure. Starbucks cafés and competitors have increasingly moved emphasis from coffee's natural richness to beverage additives such as cream, sugar, and flavorings.

Signifiers for luxury. As premium brands increasingly focus on dairy additives, sugary flavorings, European café culture, and consumer comfort, they also replace gourmet signifiers, such as dark, masculine colors and simple designs, with signifiers for luxury, including whites and pastels, feminine accents, and rounded, rather than angular, design features.

The Starbucks logo is a case in point. The original logo contained many symbolic elements associated with Starbucks' original positioning as an expert in coffee beans and roasting, including the use of brown on white, an esoteric sixteenth-century Norse woodcut of a mermaid in realistic detail, and the use of parallel lines to frame the image and the brand name and product offerings, coffee, tea, spices. The evolution of the Starbucks' logo over the years reflects the brand's increasing departure from its original, narrow gourmet positioning to its current positioning somewhere between luxury and mass culture. Between 1987 and 1992, Starbucks changed the color scheme from brown to green and black. Between 1992 and 2011, the realistic details of the siren gave way to an increasingly abstract, decorative graphic of a siren figure on a green backdrop, but the parallel lines around the image remained. In the most recent revision in 2011, management replaced the black background, the circular frame around the siren, and the brand name. The logo now consists of an abstract figure of the mermaid in white on a green background, shifting emphasis from the company's original equities in connoisseurship to its current emphasis on consumer indulgence and lifestyle.[7]

Gourmet with Luxury Accents

Since luxury culture is associated with fashion, design, and other sectors connected with appearance, gourmet brands can incorporate luxury features on packaging without subverting the brand's gourmet value proposition. For example, Intelligentsia packages Black Cat espresso in black paper with a prominent gold logo, but the brand's dominant message communicates product sourcing, integrity, and expertise. Similarly, the **Instant Gourmet** package communicates the dominant gourmet positioning of the brand by means of a dark red and brown color scheme, the coffee bean, and a "Gourmet" label. Gold accents and a swirl of flowing red add luxury elements to the packaging without contradicting the brand's overall gourmet presentation.

Furthermore, with the exception of niche brands such as Intelligentsia and Peet's that still target coffee connoisseurs through mail order and local outlets, the premium coffee category is trending toward the mass market. Starbucks has introduced coffee blends, roasts, and flavorings to their café outlets that cater to a broad public. They discount their packaged coffee at superstores such as Walmart.

Mass Brands

The mass marketing of premium brands naturally lowers their perceived value and leaves them vulnerable to competition on price from fast food chains such as McDonald's and Dunkin' Donuts and home-prepared brands such as Folgers and Maxwell House. **Instant Gourmet** is a supermarket brand that has traditionally commanded higher prices by leveraging its European, gourmet positioning. However, a semiotic audit of mass brands suggests that **Instant Gourmet** may be closer to mass brands than they intend, which threatens their legacy as a premium brand.

Folgers and Maxwell House trade on the "everyday low price" proposition. Since the recent gourmet coffee trend, these brands have displaced earlier claims about superior product quality, such as Maxwell House's "Good the

---

[7] A sample of historical Starbucks logos can be found at the company website <http://www.starbucks.com/preview>.

very last drop," and Folgers's "A good part of every day is Folgers in your cup," onto peripheral benefits such as mood enhancement and socializing. Folgers is "the best part of waking up;" it helps one "tolerate mornings," and jumpstarts the day. Maxwell House promises social belonging and community, welcoming consumers to "our house."

Signifiers for "mass." Although Folgers and Maxwell House have traditionally claimed superior flavor to generic brands, in recent years they have faced mounting competition from fine coffee brands, from espresso cafés to premium store brands. As a result, they currently focus messaging on peripheral product benefits such as the wake-up call or social bonding rather than the quality of the beans. The color scheme in advertising and packaging supports this positioning, running to primary colors, such as bright blues, reds, and yellows, rather than the earth tones associated with gourmet brands.

Coffee metaphors and coffee art abound in mass-market advertising, directing attention away from the integrity of the coffee itself to fantasy and emotion. For example, a Folgers ad includes a weird image that superimposes a steaming coffee cup over a manhole in the street, with the tagline, "To the city that never sleeps, wake up to Folgers." Maxwell House compares bitter coffee to bitter emotions, promising not only a bitter-free coffee, but a "world without bitterness." The ad includes a cup of coffee on which a smiley face seems to emerge from the coffee. Starbucks began using mass advertising in order to head off competition from the growing espresso café market. In one ad, they build a visual metaphor between coffee and social bonding by connecting two rings formed by coffee with the tagline, "Reconnect." Furthermore, the coffee pot, rather than the individual sipping coffee, represents the focus of mass brands on the social benefits of coffee.

THE **INSTANT GOURMET** LEGACY

A diachronic analysis of historical advertising for **Instant Gourmet** exposes dramatic shifts in its cultural positioning from 1984 to 2009 between gourmet, luxury, and mass. Rather than sustaining its early positioning as the instant alternative to authentic, fresh-brew premium coffee, **Instant Gourmet** advertising sought short-term gains over the years by means of attention-grabbing creative tactics that moved the brand off-course from its core positioning. A cursory timeline of the brand's positioning leading up to the "Instant Gourmet" campaign summarizes this movement (Table 2.4). Most notable is the Brewing Romance campaign from the 1990s featuring Anthony Head (see <https://www.youtube.com/watch?v=hpOBFELO0Qc>).

Table 2.4. The Shifting Positioning of "Instant Gourmet" over Time

	Gourmet	Mass	Luxury
Semiotic Dimensions	Authenticity, expertise, gourmet claim, coffee for coffee's sake, masculine. Earth tones, intellectual	Flavor at a low price. Coffee as art, as metaphor, as social catalyst. Family and community. Primary colors, *bricolage*, fun	Romance, escape, creativity. Coffee as prop in luxurious lifestyle. White, gold, pastels. Feminine, sensual
1984	"Gourmet Store Beans."		
1990s			"Brewing Romance"
2002		"Advantage You."	
2005	"100% Columbian"		
2006			"Bold Coffee, Bold Moves"
2009	"Gourmet/Instant"	"Gourmet/Instant"	"Gourmet/Instant"
2011–2013		"Four times our price, a fraction of our flavors"	

1984: A gourmet positioning was communicated in advertising that associated the brand with the authenticity and expertise of a coffee wholesaler testing the beans. The color scheme includes browns and reds.

1990s: A luxury positioning was communicated in advertising that emphasized the emotional benefits of **Instant Gourmet**. In the 1990s, McCann-Erikson wove **Instant Gourmet** into a mini-soap opera in which a British couple finds love at first sight over a jar of **Instant Gourmet** coffee. Each installment ended with a cliffhanger about the couple's brewing romance. The luxury semiotics of the campaign communicates the upscale lifestyle of the characters. The woman wears prominent gold earrings, serves coffee in gold-trimmed china, and travels to Paris.

Management credited the campaign with the 10 percent increase in sales in the first few months, but over a five-year period the campaign's impact on sales declined. Rather than act as a vehicle for sustaining the brand positioning, the entertainment value of the campaign overshadowed its strategic function. The **Instant Gourmet** brand had become a simple prop in the ongoing romantic narrative in the ads (Werder 2007).

2000s: By the year 2000, management replaced the mini-series with ads and out-of-home media that focused on product benefits such as energy and control, a positioning reminiscent of mass brands. A 2002 campaign, "Advantage You," brings to mind Folgers with the tagline, "[**Instant Gourmet**] is the charge you need to get on with your day."

2009: With the recent campaign, the various identities associated with **Instant Gourmet** come home to roost. The campaign references three cultural positionings and three value propositions for the instant coffee category, i.e. mass, gourmet, and luxury. The mass positioning is communicated in the use of coffee granules to produce the image, because it references amateur crafts such as sand painting that is popular with tourists. The gourmet positioning, communicated in the tagline and the brown and beige color scheme, is contradicted by visual signifiers for luxury and mass positionings. The tensions between these three distinct sign systems give rise to widely divergent cultural interpretations of the ad and foster confusion, rather than clarity, about the brand.

THREE SIGN SYSTEMS, THREE CULTURAL POSITIONINGS

The background research examined in detail the codes structuring meaning and value in the coffee category. It also identified specific signifiers for each cultural positioning, from mass to gourmet and luxury. The following section finds evidence that all three cultural positionings are represented in the "Instant Gourmet" campaign, begging the question, what does this ad mean?

Gourmet

The tagline, "Instant Gourmet," claims that **Instant Gourmet** is a gourmet brand of instant coffee. The dark brown package placed in the corner of the ad communicates gourmet authenticity in the clear bottle that exposes the coffee inside and the dark brown and red color scheme of the labeling.

Luxury

The luxury signifiers in the 2009 campaign ad include the central feminine figure, her dream-like gaze, suggestive of fantasy, her flowing hair, and the overall emphasis on sensuality, pleasure, and relaxation, rather than masculinity, intellectualism, connoisseurship, and authenticity.

Mass

The codes for mass brands in the coffee category were established in Table 2.3. The dominant signifier for "mass" in the ad is the overall representation of coffee as a metaphor for something else. Here coffee grains form a medium for representing a woman. As noted before, Folgers and Maxwell House resort to metaphor because they cannot claim the superior goodness of their coffee beans by comparison with high-priced premium brands. Furthermore, the assemblage of photography, coffee grains, and the coffee jar falls into the realm of *bricolage*, a form of folk art in which amateurs cobble together natural materials and found objects into craft art and home decorations.

IMPLICATIONS FOR BRAND EQUITY

Figure 2.5 illustrates the perils of cultural ambiguity, because it positions **Instant Gourmet** in a nebulous space that is neither gourmet nor luxury. By mixing and matching the signifiers for mass, gourmet, and luxury discourses in a single ad, the "Instant Gourmet" campaign not only communicates ambiguity and confusion, it also raises doubts about the integrity, reliability, and perceived quality of **Instant Gourmet** as a premium brand.

Furthermore, the ad's ambiguity cannot simply be passed off as a glitch in the creative execution, because it represents the culmination of years of unfocused strategy that centered on short-term creative tactics at the expense of the long-term brand value. As I explain in case after case in *Marketing Semiotics* (2012), the lack of focus depletes brand equity because it erodes the brand's credibility, customer loyalty, and perception of quality. This principle seems to be operable in the **Instant Gourmet** case, because in 2011 management began positioning the brand as a lower-priced alternative to Starbucks' instant Via brand with the claim, "Four times our price, a fraction of our flavors." Competing on price is a clear indication that the brand's inconsistent cultural positioning has diluted its distinctive identity as a premium brand instant coffee, which will inevitably translate into lower market value.

THE "INSTANT GOURMET" CAMPAIGN

By contextualizing the advertising analysis in the system of codes structuring the meaning and representation of value in the coffee category, the strategic semiotic study provided material and objective criteria for decoding the "Instant Gourmet" campaign. Findings exposed mixed messages in the ad and a confused brand positioning somewhere between gourmet, luxury, and mass.

The study had the additional benefit of tracking inconsistencies in the brand positioning over time. From its original positioning as the gourmet brand for demanding customers, **Instant Gourmet** moved to more of a luxury positioning in the 1990s campaign where coffee was merely a prop for the more prominent narrative about a brewing romance. When this tactic lost steam, management tried to refocus on product benefits, but their campaign echoed the messaging associated with mass brands such as Folgers and Maxwell House. The **Instant Gourmet** positioning moved back and forth a few more times before 2009 and the launch of the "Instant Gourmet" advertising campaign.

By 2009, the **Instant Gourmet** brand had moved between gourmet, luxury, and mass so frequently that it lost focus. The lack of strategic focus accounts for the multiple, conflicting discourses in the "Instant Gourmet" coffee campaign itself, and led ultimately to the brand-destroying tactic in 2011 of competing on price with Via.

The case illustrates a stage in the strategic planning process that audits the brand's equities as represented in advertising and aligns them with the structures of perceived value in the category. The next phase would assess consumer responses to current offerings in the coffee category with an aim to finding a new cultural space for **Instant Gourmet** that would play with the tensions between gourmet and luxury and move the brand away from associations with mass brands. This process involves projecting additional binary dimensions over the semiotic square in Figure 2.5 based upon findings from the consumer study. An example of the multidimensional semiotic square can be found in Figure 2.3 relating to the men's luxury suit example.

Conclusion

The central question for strategic semiotic research in advertising is not, "What does this ad mean?" but, "How does this ad extend the brand heritage, defend it against competitors, and relate to popular culture?" These questions determine the scope and focus of strategic semiotic research, including collecting, analyzing, and presenting data. It extends the data set to historical and competitive advertising for the brand and category. It embeds the textual analysis in the broader search for the cultural and category codes structuring patterns of meaning across the data set. And it submits findings to a binary analysis that exposes the semantic tensions between the brand, competitors, and the cultural paradigms shaping a product category.

3 Brand Metaphor

Metaphor deserves an entire chapter because of its far-reaching importance in consumer culture. It has been said that one hears more metaphors in a day at the market than in the entire text of Virgil's *Aeneid* (Genette 1993 [1968]: 12). By finding synergies between far-flung ideas, metaphors make poets of us all and inject energy and emotion into everyday communication. By drawing analogies between things, metaphors expand the imagination and present unfamiliar ideas in the form of things we know. Cognitive linguists such as Jakobson (1990 [1956]), Lakoff and Johnson (1980), and Sapolsky (2010) claim that metaphor structures the most basic symbolic functions of the mind.

Metaphors abound in advertising, where they transform ordinary things such as blue jeans into objects of desire. Who can forget that nothing comes between Brooke Shields and her Calvin's? However, this chapter is not concerned with advertising metaphors alone, but with the broader implications of metaphorical thinking for managing brands. Since metaphor shapes consumer perceptions of the world, the marketplace, and their possessions, managing the brand metaphor is tantamount to managing brand value.

In order to account for the broad reach of metaphor in marketing, I open the chapter with a clarification of the form and function of rhetoric in semiotic theory. I challenge the current scholarship on advertising rhetoric, which limits metaphor to a local trope formed by a comparison between two signs in the isolated advertisement. As discussed in Chapter 2, brand meaning is formed over time by the repeated association of the brand with a particular set of meanings. Likewise, the brand metaphor consists of the long-standing, repeated comparison between the brand name and logo and a given meaning set. I propose an alternative to trope theory that accounts for the role of metaphor in the construction of discourse. Discourse theory builds upon, rather than resolves, the tensions between meaning and reference, subject and others, proximity and distance, text and hypertext in the brand discourse.

I examine these tensions in relation to the brand's positioning in the category, the metaphors consumers construct to associate meanings with brands, and media metaphors that link one medium to another in multimedia, hypertext marketing campaigns. The chapter also presents actionable methodologies for leveraging the power of metaphor to build competitive and relevant brand strategy.

To orient the theoretical discussion to research practice, the chapter includes numerous examples that illustrate the importance of brand rhetoric for marketing and media strategy.

Case Preview: Finding a Brand Metaphor for the Ford Escape

The case study presents the metaphor elicitation technique and semiotic research process that were used to develop a brand metaphor for the launch of the Ford Escape in the year 2000. The case illustrates the sustainability of the brand metaphor over time, because it continues to guide marketing strategy for the Escape after these many years. The chapter also includes a detailed analysis of the role of rhetorical operations in structuring Red Bull's hypertext marketing campaign, Flugtag. Metaphorical and metonymical operations motivate semantic links between the brand metaphor and multiple media and social spaces in these interactive, multimedia events. The implication of social media and semantics is based upon a web-based model of the "semantic net" linking users, computers, and documents in a web-based system.[1]

The Aristotelian Tradition in Advertising Research

This broad, strategic approach to metaphor stands in contrast to the dominant, Aristotelian tradition in advertising research, which focuses on the effects of isolated tropes on consumer persuasion.[2] Trope theory limits the force of metaphor to "artful deviations" from the "proper" or codified meaning of things. Proponents of trope theory such as Scott (1994a) and McQuarrie and Mick (1996, 2003a) focus on the substitution of one sign for another in figures taken in isolation from the broader media and cultural contexts in which they occur. Metaphorical tropes substitute one sign for another on the basis of analogy. When consumers state, "My car is my baby," the metaphor deviates from the proper meaning by condensing two apparently disparate semantic fields, cars and babies, into a single, polyvalent concept.

TROPE THEORY

The advertising research literature focuses on a narrow interpretation of Aristotle's (2004) *Rhetoric*, focusing on his taxonomy of rhetorical tropes used by speakers to sway public opinion.[3] Aristotle classified dozens of tropes according to their unique effects on the audience, from metaphor and metonymy

---

[1] For instance, Berners-Lee and Cailliau 1990; Rada 1991; Wang and Rada 1998.
[2] See Scott 1994a, b; McQuarrie and Mick 1996, 2003a, b; Scott and Batra 2003; Jeong 2008; Phillips and McQuarrie 2010.
[3] For example, Mick and Politi 1989; Scott 1994a; McQuarrie and Mick 1996, 1999, 2003a, b; Scott and Batra 2003; Jeong 2008; Phillips and McQuarrie 2010.

to ellipsis and zeugma. As a result, much of the literature on metaphor in marketing focuses on the effects of individual tropes on advertising persuasion.

Since trope theorists limit analysis to the single ad, they forego consideration of the strategic effects of the ad's tropes on the brand image and competitive edge. They take for granted that persuasion, rather than branding, is the "distinctive feature of advertising" (Phillips and McQuarrie 2004: 113). Thus, rather than question the limits of trope theory for marketing, writers such as McQuarrie and colleagues devote a research stream to refining their methodology.

Under the aegis of persuasion, trope theorists examine how consumers process tropes (Phillips 1997, 2000), and track changes in the rhetorical style of print ads change over time (Phillips and McQuarrie 2002). They develop typologies of tropes based on their semantic structure, i.e. similarity or contiguity, degree of complexity, i.e. metaphor or simile, and medium of communication, i.e. visuals vs. language.[4] For example, metaphor structures dissonance between words, as in "my truck is my husband"; between visual elements (Jeong 2008), as in Comcast's image of a large potato resting on a couch, i.e. "couch potato," and between word and image, as in Nike's "I am the bullet in the chamber," superimposed over an image of Oscar Pistorius running.

If one agrees that metaphors are simply deviations, one also assumes two basic principles of trope theory. First, that metaphors are frivolous supplements to the literal meaning of things. Second, that metaphors are transgressions of linguistic code because they introduce ambiguity, nuance, and figurative play into discourse. This chapter sets out to prove that metaphor is not frivolous, because it plays an important role in symbolic consumption, cultural branding, and integrated media strategy. Nor is metaphor "deviant" by introducing ambiguity into discourse. On the contrary, metaphor exposes the inherent instability and polyvalence of meaning in semiotic practice.

From Trope Theory to Metaphorical Discourse

Although striking metaphors increase media breakthrough and memorability in advertising campaigns, metaphor's impact on brand value is broader and deeper than the effects of any single trope. The capacity to make metaphors is the cornerstone of symbolic consumption, where consumers use goods as social markers and emotional rewards (Douglas and Isherwood 2002 [1979]). Brands are metaphors because they substitute products for emotional benefits such as status, identity, and even relationship.[5] Brand metaphors sustain the

---

[4] See McQuarrie and Mick 1992, 1996, 2003a, b; Phillips and McQuarrie 2004.
[5] See D. Aaker 1991; Fournier 1998; J. Aaker et al. 2004.

brand message from one medium to the next in the multimedia campaigns and form bridges between the brand heritage, cultural trends, and advertising semiotics.

For discourse theory—a "good" metaphor anchors analogy in the context of the brand's legacy and competitive environment. In contrast, trope theory focuses on the rhetorical structure of isolated ads, which may obscure potential conflicts between the trope's meaning and the brand positioning. A case in point is the following metaphor in a recent ad for Nationwide Insurance (The McKinney Advertising Agency 2013).

What's Wrong with this Metaphor?

In a 2013 survey, Nationwide Insurance Company found that 25 percent of consumers refer to their cars as "their babies." To leverage this insight in advertising for the brand, they developed an advertising campaign that used special effects to substitute a car in the ad with an image of a large baby (Figure 3.1). They motivate the comparison on the basis of the shared characteristic, "precious," referred to in voice-over, where a brand spokesman says "What's precious to you is precious to us."

Situational cues transfer car-like meanings to the baby. The man parks his "baby" in the garage, he sprays it with a hose in the driveway, and finds it crashed into a fire hydrant.[6]

Figure 3.1. A Visual Metaphor for Nationwide Insurance

---

[6] The ad can be viewed on YouTube: <http://www.youtube.com/watch?v=ryNtVK55OUY>.

The Nationwide ad provides an object lesson in the limitations of trope theory for creative strategy and illustrates the importance of context on the meaning of metaphor. First, in contrast with verbal metaphors, visual metaphors resist assimilation into the logic of visual discourse because of the stubborn materiality of the image. Whereas a verbal metaphor would attach baby-like nuances to the car, in this ad, the baby never ceases to be a baby. As a result, the ad does not transfer baby-like meanings to the car, but transfers car-like meanings to the baby.

Furthermore, though tropes like this may add shock value and memorability to the isolated campaign, it does not necessarily support the brand's historical positioning and message. Although the metaphor could be viewed as a visual gag, it also dehumanizes the baby and borders on cruelty, because it places the baby in unsafe situations. The baby is sprayed with cold water, stored in the garage, and put in harm's way. Next, though the car/baby trope grabs our attention, it does not support the Nationwide Insurance brand legacy. In fact, treating a baby like a car may actually tarnish Nationwide's core equities in family values and driver safety.

The Nationwide example illustrates the potential risks of trope theory for brand equity. It represents an all-too-common creative strategy aimed at grabbing attention in the cluttered media environment while ignoring its effects on the brand.

From Poetic Sign to Poetic Function

By defining metaphor as a supplement to and deviation from the proper sense, trope theorists assign a kind of transcendent stability to linguistic code—or what some would call the "standard meaning" of discourse. By assuming that metaphor is a supplement to and even a violation of the code, trope theorists obscure the inherent ambiguity and volatility of the standard meaning in everyday practice.

In contrast to trope theory, discourse theory acknowledges the role of metaphor in the very production of discourse. As a cognitive operation, metaphor is responsible for symbolic consumption, brand meaning, the brand relationship, and the integrity of hypertext marketing campaigns.

The discourse theory of metaphor has evolved over the years from a focus on poetic signs to the poetic function of discourse. It draws upon the basic concepts of structural linguistics, but moves emphasis from the logic of the sign to the potential creativity of discourse.

Saussure emphasized that codes, rather than Nature, structure signs. Consequently, the relationship between signifier and signified in the linguistic sign is arbitrary. For example, there is no intrinsic association between the sounds /car/ and the idea of a car. By emphasizing the arbitrariness of the sign, Saussure aimed to logically separate the structure of meaning from any affinity with Nature and advanced the notion of language as a system of codes. The arbitrariness of the sign also focused structural linguistics on the centering effects of the code on the inchoate flow of human thought. However, the arbitrariness principle also obscures the creative potential of active discourse, which puts into play tensions between the meaning of signs and reference to the context. Although Saussure shed light on the mimetic relation of words to their meanings in anagrams (see Starobinski 1980), it would fall to the Russian Formalist Roman Jakobson to develop a theory of the poetic sign that both transcends linguistic code and relies upon the context for its precise meaning.

THE POETIC SIGN

Poetic signs contrast with linguistic signs inasmuch as each term of the poetic sign is itself a discrete sign, i.e. "car" and "baby," each with its own field of associations (Figure 3.2). As a result, poetic signs such as metaphors do not simply replace one sign for another, i.e. "baby" for "car" but superimpose one semantic field over another in the mind.

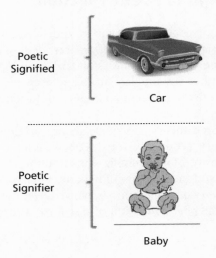

Figure 3.2. The Poetic Sign

In the statement, "My car is my baby," the poetic sign assembles a complex system of similarities and contrasts between car-like and baby-like characteristics. It is up to metaphorical *discourse* to structure the precise links between the two fields of meaning by highlighting similarities over contrasts between the two. There is no intrinsic similarity between cars and babies; the association is entirely motivated by consumers' emotional attachment to their cars.

Making metaphors changes the focus of rhetoric from the poetic sign to the poetic function of discourse. The poetic function contributes to the intrinsic ambiguity and creativity of meaning production because it keeps in play the tensions between poetic signifier and signified, increasing the semantic range of metaphorical discourse.

THE POETIC FUNCTION OF DISCOURSE

Roman Jakobson introduced Saussurian linguistics into Russia in the 1910s in the formative years of the Russian Formalist Movement and spawned the structuralist movement in linguistics and poetics across the globe as he moved from Moscow to Prague, then Paris and the United States. In the notion of the poetic function, Jakobson (1960) identified the intrinsic creativity of meaning production, which accounts for the "thoroughgoing symbolic, multiplex, and polysemantic essence" of ordinary discourse (p. 370).

In order to analyze the broader poetic function of discourse, Jakobson (1990 [1956]) traced the basic structures of rhetoric, discourse, and cognition to two primary rhetorical operations: metaphor and metonymy. By shifting focus from rhetorical tropes to the formal operations structuring discourse, Jakobson not only identified universal characteristics of thought and representation; he also provided means of accounting for the discursive structure of non-verbal media as cinema, which create meaning without the aid of grammatical or syntactical codes (Table 3.1).

By privileging the two "master tropes," metaphor and metonymy, Jakobson did not intend to eliminate the other tropes from structural poetics, but to

Table 3.1. A Discourse Model of Rhetoric

	REPRESENTATION	
Figure	metaphor	metonymy
Relationship	similarity	contiguity
Discourse	paradigm	syntagm
	COGNITION	
Mental Operation	selection	combination
Psychic Drive	condensation	displacement

find a unifying binary that accounts for the cooperation of rhetorical, discursive, and cognitive processes in meaning production. Metaphorical operations structure rhetorical figures based on analogy and structure the axis of selection and substitution in paradigms. Metonymical operations structure rhetorical figures based on contiguity, the combination and alignment of elements in statements and account for the condensation of similar terms in creative thought. In this general binary, Jakobson accounts for the dialectical implication of cognition and representation in meaning production and challenges the limited view of rhetoric as "artful deviation."

The poetic function extended the role of rhetoric beyond its decorative effects in poetry and led to inquiry about its role in the organization of the psychic drives and the production of discourse. The implication of mind and meaning also accounts for the dialectical relationship between culture and consumption.

The Psychic Drives

Lacan (1977 [1953]) extended Jakobson's binary to Freudian (1965 [1899]) psychoanalysis. Lacan proposed that the psychic drives of condensation and displacement structure the unconscious the same way metaphor and metonymy structure discourse. He also suggests that the drives not only structure the strange organization of dream thoughts but account for the psychological and emotional dimensions of symbol formation. By associating metaphor with psychic condensation and metonymy with psychic displacement, Lacan's theory accounts for the underlying psychological motivation of rhetoric that moves thought from the realm of the literal meaning to the realm of the consumers' imaginary, symbolic associations with their possessions.

In the next figure I illustrate the complexity of metaphorical discourse because it accounts for the role of psychic projection in the production of symbols (Figure 3.3). Cars contrast with babies in terms of *material* oppositions such as inanimate/animate, powerful/vulnerable, and automated/living. However, consumers bridge these contrasts by means of projective identification. In the statement, "my car is my baby," metonymy, in the form of psychic displacement, moves the focus from the material dimension of cars to their symbolic relationship to consumers and motivates the personification of cars in consumers' minds. Personification works best in language, because the mental concepts associated with cars and babies merge in the consumer's imagination.

In comparison with verbal metaphors, visual metaphors tend to resist assimilation in the imagination due to the stubborn materiality of the image. Silent movie directors use editing or *montage* to make comparisons between two shots. In *City Lights* (1931), for example, Chaplain communicates the fresh beauty of a flower girl by joining a close-up on a rose and a close-up

"My car is my baby."

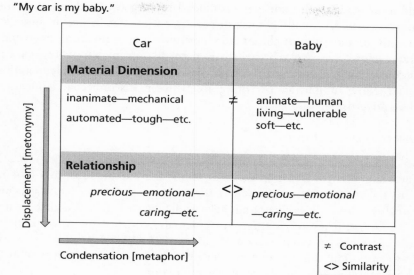

Figure 3.3. The Play of Difference and Similarity in Metaphor

of her face (see Oswald 1981). The metaphor does not jar the imagination because it is motivated by a metonymy joining the rose and the heroine in the story who sells roses on the street.

In contrast to the flower metaphor, the baby metaphor in the Nationwide ad image magnifies disjunctures between car and baby and disrupts the realism of the image. The baby is three times larger than the man, which is reminiscent of the giant characters in science fiction films. Although the voice-over suggests a bridge between baby and car in the notion of "precious," the ad does not personify the car, but treats the baby like an inanimate, mechanical object, not a precious object. They place the baby in dangerous, car-like situations, including a car accident.

These stylistic shortcomings have more than esthetic interest for marketers, because they conflict with the brand's historical equities in safety, reliability, and family values. Furthermore, the strange visuals jar with the brand's traditional focus on realism. They remind one of Nationwide's competitors, Progressive and GEICO, brands that consumers associate with weird humor and visual gags. For Nationwide, however, weird humor may only erode the brand's credibility.

Strange metaphors are not new to advertising. Advertisers use them to break through the cluttered media environment and create awareness of the brand. In the best cases, weird metaphors also support the brand's traditional positioning and esthetic style. For instance, GEICO's talking pig and gecko distinguish the brand from the industry leaders, State Farm and Allstate, by adding warmth and humor to a traditionally boring and staid industry. They are consistent with GEICO's use of parody, satire, and fantasy in historical advertising and support the brand's positioning as a practical, everyman's brand. However, even weird rhetoric demands an anchor in the logic of discourse. In the next section, I discuss the role of rhetorical operations to structure an illusion of contiguity between disconnected contexts in video advertising.

Discursive Structures

As discussed in Chapter 1, syntactical and grammatical codes regulate the linear alignment of words on the syntagmatic axis and the substitution of one term for another on the paradigmatic axis of discourse. In contrast, non-verbal systems, such as cinema and television advertising, have no fixed syntax or grammar. They rely entirely on cinematic codes structuring similarity and contiguity in visual discourse (Metz 1981 [1977]). Cinema semiotics draws important implications from Jakobson's (1990 [1956]) theory of meta-phorical and metonymical operations in discourse.

For example, the cross-cut is an editing code that creates an illusion of a single, continuous space from a series of discontinuous shots in a film sequence. The code is based upon a visual metonymy structuring continuity between a character looking off screen and a return shot of the object of their look. The logic of continuity editing depends upon two elements: a formal metonymy linking the character looking with the object of their look, on the syntagmatic axis, and the match between the spatial contexts of each shot, on the paradigmatic axis.

In farce, science fiction, and surrealism (Oswald 1981), the logic of the cross-cut can also force an illusion of continuity between the most implausible elements of visual discourse. In GEICO's "Pyramid" ad (the Martin Agency

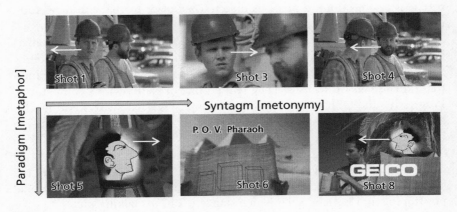

Figure 3.4. The Pyramid Sequence

2013), for instance, a pattern of cross-cuts forces a false continuity between the contemporary space of the story and a completely discontinuous sequence in ancient Egypt (Figure 3.4). Man A makes the ridiculous statement to Man B, "Did you know that the Pyramids were a mistake?" The image cuts to man B, dubious, looking off-screen. The "return shot" cuts to a Pharaoh in ancient Egypt, checking out a blueprint that calls for rectangular, not pyramidal, structures. By forcing an implausible spatial contiguity between the two disparate contexts—the workers on a modern street and a Pharaoh in ancient Egypt—the editing motivates the absurdity and humor of the gag. Above is a summary of the sequence (Figure 3.4). [The actor playing the Pharaoh did not give permission to use his image in shots 5 and 8, so it has been replaced by a stock image.]

Shot Summary of the GEICO "Pyramid" Sequence

#1. Man A looks screen left at a GEICO ad atop a taxi. Man A looks right at Man B, says:
"Did you know that fifteen minutes could save you 15% or more on car insurance?"
#2. Man B looks left, dismisses the man, says: "Everybody knows that."
#3. Man A looks right, says: "Well, did you know the ancient pyramids were actually a mistake?"
#4. Man B looks left, dubious. CUT to a Pharaoh in ancient Egypt.
#5. Pharaoh looks right. In the next shot, not shown here, he looks down, as if to the next shot.
#6. Shot of the blueprint of square structures, Pharaoh's point of view, matches the eye-level of the spectator's gaze.
#7–8. Pharaoh sighs, looks screen left toward his servant.

The complete sequence of shots shows how continuity editing weaves the nonsensical statement about square pyramids into the logic of the ad narrative and also increases the force of the gag by matching the spectator's look with the look of the Pharaoh as he realizes the "mistake" on the blueprint.

Culture and Consumption

Linguists such as Jakobson (1990 [1956]), Lakoff and Johnson (1980), and Danesi (2013) have shown that rhetorical operations account for the transfer of meaning between culture and signs, because rhetoric has a cognitive as well as formal function. Rhetorical operations also motivate the cultural meaning of brands. From the perspective of semiotics, consumer culture is not a metaphysical entity (McCracken 1986), but a system of codes organizing the meanings and rituals associated with a product category or consumer segment (see Eco 1979: 66). The brand system consists of the long-standing

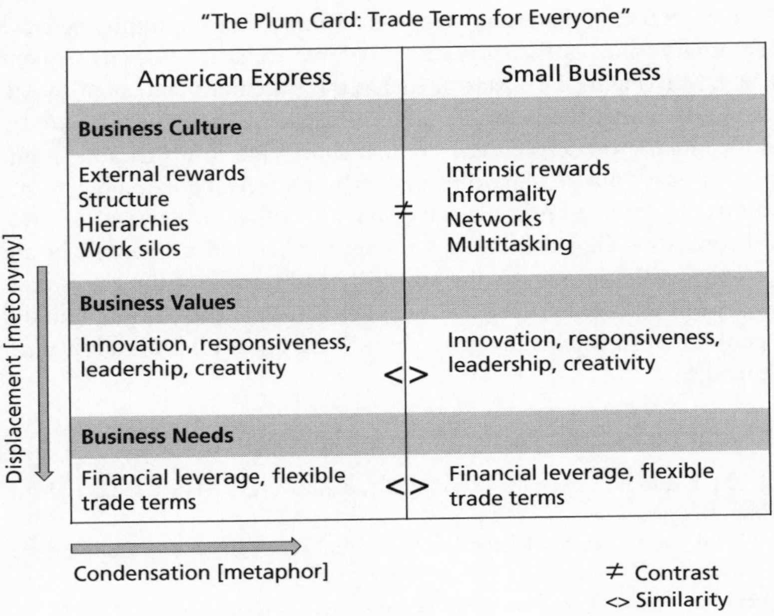

"The Plum Card: Trade Terms for Everyone"

American Express	Small Business
Business Culture	
External rewards Structure Hierarchies Work silos ≠	Intrinsic rewards Informality Networks Multitasking
Business Values	
Innovation, responsiveness, leadership, creativity <>	Innovation, responsiveness, leadership, creativity
Business Needs	
Financial leverage, flexible trade terms <>	Financial leverage, flexible trade terms

Displacement [metonymy]

Condensation [metaphor]

≠ Contrast
<> Similarity

Figure 3.5. The Brand Metaphor: Between Culture and Consumption

equities associated with the brand name over time. To find a relevant cultural positioning for brands, the semiotic research process identifies similarities and contiguities joining the brand legacy and emergent trends in consumer culture. The research design includes qualitative research with consumers and an audit of the brand identity as represented in the brand's historical advertising. I discuss cultural branding at length in Chapter 4.

For example, American Express commissioned semiotic research to develop a brand extension strategy for a new financial product targeted to small business owners. The research design included ethnographic research with small business owners and an audit of the American Express brand, as communicated in corporate communications and historical advertising. As shown in the grid in Figure 3.5, American Express faced the challenge of finding common ground between the brand's corporate culture and the entrepreneurial culture of small business.

The primary brand differed from small business culture on the basis of binaries such as external versus intrinsic rewards, structure versus informality, hierarchies versus networks, and work silos versus multitasking. The American Express brand identifies with small business (association by similarity), because they share business values. American Express also serves small business (association by contiguity) by offering financial leverage and flexible trade terms for making credit card payments.

The tagline plays an important role in new product development because it anchors the brand in a brand metaphor that bridges distances between the primary brand and the extension. The brand metaphor acts as a catalyst for condensing the primary brand and the extension in a new cultural space. The tagline for the American Express Plum card, "Trade terms for everyone," communicates the shared business needs of two business entities—big Blue and the small business owner—while maintaining the distinctive identity of small business.

METAPHOR AS VERB

By expanding the scope of rhetoric from the poetic sign to the relations between figures and discourse, Jakobson highlighted a discursive function of metaphor that transcends the isolated trope and forges connections between disparate fields of meaning, between symbols and the unconscious, and between culture and consumption. By highlighting the poetic function of everyday discourse, Jakobson also acknowledged the intrinsic polyvalence and instability of meaning and subjectivity in semiotic practice.

Jakobson's poetics also fostered debates in post-structural linguistics (Benveniste 1971 [1966]), psychoanalysis (Lacan 1977 [1953]), and philosophy (Ricoeur 2003 [1975]) that build upon the underlying principle that metaphor an act of predication that constructs, rather than accessorizes, discourse. Ricoeur (2003 [1975]) brings the discussion of metaphor full circle from Aristotle to post-structuralism when he reminds us that the Aristotle, in the *Poetics*, referred to metaphor as a verb, a mental operation, and a figure of speech. Quoting Aristotle, "The greatest thing by far is to be a master of metaphor...to metaphorize well implies an intuitive perception of the similarity in dissimilars" (p. 25).

The Brand Metaphor

In a very general sense, brands are metaphors because they satisfy the emotional needs of consumers for things like self-esteem, social acceptance, and relationship by means of symbols (D. Aaker 1991; J. Aaker 1997; Fournier 1998). Brand metaphors are positioning statements in brief. They transcend the isolated trope in advertising because they represent the system of meanings associated with the brand's identity and heritage. When Coke (2011) invited consumers to "open happiness," they not only replaced the word "bottle" with the trope "happiness" but also sustained and supported Coke's historical positioning as a lifestyle beverage that promises the "good life," "smiles," and the "real thing."

Metaphorical discourse is a building block of brand management because it structures the associations consumers make between the brand name and the brand's symbolic equities, such as the brand story, image, and personality. Furthermore, the capacity to "metaphorize"—to make metaphorical connections between dissimilar things—enables consumers to build brand relationships or use brands to resolve, symbolically, their emotional needs. When someone exclaims, "I love my Audi," they draw upon this capacity to personify the brand and form a symbolic relationship to it.

Metaphor, in conjunction with metonymy, also structures the logic of non-verbal discourse and transfers meaning between the brand heritage, the culture of consumers, and representation in promotional advertising. Brand metaphors reflect the rhetorical complexity of the brand system and its potential to generate new products, media campaigns, and markets. They also provide a compass for moving the brand message and engaging consumer attention across complicated, multimedia marketing campaigns.

Researchers such as Zaltman (1996) have used metaphor elicitation techniques for many years to probe deeply into consumers' imagination and gain insights into their perceptions of brands. In the next section, I propose a distinctive approach to metaphor elicitation and rhetorical analysis that not only applies to existing brands, but also forms the basis for developing brand associations for new products that are still in the development stage. The case in point concerns a project for the Ford Motor Company where the Marketing Semiotics company used metaphor elicitation techniques to define the semiotic dimensions of the subcompact SUV category and identify a unique cultural space for the U204, a prototype for the new vehicle which would become the Ford Escape.

Case: Launching the Ford Escape

In 1998, the J. Walter Thompson agency in Detroit commissioned strategic semiotic research to develop a consumer insights platform for positioning a new, subcompact SUV from Ford, the U204, a prototype for the Ford Escape. The vehicle was targeted to women at two critical transitions in the family life cycle: new mothers and empty nesters whose children were transitioning out of the home. Respondents were screened on the basis of attitudinal characteristics they shared with Ford loyal buyers.

The case illustrates how metaphor elicitation techniques can be used to identify a positioning for a brand that had no name, no advertising, and no prior research, in an emerging, ill-defined automotive category—the crossover. The resilience and sustainability of the Escape brand positioning for almost fifteen years reflects the reliability of this approach for brand management.

THE CROSSOVER CATEGORY

Jeep created the subcompact category with the Cherokee in the 1980s, followed by Honda's CR-V and the Toyota RAV-4. At the time of the study, the subcompact category straddled the car and truck categories. Although the subcompact was built on a car rather than a truck chassis, the category was trading on its associations with larger, truck-based sports-utility vehicles such as the Ford Explorer and the Chevrolet Blazer, rather than leveraging their advantages as nimbler, safer, and more economical vehicles.

With the RAV-4 and CR-V, Toyota and Honda took a somewhat different tack and positioned the crossover as a lifestyle vehicle that combines the informality of the SUV with the agility and safety of a car. The crossover has gained momentum in recent years, as the big, tough, and masculine automotive culture of 1990s has given way to the metrosexual, socially responsible, digital culture of Millennials who were coming of age in the 2000s (Strauss and Howe 2000). In addition, rollover accidents, environmental activism, and rising cost of gasoline created demand for safer, more fuel-efficient and economical SUVs.

As with any brand extension, the new product positioning would build upon synergies between Ford's global brand positioning, "No Boundaries," and unmet needs of consumers in the crossover category. The crossover is a kind of metaphor for the lifestyles of Ford's consumer target who were transitioning between life stages. At one end of the spectrum, young mothers were trading their independence and sports cars for diapers and SUVs. At the other end, empty nesters were trading their station wagons and large SUVs for more self-directed lives and smaller cars.

In the metaphor elicitation exercises, respondents consistently imagined an ideal brand that would satisfy their needs for self-expression, independence, and personal space by means of forward-looking engineering, styling, and messaging. Although their active lifestyles were more suited to the informality, engineering, and storage capacity of the SUV, respondents rejected the standard SUV as a family vehicle rather than a personal space. Empty nesting women even refused to share their vehicles with spouses and teenage drivers. Their ideal vehicle would move them through this life stage transition by resolving the tensions associated with change.

THE RESEARCH DESIGN

The research design called for an advertising audit of competitive brands, focus groups with current owners of subcompact SUVs, and ethnographic interviews with consumers in their homes. The focus group protocol was laddered (Reynolds and Gutman 1988) to move respondents from direct questioning about lifestyle choices and brand preferences to projective techniques that elicited free associations, fantasies, and consumer metaphors. Metaphor elicitation was also incorporated into the ethnographic interviews, particularly in relation to stimuli provided by respondents, such as photo albums.

Laddering

Laddering not only structures the interview sequence from low to high emotional intensity, but builds the findings from one phase of the interview upon insights gained in the previous phase. For this reason, laddered questioning demands the moderator's creative participation. For example, metaphors are usually motivated by metonymies linking them to something in the speaker's environment (Genette 1972b). The skilled moderator probes respondents to expand upon a metaphor such as "my car is my baby," by linking it back to earlier consumer statements and observations. For example, babies may be a focal point in respondents' lives and may represent positive as well as negative emotions.

I present a more detailed discussion of focus group design and ethnographic methodologies in Chapter 6. For the purposes of this chapter, I will focus here on the metaphor elicitation techniques used in the study.

Metaphor Elicitation

The metaphor elicitation exercises highlighted the powerful symbolic role that cars play in consumers' lives. Cars lift them up during a long commute. They empower them to move about, to get away, and to explore. Cars bring people together and share in the most important events in consumers' lives. Cars are lived environments that drivers personalize with music, scents, and styling. These observations confirm Nationwide Insurance's findings, mentioned above, that consumers tend to form deep personal attachments to their cars.

Elicitation techniques such as sentence completion, image association, and storytelling brought to the surface a consistent set of brand associations. The metaphorical associations consumers made with the CR-V, the RAV-5, and the Jeep Cherokee reflected their perceptions of the distinctive positionings and personas of each brand.

The Competitive Set

The competitive brand positionings described below summarize brand perceptions that were consistent across sixteen focus groups and twenty-four ethnographic interviews (Table 3.2).

Table 3.2. Competitive Analysis: The Subcompact Category

	Cherokee	RAV- 4	CR-V	Brand X
Brand Metaphor	Cowboy. Rugged, rough ride. Masculine, and adventurous	"Cosmo girl." Strong, fashion conscious, independent, feminist	Engineer. Gender-neutral, smart, practical, and reliable	Small business owner or charity organizer. Socially responsible, self-directed, conservative, intelligent, and stylish

Respondents personified the Jeep Cherokee as a rugged, rough-riding, masculine, and adventurous cowboy. Jeep's iconic history as a World War II military vehicle shaped the brand's rugged persona and also set the tone for the off-road market in the 1990s. Historical advertising shows mud-splattered Jeeps navigating rugged terrain and challenges consumers to leave the beaten path, camp out, and "Play Dirty."

In contrast to the Jeep, Toyota targeted the RAV-4 to independent, even feminist women who expressed their femininity in the design features of the vehicle. Respondents personified the Toyota RAV-4 woman as the "Cosmo girl," based on the *Cosmopolitan Magazine* ethos—strong, fashion-conscious, and independent. The curvy, feminine styling, bright colors, interior comfort, and easy handling are testimony to the brand's claim that "It's one thing to climb a mountain. It's quite another to look good when you do it" (Agency: Saatchi & Saatchi 2001).

The Honda CR-V emphasizes functional attributes such as superior engineering, durability, and safety, and asks consumers to ponder the question, "Where would we be without engineers?" (Agency: Wieden & Kennedy 2003). Respondents personified the CR-V as a gender-neutral, practical, and reliable engineer. The boxy design and functional colors reinforce the brand's focus on rational benefits.

The Ideal Brand

The metaphor elicitation exercises provided a model for developing new concepts for the U-204. At the end of each exercise, respondents were asked to create their own personal brand, i.e. Suzie's brand that would satisfy needs that current brands did not satisfy. By associating words, pictures, and stories with the unnamed brand, respondents generated metaphors and personifications that differentiated their ideal brands from current offerings in the subcompact category. The semiotic analysis of the results exposed a consistent set of brand associations. The ideal brand might be male or female, and either a small business owner or charity organizer. He or she would be socially responsible, self-directed, conservative, independent, intelligent, and stylish. Respondents wanted design options that would enable them to express their personal esthetic and style.

I present below a summary of the strategic analysis used to translate research findings into a strategic positioning for the brand that would become the Ford Escape.

The Strategic Semiotic Analysis

Contrary to expectations, research identified a unique brand positioning for the U-204 that ran counter to the family-centered positioning of the popular Ford Explorer. The positioning nonetheless aligned consumer needs with Ford's "No Boundaries" campaign, stood out from competitors, and claimed a bolder, more assertive definition for the crossover category. To tease out the complex intersections between the Ford brand, the crossover category, and the unmet needs of consumers, researchers mapped these dimensions on the semiotic square.

THE SEMIOTIC SQUARE

The semiotic square has been aptly called the "map of logical possibilities" (Katilius-Boydstun 1990) because it deconstructs local binaries such as Good versus Evil into relations of contraries, contradiction, and implication. Since the semiotic square expands the range of potential meanings associated with a cultural binary, such as [Car/Truck], it can be used to find metaphorical associations between apparently disparate dimensions of a product category. For example, by implicating the [SUV/Car] binary in its contrary, [not-SUV/not-Car], the semiotic square makes room for a new automotive category, the crossover, which merges equities from each category (Figure 3.6).

As a system of logical possibilities, the semiotic square is a useful tool for creative ideation. The research team may generate numerous concepts from the original analysis, submit the concepts to focus groups for evaluation, and continue breaking them down through the binary analysis until they find a concept that fits. The semiotic analysis also has the potential to map intersections between multiple cultural variables on a single grid.

For example, to identify a distinctive cultural space for the U-204 within the SUV market, researchers deconstructed the rhetorical associations linking the automotive term, crossover, to respondents' transitional life stage. The metaphor is motivated by the idea that the women were all "crossing over" from one life stage to another. However, this metaphor does not completely describe the small SUV because "crossing over" signifies movement from one static point to another, as between the two sides of a river, rather than ongoing movement. Likewise, the crossover category itself was static in 1998 because it had not yet found a coherent identity in the SUV category.

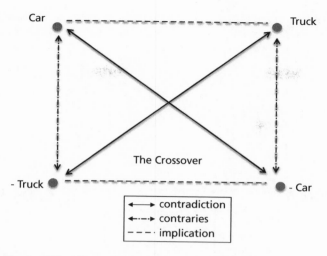

Figure 3.6. The Semiotic Dimensions of the Automotive Category

POSITIONING FORD IN THE CROSSOVER CATEGORY

Researchers identified a distinct rhetorical space for the U-204 within the Crossover category by aligning the Crossover/Cross Over metaphor with the dynamic, forward-thinking theme of Ford's "No Boundaries" global positioning. They then mapped a binary analysis of the verb, "to cross over," against the verb, "keep moving," on the semiotic square (Figure 3.7).

I draw attention to the right quadrant of the semiotic square (Figure 3.8) and the binary of implication, [Keep Moving/−Cross Over]. In the semiotic analysis, the process of negation does not cancel or diminish the negated term of a binary, such as the "Cross Over" metaphor, but changes the meaning of the term by framing it in a new context, a context defined by the other term of the binary. The "Keep Moving" framework shifts the focus of "crossing over" from a static movement between two life stages to a moment in consumers' forward-moving life projects. This shift in focus aligned the Ford "No Boundaries" positioning with the unmet consumer needs identified in the research. It also opens up a new rhetorical space for the crossover category that integrates the personality of the truck-based SUV with the agility and comfort of the car-based crossover.

By expanding the range of possible relationships between variables in a category, the semiotic square has important implications for identifying a distinctive rhetorical positioning for brands. From an automotive standpoint, the negation of the "Cross Over" metaphor does not mean that Ford repudiates the crossover category per se. Instead, the implication of [−Cross Over] in [Moving Forward] opens up a rhetorical space within the category that is *both* a "crossover" from an engineering standpoint, but not a crossover in the current (at that time 1998) static definition of the term in the marketplace.

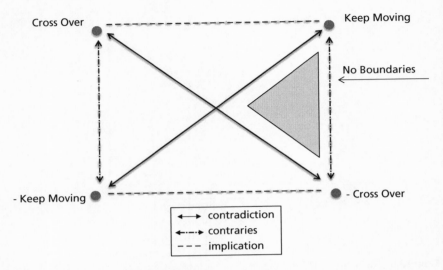

Figure 3.7. Ford's Rhetorical Space in the Crossover Category

A DISTINCT RHETORICAL POSITIONING FOR THE ESCAPE

In addition to communicating stasis rather than movement, "crossing over" also bifurcates the transitional life stage into either/or identities, which would force one to choose between self and family, or between past and present identities. To position the new product as a vehicle for moving consumers through the life stage, these tensions had to be integrated into a bold and coherent brand positioning for the U-204 within the crossover market. Researchers therefore superimposed the [Self/Family] binary over the [Cross Over/Keep Moving] binary on another semiotic square (Figure 3.8).

The analysis begins with the upper right hand quadrant of the grid. A binary of implication, [Crossover/− Keep Moving], is superimposed over the [Self/Family] binary. In this cultural space, "crossing over" means from point A to point B, but not beyond. It is "not-moving." For consumers in transition, it also means choosing between Self and Family, leaving behind some part of their identities in order to move into the next life stage. Researchers naturally moved away from this quadrant for positioning the new Ford brand.

Next attention is drawn to the upper right quadrant of the category. The binary structure that implicates "Keep Moving" in the negative term, [−Cross Over], reflects broader tensions within the crossover category and consumer segment in the areas of mobility and personal identity. By aligning the brand extension with Ford's dynamic "No Boundaries" strategy, researchers challenged the current association of crossing over and crossovers with stasis and

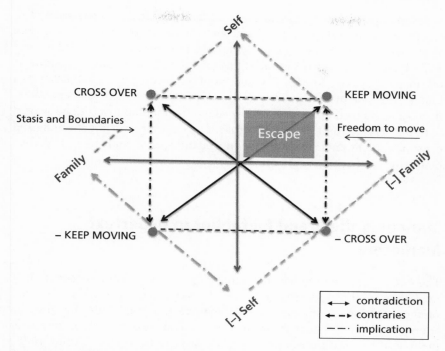

Figure 3.8. A Bold Rhetorical Positioning for the Escape

boundaries, introducing equities normally associated with larger, truck-based SUVs. Next, "Keep Moving" is also superimposed over the [Self/−Family] binary.

As said before, negation does not mean repudiation. The implication of Self in the negative proposition, [−Family], does not mean that one must reject family to assert oneself. On the contrary, just as the negation of the Cross Over metaphor challenged current perceptions of the crossover category, the [Self/−Family] binary challenges rigid interpretations of Family as binding and limiting. This cultural space integrates the Family concept into consumers' self-directed life projects. It also suggests that the new brand is gender neutral as far as the [Self/Family] binary is concerned, since both men and women experience tensions between their commitments to family and personal goals.

IMPLICATIONS FOR SEMIOTIC RESEARCH PRACTICE

In summary, the semiotic analysis exposed a distinct rhetorical space for Ford in the crossover category that aligned the Escape with Ford's global "No Boundaries" positioning, emergent trends in the automotive category, and the unmet needs of consumers for power, agility, and self-directed, integrated lives. Over the years, the Escape has followed through on its commitment to forward-looking, relevant branding and engineering. The Escape leads the

Ford line-up for innovation in areas such as hybrid technologies, mobile communications, safety, and fuel efficiency. It currently targets men, as well as women, and is one of the best-selling cars in the class on the road.

The case also has broad implications for the role of semiotics in strategic research and creative strategy. The success of the Ford Escape was built upon a brand metaphor that emerged from creative research with consumers, rather than being imposed upon the brand by attention-grabbing advertising rhetoric.

In the next section I focus on the role of metaphor in moving meaning and consumer attention across multiple media and spatial contexts in hypertext marketing.

Managing the Brand Metaphor in Hypertext Marketing

The new media environment has shifted the site of meaning production in marketing from the advertising text to the movement of meaning and consumer attention in the multimedia hypertext. It demands, in turn, an approach to rhetoric that transcends the individual trope and accounts for the role of rhetorical operations to form passages from one medium to the next, one media event to the other, in hypertext marketing.

The Hypertext

Hypertext marketing differs from traditional integrated marketing strategy (Schultz and Schultz 1998) inasmuch as it not only integrates a single brand message across multiple media, but draws upon interactive platforms that modify and even generate new brand messages. The marketing hypertext actively engages consumers in the production of the brand message, which in turn provides content for new advertising, which then leads to more consumer participation, and so on. It is modeled after the web-based hypertext model of user browsing, a dynamic, multimedia, and inter-nodal movement of semantic links within the worldwide web network.[7]

Hypertext marketing has the advantage of putting marketers in direct contact with consumers, but it also poses challenges because it transfers some control over the brand metaphor to consumers and the vicissitudes of the social media. Hypertext campaigns succeed to the extent that they translate the brand metaphor into actionable, performative media events that stimulate consumer

---

[7] Berners-Lee and Cailliau 1990; Rada 1991; Wang and Rada 1998; Neumüller 2000.

participation in a shared, integrated media activity. Rhetorical operations play an important role in this process because they create semantic links that integrate the brand metaphor across media and over time (Neumüller 2000). Spatial metaphors play a particular role in constructing links between various media in the virtual space of the campaign.

RHETORICAL OPERATIONS AND COGNITION

As a mental operation, metaphor condenses disparate meanings, emotions, and spaces around a single idea or positioning (Genette 1972b). For example, Coke's "open happiness" metaphor is based upon a series of metonymies that form continuities between the bottle, the fizz, and the brand experience in a dense semantic system. Rhetorical operations not only enable consumers to make sense of hypertext campaigns but also have the potential to *generate* hypertext messaging.

Hypertext marketers tap into consumer creativity by unpacking the rhetorical associations condensed in the brand metaphor. A case in point is Red Bull's Flugtag campaign, a sponsored event that motivates and is in turn motivated by consumer engagement in the brand at multiple points of media contact.

SPATIAL METAPHORS

The discourse theory of rhetoric accounts for the cognitive processes that enable consumers to integrate disparate semantic fields together in meta-phorical discourse. They also structure a sense of contiguity between disparate time and space contexts in hypertext campaigns. Spatial metaphors structure pathways from one text to another, one medium to another, and one con-sumer space to another, keeping in play the movement of meaning between texts, consumers, and mediums over the course of the campaign. Rhetorical operations assure the continuity of brand meaning across the many stages of the campaign. They also integrate the different spatial dimensions of the hyper-text by bridging distances between discrete media events. In this way, hypertext rhetoric employs the same strategies as spatial metaphors in literature. In Proust, for instance, spatial metaphors collapse distances between the space-time of the narrator's immediate perceptions and his memories of places and times past, along the paths of similarity and contiguity (see Genette 1982 [1966]).

The Red Bull Flugtag Campaign

Red Bull's annual Flugtag event invites consumers to form teams and compete in the construction and deployment of "flying" machines in sponsored events throughout the world. The campaign takes place over several months and integrates the brand message across multiple media, including print and television ads, direct marketing, the company website, sponsored events in real time and space, and social media marketing. The campaign engages consumers—as actors and spectators—in the brand culture of extreme professional sports, cutting edge rock music, and risqué humor by leveraging rhetorical associations between the Flugtag event and the central brand metaphor, "Red Bull gives you wings." The event literally gives wings to participants and extends Red Bull's reach in the social media. Rhetorical operations integrate brand symbols, consumer performance, and multiple media in an amusing brand gag.

For the Flugtag event, Red Bull recruits consumer teams on the brand website to build and navigate homemade "flying machines" powered by humans, not rocket science. Contestants build the machines to prescribed dimensions for size and weight. Competitions draw sometimes hundreds of thousands of spectators to Red Bull Flugtag events on the waterfronts of large cities, where the flying machines are launched off a pier about 30 feet above water. Contestants compete on the basis of the team's design and showmanship and the number of seconds their machines can sustain flight before falling into the water.

RED BULL'S RHETORICAL STRATEGY

Red Bull's tagline, "Red Bull gives you wings," draws from a conventionalized metaphor whose meaning has become codified through popular usage. The metaphor "gives you wings" first appears in the Bible (Isaiah 40:30–41:1) and is used in hymns and even secular music to signify, "inspire," "lift up," and "motivate." It is an apt metaphor for the brand's energizing ingredients, its intense, risk-taking persona, and its association with extreme sports and cutting edge rock music. Online advertising captures extreme athletes in mid-air, defying gravity with skis, bikes, and parachutes, performing in Red Bull sponsored events. The website also references Red Bull sponsored musical events.

The Flugtag event deconstructs the commonplace meaning of the "wings" metaphor by shifting focus from the metaphorical to the literal meaning of the statement: the event challenges contestants to fly. In reality, people do not have wings, nor, by extension, do they fly. Flugtag events seem destined to disprove this obvious truth by giving contestants "wings." The contradiction between flying/not flying structures the ironic tone of the entire campaign, such as the contrast between the earnest hard work of contestants and the inevitable failure of their machines to fly. There is a slapstick quality to the spectacle itself, since the machines and teams splash into the water within seconds of takeoff. The absurdity of this rhetorical twist is consistent with the satirical humor of Red Bull's online advertising, such as the famous Flying Pigs campaign, which also plays on a cliché, "If pigs could fly...."

Red Bull's media strategy builds upon the interface between consumers and the company website, sponsored events, social media, and online videos. Red Bull's strategy not only forms associations with edgy Millennial culture, but contributes to that culture by sponsoring teams and musical artists. Traditional advertising in print and video primarily serves to send consumers to the website.

THE RHETORICAL SYSTEM OF THE FLUGTAG HYPERTEXT

The associations in Figure 3.9 suggest something of the complexity of the rhetorical structure of hypertext marketing. Rhetorical operations form the junctures between the various media touch points. They also twist the tone of the discourse from sincere to ironic, playing on the contrasts between what is said and what is referred to in the ad. Rhetorical operations structuring similarity and contiguity also motivate the integration of the brand message across media, and generate the production of new brand messaging, including traditional advertising and consumer sharing on Facebook.

On the grid below, the arrows leading from one media touch point to another oversimplify the multidirectional movement of meaning between media events and consumers in semiotic performance. The arrow [>] refers to a metonymical link and the equal sign [=] refers to a metaphorical link.

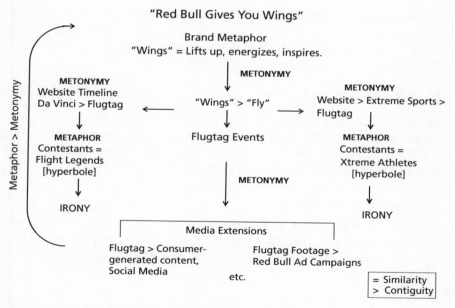

Figure 3.9. The Rhetorical System of the Flugtag Hypertext

Tagline > The Flugtag Campaign

The web of associations begins with a metonymy of cause and effect between the statement "gives you wings," and the effects of wings, "flying." Furthermore, tensions between the meaning of the metaphor "lifts you up," and reference to the context, an amateur flying event, are responsible for the irony of the campaign.

Flugtag = Flight Heroes

The brand website extends the metaphor by suggesting hyperbolic comparisons between Flugtag and famous aeronautical achievements. The event webpage positions Flugtag on a timeline of aeronautical history leading from Da Vinci's aeronautical research to the Wright brothers' flying experiments. This metonymy motivates a comparison between these pioneers in aviation to Flugtag contestants. The comparison is a hyperbole or exaggeration that is disclaimed by the humor of the timeline's title, "A Rich History. Sort of." The contradiction between what is said, i.e. Flugtag contestants are like aviation heroes and what is referred to, i.e. an amateur event where contestants promptly splash into the water forms the ironic tone so characteristic of the Red Bull brand.

Flugtag = Extreme Sports

The juxtaposition of Flugtag with extreme sporting events on the website motivates a similar hyperbole comparing Flugtag contestants to professional athletes. The comparison is ironic because it is in contrast to the actual slapstick nature of the Flugtag sporting event.

Flugtag > Shared Media

The interactive nature of the website also forms the basis for extending the Flugtag event, along the lines of metonymy, into consumer-generated and traditional marketing messages. Contestants and spectators can share photos and comments on Facebook and other media.

Flugtag > Advertising Content

Additionally, management extends, along the lines of metonymy, the Flugtag event into new media messaging, when they incorporate video footage captured at Flugtag events into the content for traditional television and print advertising.

Media Extensions > Red Bull Brand

Flugtag events generate social media and advertising messaging. These messages influence, in turn, consumer perceptions of the Red Bull brand. The arrow leading from the Media Extensions at the bottom of the grid to the Brand Metaphor at the top represents the dynamic flow of meaning between formal marketing actions and consumer feedback on the on-going construction of the brand metaphor. It also illustrates the role of rhetoric in this process.

Conclusion

By identifying the much broader implications of rhetoric for structuring meaning and consumer attention in non-verbal discourse, structural semiotics accounts for the formal and mental operations that link one message to another, one medium to another, in hypertext marketing. Furthermore, to develop a hypertext strategy for brands, semiotic research follows these associative paths to unpack the brand metaphor, extend its elements into multimedia events and messages, and engage consumers in the hypertext performance. Hypertext research builds upon an audit of the brand metaphor as represented in historical advertising and corporate communication. Qualitative research is used to unpack the brand metaphor with reference to consumers' media preferences and practices and the rhetorical associations they link to the brand name and logo.

Although hypertext marketing presents a new set of challenges for brand management, the fundamental challenge for marketers remains the same. Regardless of the medium, marketers must identify and clarify the brand metaphor, its competitive advantage, and its relevance for contemporary consumer culture.

As a discursive function and cognitive operation, metaphor taps into the creative and emotional centers of the brain that lead to innovative connections between signs and meaning in the marketplace. It is the marketer's challenge to leverage these connections in developing brand strategy, by tapping into the metaphorical thinking of consumers about their brands in the early stages of the planning process.

4 Servicescape Semiotics

This chapter summarizes the basic concepts and methods used in semiotics-based research in the field of retail design. The chapter underscores the role of theory in semiotics-based research and its ability to generate innovative, culturally relevant concepts for both marketing practice and marketing science. In addition to illustrating the application of semiotic theory to the analysis of servicescapes, the chapter also illustrates the importance of situating the servicescape in the broader contexts of service trends in the category and the culture at large. The chapter also addresses an emerging issue in contemporary servicescapes related to the virtual spaces consumers visit via their mobile apps and Internet platforms while shopping and waiting in line.

The chapter includes a discussion of the semiotics of space and its distinctive approach to servicescape research, a case study for Domino's Pizza Company, and a discussion of the implications of the Domino's case for reinventing pick-up service and integrating consumer technology into bricks and mortar service sites. The semiotic analysis led to innovations that transformed Domino's pick-up sites from a "lean" service environment (Bitner 1992), whose main function consists of food preparation and pick-up, to a hybrid form that combines function with pleasure. The study also identified ways to extend the retail design strategy to consumers' virtual spaces by enhancing Domino's mobile application. Customers can now watch on their smart phones a video of the pizza at various stages of preparation and baking while they wait for their orders.

In order to orient the theoretical discussion that follows to research practice, I begin the chapter with a preview of the Domino's case.

Case Preview: A Paradigm Shift at Domino's Pizza

Since 1973, Domino's Pizza, "the pizza delivery experts," has positioned its brand and operations around the promise to deliver freshly baked pizza to the customer within thirty minutes of placing an order. Since Domino's and competitors such as Pizza Hut and Little Caesars relied upon delivery rather than in-store customers for the bulk of their business, customers came face to face with the brand in the form of the delivery person rather than at the store. Consequently, the service-sites themselves were traditionally simple functional structures rather than destinations.

The Domino's case illustrates how a food service category had to adjust its value proposition and retail design to adapt to changes in consumer lifestyles and service technologies. Not only do consumers have less money to spend on tipping the delivery person, they are also spending less time at home and have become increasingly mobile. These factors have reduced demand for home delivery and have increased the volume of orders at pizza pick-up sites by about 30 percent (York 2013). Furthermore, rather than calling in the orders from home, customers place orders from mobile apps while in transit between work, home, and other locations.

Up to this time, the pick-up station had been a bare bones operation dedicated to cooking and packaging delivery orders. However, the increase in pick-up service meant that customers would come face to face with the brand at the pick-up site. This prompted Domino's to improve the décor of the service sites in the early 2000s. Management also enhanced their mobile app to allow customers to order personalized pizzas from their smart phones and track the various stages in the preparation and packaging of their orders, in video format. In spite of these improvements, however, customer satisfaction fell short of expectations. They commissioned semiotics research in order to develop concepts for a complete overhaul of the pick-up site. In the full-length case analysis, I illustrate how servicescape semiotics produced innovative design concepts leading to a hybrid form of food service and extended the servicescape into the cyberspaces that consumers access through their mobile apps.

SERVICESCAPES IN SEMIOTIC PERSPECTIVE

Semiotic servicescapes, in a very general sense, are "built environments in which retail transactions take place" (Bitner 1992). Environmental psychologists define the built environment as a topology of material stimuli that elicit measurable sensory responses from consumers. Semioticians, on the other hand, conceptualize the built environment in terms of the cultural codes that endow it with meaning. These codes form the normative aspects of retail culture that contribute to the collective assumptions and expectations of consumers about a shopping site. They also structure the symbolic interface between the buyer and the brand that may or may not include transactions.

The Semiotic Research Perspective

Servicescape semiotic research differs from psychological approaches inasmuch as it takes into account the cultural and strategic dimensions of retail space.

THE CULTURAL PERSPECTIVE

Environmental psychologists use empirical testing and observation to study the effects of specific design elements, such as atmospherics or product placement, on consumer behavior (for example, Donovan and Rossiter 1982; Bellizzi, Crowley, and Hasty 1983; Bellizzi and Hite 1992; Baker, Levy, and Grewal 1992; Houston, Bettencourt, and Wenger 1999; Fiore, Yan, and Yoh 2000; Baker, Parsuraman, Grewal, and Voss 2002). Their findings transcend the cultural and strategic implications of store design because empirical testing isolates any given service site from its context in the competitive set and category trends. Underhill's (2009 [1999]) study of shopping behavior is a popular example of this approach.

In contrast, semiotics-based research begins by identifying patterns of spatial semiotics structuring the servicescapes of a large group of stores in a category, such as fast food. These patterns are then compared and contrasted with the codes structuring peripheral categories such as casual dining and even retailing generally. In this way, the semiotician articulates a kind of servicescape "grammar" or code system for the retail category, identifies emergent codes or trends in the category and retailing culture generally, and makes recommendations for store design based upon this cultural context.

STRATEGIC DIMENSIONS

Servicescape semiotics also differs from psychological studies because it accounts for the strategic marketing function of retail space. Semiotics takes into account the implications of architectural design for sustaining the brand message, experience, and perception and its distinctions from competitors. In effect, semiotics-based research approaches servicescapes as discourses that integrate all of the semiotic elements in a store, from layout and furnishings to lighting and traffic flow, into a single brand message and experience.

Furthermore, the servicescape must integrate all of the design elements, from layout and furnishings to lighting and traffic flow, around a single brand message and experience. Inconsistencies between the brand message communicated in advertising and the brand experience of the store foster ambiguity and undermine consumer trust. The importance of this principle cannot be overstated. For example, in department stores, contrasts between luxurious product displays and drab, poorly lit fitting rooms communicate ambiguity and tarnish consumer perceptions of the brand. In contrast, the McDonald's flagship store in Chicago dramatically illustrates how design integration pulls together a theme and a brand statement, because every inch of the site, including trash cans and restrooms, relates back to the overall design theme and McDonald's commitment to consistent service.

Strategic semiotic research also examines the ways layout and design either help or hinder new product trial and customer loyalty. For example, McDonald's commissioned semiotics research to find out why customers were consistently choosing the traditional burger and fries menu rather than new menu offerings. A semiotic analysis of traffic flow, signage, and furnishings in the store identified physical and psychological barriers between customers and the point of purchase that discouraged new product trial and returned customers to their default choice: burger and fries. These insights confirm research findings that consumers' emotional responses to a service environment influence their perception of the products offered there (Obermiller and Bitner 1984; Bitner 1992).

Semiotic Dimensions of Servicescapes

The semiotic servicescape, like all design systems, includes material, conventional, contextual, and performative dimensions (Figure 4.1). Although these dimensions work together in the design system, in the section below I define these dimensions and summarize their implications for designing semiotics-based research.

MATERIAL DIMENSIONS

The material elements of stores include movable and immovable structures and furnishings, architectonics, and the decoration of the exterior and

MATERIAL
Objects, architecture, design, traffic flow.

CONVENTIONAL
Codes structure the meaning of the material elements.

CONTEXTUAL
Codes mean different things in different markets.

PERFORMATIVE
Codes implicate consumers in servicescapes.

Figure 4.1. Four Dimensions of Servicescape Semiotics

interior structures, as well as the social groupings mapped by these elements, such as traffic flow. They include both the tangible objects and structures used in a store and the organization of those elements in a service layout.

Architecture

Architectural elements include the exterior and interior infrastructure of a store, including the outer walls, façade, entrance, and windows. The interior structure includes architectural design, partitions and walls, ceiling height, windows, and the organization of traffic flow and sociality as a function of the layout.

Décor

Décor includes design elements that enhance the surfaces of the walls, ceilings, and furnishings, such as the color scheme, video screens, lighting, hanging fixtures, pictures, and decorative signage. Although decorative elements do not necessarily reproduce the brand logo, the décor must extend the brand identity throughout the store in order to integrate the customer experience with the brand, from the color palette and mood lighting to any artwork or video content.

Furnishings

Furnishings include movable units such as tables and chairs, and stationary units such as counters, kiosks, and service stations. The placement of furnishings reinforces the overall traffic flow and contributes to the social disposition of customers around various focal points, including product displays, cashier, payment queues, food preparation areas, television screens, fireplaces, and other structures.

Signage and Merchandising Cues

Merchandising cues include visual elements related to the sales function, including product displays, promotional signage, menu boards, and brochures. Other signage includes branded imagery, signs, and logos.

Consumer Technologies

Depending on the service sector, retailers may add consumer technologies, from video screens to wireless service and online catalogues, to entertain consumers, highlight a new product line, or bridge the gap between their online and in-store businesses. Furthermore, consumers' personal technologies also contribute to their experience of a store, because they spend a growing amount of time switching between the real space of the site and a virtual "fourth space" accessible by means of their smart phones. Retailers may occupy this space through mobile applications for making orders and viewing the brand offerings.

CONVENTIONAL DIMENSIONS

The semiotics of space is structured by cultural codes, in the manner of a language. Spatial codes account for Panofsky's (1991) observation that "homogeneous space is never given space, but space produced by construction" (p. 30). The codes structuring visual perspective lend an artificial linearity and continuity to the *representation* of visual perception that masks the natural distortions and discontinuities apprehended by the naked eye. Like other code systems, visual perspective supports the normative, rather than individualistic, ideals of a culture. In the same way that drivers agree on the meaning of Stop signs because they have internalized the traffic codes regulating driver behavior, consumers read servicescapes through the lens of the cultural conventions that structure the spatial semiotics of their lived environments, including similar stores in a retail category, other commercial sites, and also non-commercial sites such as home, theater, and places of worship.

The Binary Nature of Codes

Like all semiotic codes, servicescape codes are binary structures that frame the meaning of a design element, such as mobility, in the logic of its contrary, immobility, and implicate any given binary in a paradigmatic set of codes related to the culture and product category. For example, cultural codes explain why Germans, who prioritize order, are more likely than Americans, who prioritize spontaneity, to fix chairs to the floor to prevent changes to the layout of a public room. Category codes implicate the binary movable/immovable in the conventions associated with one type of store or another. They also influence the perception of value in each sector. The fixed placement of tables and chairs in fast food restaurants communicates a lower degree of consumer control than the furnishings in upscale restaurants where consumers move the chairs to suit the situation. The paradigmatic series would look something like this: movable/immovable; spontaneity/control; restaurants/fast food; upscale/cheap.

Spectacle

The architectural design of commercial sites is steeped in time-honored codes for organizing public space, such as the semiotics of spectacle. Spectacle is a particularly apt metaphor for servicescape design because stores, like theaters, use theatrical conventions to draw consumer attention to specific focal points in the store and engage them in the brand story. The spectacle analogy highlights the strategic potential of theatrical codes for engaging consumers in the brand (Firat and Venkatesh 1995; Peñaloza 1998; Sherry 1998; Kozinets et al 2004).

The semiotics of retail spectacle avoids judgments about the uses and abuses of spectacle by marketers (Debord 1994 [1967]; Firat and Venkatesh 1995; Ritzer 2009). Semiotics takes into account the cultural codes structuring the "spectacular disposition" of public spaces that predisposes consumers to adapt to the spectacularization of the retail sector. These codes include optical illusions rooted in Quattrocento Perspective in the fifteenth century which match the attention of spectators and consumers with a focal point in a painting, a proscenium stage, and a service structure (see Panofsky 1991). The success of the retail spectacle for marketers testifies to the enduring power of spectacle to organize the attention and sociality of groups in relation to design semiotics (see Shields 1991; Willis 1991; Oswald 1996).

Design codes not only structure the physical environment of social events, but anchor these structures in social relationships defined by culture and ideology. As Foucault (2001 [1977]) claims, "spatial anchoring is an economic-political form" (cited by Blommaert 2013). For example, the proscenium traditionally structures relationships of domination and control between the faithful before the altar, the accused before the Bench, and spectators before the stage. In service sites, the proscenium also frames the relationship between service and consumer spaces in the store as a relationship of power. In contrast, alternative design forms such as the circus or the carnival organize a more fluid relationship with consumers, as I discuss below in detail.

Proscenium space. The proscenium frame is a cultural code that sets aside a given space from the natural environment and marks it as a representation. The proscenium articulates the divide between the content and contexts of paintings, film images, and the proscenium stage. Retailers adopt this code when they frame service counters and product displays with proscenium structures. They also set in motion a dialectical relationship between consumers as spectators and the servicescape as spectacle. Proscenium codes shape this relationship in a very specific ways.

In the theater, the proscenium wall frames the action on stage behind an invisible "fourth wall" that forms a symbolic barrier between the performance and the audience. Proscenium codes also create a sense of continuity and empathy between the audience and the performance by means of optical illusions. The placement of seats and other design elements organize the visual field along parallel lines moving from the audience out front toward a point on the horizon in the deep space of the stage (Figure 4.2). This visual structure focuses consumer attention toward the stage and engages the audience in the scene as it unfolds. To maintain this illusion, another proscenium code prohibits performers from looking back through the fourth wall at the audience.

Figure 4.2. The Proscenium Stage

During its heyday in the nineteenth century, the proscenium stage reflected the strict social hierarchies organizing high culture in Victorian society between sacred and profane spaces of the theater. The proscenium structures a paradigmatic series of cultural binaries that position spectators against actors, passive recipients against active producers of discourse, and reality against illusion. The audience is stratified in turn into seating areas assigned by social class (Smith 1996).

In servicescapes, as in the theater, proscenium codes structure consumer identification and engagement with the (brand) story. The visual design of theme parks such as Disney World illustrates how management uses theatrical conventions to control consumer perceptions and movements in branded servicescapes (see Willis 1991; Oswald 2012, Chapter 6). Even in the more functional layouts of supermarkets, the frames around flower displays, cosmetic kiosks, and delicatessen areas reproduce the spectacular structure of the proscenium stage by means of these codes.

Proscenium codes can also be used to disadvantage if they structure rigid relationships between the service and consumer areas of the site and discouraging consumer spontaneity and control. For example, in fast food restaurants the proscenium frame around the service counter not only creates a physical barrier between consumers and service staff but also symbolizes the impersonal and inflexible nature of fast food service in general. For this reason, in theater as in commerce, designers have opened up the fourth wall, extending the "thrust" stage into the audience and service displays into the consumer spaces of stores.

The circus. Not all servicescapes or spectacles draw their design schemes from the proscenium stage. The circus, for example, is a popular form spectacle that takes its name from the circular organization of the audience around the performance. In lieu of the proscenium wall and elevated stage, a permeable, movable ledge separates spectators from the spectacle on the ground level of an amphitheater. The circular structure levels class differences because it provides everyone with an equal perspective on the event. Travelling circuses in the United States were housed in temporary tents, underscoring the informality and flexibility of circus space.

Circus elements appear in retail spaces that organize consumers' movement and attention around a central mall, circular kiosks, and rounded product displays rather than directing them to a single point in the deep space of a store or display case. By releasing the visual field from the geometric logic of the square, circular structures reproduce the equality and informality of circus space and emphasize pleasure over function. Since rounded displays stand out from the wall, they also extend the service space into consumer space, lowering barriers between customers and management and increasing consumer choice and control.

For example, circular kiosks and service islands liberate the service counter from the rigid, binary structure of the proscenium design. The circular design moves traffic and consumer vision around a central counter, adding an element of spontaneity and fun to the design of quick food service, which includes pre-packaged salads and sandwiches. For this reason, the free-standing, boat-shaped design of the service island at the new Lurie Children's Hospital supports the playful, child-centered architecture of the building (Figure 4.3). This design scheme also offers consumers more freedom and control over the service experience by moving food displays to the exterior of the counter, within reach of shoppers.

Carnival. Originating in medieval liturgical holidays, carnival festivals represent a release from routine and social hierarchies. Unlike the circus, carnival actually collapses the social and spatial hierarchies structuring public space. Carnival deconstructs the formal and ideological boundaries separating spectacle from life by moving the performance into the street, dressing the audience in costumes, and mixing performers in with the crowd.

Figure 4.3. The Quick Service Island at Lurie Children's Hospital, Chicago

As a semiotic concept, the "carnivalesque" (see Bakhtin 2009 [1965]) characterizes the deconstruction of rigid binaries, formality, and logic. In servicescape design, the carnivalesque may be expressed in a physical layout that represents tensions between design norms and spontaneity that encourages consumer agency and creativity. Nike introduced carnival elements into its flagship store in London, for instance, when management moved the cash counters out of sight in order to make room for customers to play basketball, watch movies, and explore Niketown. In addition, retailers like Whole Foods play with the boundaries between commerce and daily life when they use retail space to engage in social causes, consumer well-being, and education. They create an atmosphere in which service staff and customers mingle, share recipes, and exchange information about products. By extending its social reach into customers' daily lives, Whole Foods transcends its commercial function and engages with the surrounding community.

Flat space. I use the term "flat space" to name an emergent paradigm in retail design that actually deconstructs the traditional orientation of consumer experience to binary structures such as the service counter. Unlike the carnival space, which structures tensions between cultural norms and consumer creativity, "flat" spatial design does not transgress spatial codes so much as it reorients the experience of space to the personal space of consumers in the store. In Apple stores, for example, sales staff make transactions by means of credit card apps on their iPhones. This design strategy deconstructs the traditional focus of retail service around a central counter into multiple, moving points of purchase throughout the store.

Flat servicescape design used by high tech brands reflects broader cultural trends in social organization. Friedman (2005) uses the term "flat" to describe a leveling in the competitive environment in the global economy. A more profound change relates to the ways digital communications have a "flattening" effect on the traditional hierarchies structuring social relationships, knowledge acquisition, and power in global consumer culture. For example, online friendship groups and brand communities transcend status hierarchies represented by family, physical address, and income. Chat groups, blogs, and online resources such as Wikipedia blur the boundaries between personal opinion and "official" knowledge. A few insurgents with a Twitter account can undermine the authority of the nation state, as witnessed in recent popular uprisings in Tunisia, Libya, and Egypt.

Although management may adopt a flat retail design to bolster the brand's association with radical post-modern culture, the lack of anchor to traditional design codes may prove to actually disorient shoppers rather than engaging them in the brand world. This may have prompted Apple recently to plan a complete redesign of their global flagship stores. In politics, as in marketing, flat environments may foster confusion rather than pleasure.

Category Codes

The binary codes structuring public spaces resemble grammar inasmuch as they form the unspoken, abstract rules that regulate the organization of social groups in the marketplace. They also form a kind of blueprint guiding the consistent organization of service spaces within a retail category. Category codes structure the standard layout for all stores in a retail category and account for the collective expectations of consumers in relation to that category. Category codes, for instance, dictate that checkout queues at superstores are usually placed in the front by the exits, while cashier counters in fast food restaurants are placed in the depth of the store by the kitchen. These conventions translate into the specific codes responsible for the social organization, meaning, and consumer behavior associated with any given design element, such as traffic flow or product placement.

In fast food restaurants, for example, the service counter, framed by a proscenium wall, divides the site into the service spaces behind the counter and the consumer spaces in front (Figure 4.4). This rigid binary structure generates a cultural paradigm of oppositions between service and consumers,

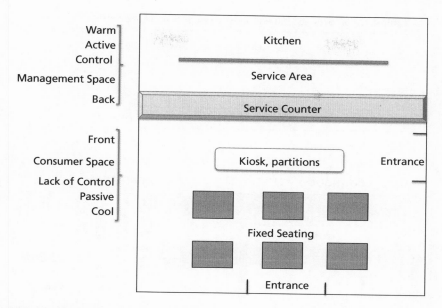

Figure 4.4. The Fast Food Service Paradigm

such as active/passive, control/lack of control, and warm experiences/cool experiences.

The main action in fast food restaurants takes place in the kitchen and serving areas behind the counter, where the staff prepare and package food orders and complete transactions. Partitions and furnishings block the kitchen area from customers' view. Even the menu is placed at a distance behind the counter, and customers have little flexibility in menu choice. Service staff control the delivery of food because there are no opportunities for impulse purchases in front of the counter. The rigid organization of furnishings in the dining area itself, where tables and chairs are often screwed into the floor, reinforces the lack of creativity and flexibility allowed to customers in the fast-food space.

Design codes also communicate the value proposition associated with the category. For example, the functional structure and décor of superstore environments such as Walmart communicate the priority given to low price over esthetics in this sector. In contrast, the emphasis on design and atmospherics at boutiques and gourmet shops communicates the priority given to consumer pleasure and luxury in these sectors (Table 4.1).

The value proposition of a service category is also communicated in the layout and traffic flow of different stores. In superstores, where the checkout counters are located at the exits, the layout emphasizes the moving of consumers to the transaction as efficiently as possible. At boutiques, in contrast, the checkout

Table 4.1. Paradigmatic Dimensions of Boutiques and Superstores

	Boutiques	Superstores
Value proposition	Luxury & Pleasure	Low Price & Convenience
Perception	Illusion	Reality
Relationship	Personal	Distant
Design	Esthetics	Function

©2013 marketing semiotics

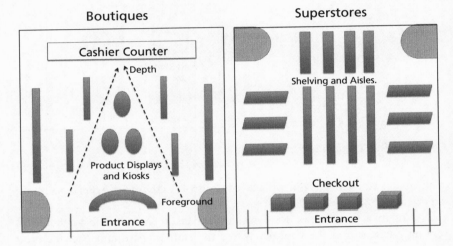

Figure 4.5. The Contrasting Layouts of Boutiques and Superstores

counter is traditionally located in the depth of the store, directing the line of vision and traffic flow from the entrance toward a vanishing point in the back. The organization of the boutique along the lines of theatrical perspective underscores the entertainment value of such stores (Figure 4.5).

In summary, the physical structure of boutiques and superstores represents a cultural paradigm organizing both the customer relationship and the value proposition associated with each type of store.

CONTEXTUAL DIMENSIONS

Design codes form a reference point for all servicescapes in a category. However, they are not carved in stone. They evolve over time in line with cultural change and trends in the retail category itself. Furthermore, since codes are culture-specific, the standard design for a retail franchise in North America may confuse or alienate consumers in emerging markets such as China and India.

Cultural Change

The rigid organization of space in the proscenium theater reflects the rigid social hierarchies ordering European social life in the nineteenth century. Likewise, modifications in the proscenium style evolved in line with the growing informality of social life during the twentieth century. Designs such as the thrust stage and theater-in-the-round integrate the space of the audience into the space of the performance and expose the mechanisms at work in the production of theatrical illusion. By giving spectators multiple perspectives on the action, these new forms also deconstruct the one-dimensional organization of the visual field along the lines of perspective. These changes in the form and meaning of theatrical space have influenced innovative trends in retail design.

Category Trends

In all retail sectors, there has been an increasing emphasis on relaxing the barriers between the customer and service spaces of stores, reflecting the growing empowerment of consumers in modern consumer culture. For example, the cosmetic displays in department stores and boutiques no longer conceal products in the sacred space behind the service counter. Instead, they encourage consumers to try on products for themselves, without the mediation of the sales clerk. Even the traditionally functional spaces of supermarkets have moved produce into rounded kiosks and display cases that reach into consumer space and invite them to try the goods on display. In some stores, such as the Treasure Island store in Chicago (Figure 4.6), mirrors and backlighting enhance the presentation of fruits and vegetables as if they were fashion items in a boutique.

The External Environment

The external environment, including the esthetic and cultural contexts, also plays a role in the design and perception of service sites. The store location affects the perceived value of a franchise in the same way it affects the value of a home. A strip mall full of cheap stores lowers the perceived value of restaurant franchises. Conversely, when, McDonald's aligns restaurant design with the architecture of upscale neighborhoods they raise the perceived value of the brand.

Furthermore, global franchises encounter tensions between western traditions and the expectations and traditions of local customers as they relate to architecture and design. A 2002 study of Chinese consumers at McDonald's stores in Shanghai (Eckhardt and Houston 2002) exposes tensions between the seating arrangements for two at McDonald's and the traditional dining arrangements in China that include larger social groups. Such cultural contrasts are not

Figure 4.6. Treasure Island Thrust Stage

simply opportunities for local populations to "embrace a new set of ideals" (p. 69); they also create barriers to brand acceptance in emerging markets.

PERFORMATIVE

The performative dimension of servicescapes takes into account the actions of management and consumers to manipulate design codes in the execution of brand strategy, sociality, and creativity in a service environment. The relation of performance to codes parallels the relation of speech to linguistic codes ("la langue") in Saussure's (2011 [1916]) theory of structural linguistics.

Management Actions

The performative function enables management to bend category codes along the lines of the esthetics and mood state proper to the brand. The extent of these modifications depends upon the degree to which the retail design contributes to the perceived value for consumers. The functional design of supermarkets and big box stores reflects their association with low price and convenience, leaving little room for design innovation. These kinds of stores are more or less interchangeable with other stores in the category, save for decorative elements such as logos, color schemes, and signage.

Themed franchises form the more esthetics-driven end of the spectrum because the design itself adds to their value proposition. The settings of casual dining franchises such as Olive Garden, Red Lobster, and Rainforest Café recreate themed environments that complement the meal with a vacation fantasy. In similar fashion, themed boutiques such as Victoria's Secret and Urban Outfitters use architectonics, décor, and music to draw consumers into the brand narrative and product line.

Consumer Actions

The performative dimension also includes the ways in which consumers engage with retail design and, in some cases, navigate the movement between the physical space of the store and virtual sites on consumers' mobile phones. Servicescape design determines the nature and flexibility of consumer "agency," that is, consumers' freedom to construct their own experiences of retail spectacles (Kozinets et al. 2004). The physical design also structures the focus of consumer attention in the visual field of the store, which affects their psychic engagement in the brand spectacle.

Design factors. The design schemes associated with the proscenium stage, the circus spectacle, the carnival, and flat space construct different degrees of flow, control, and spontaneity in the shopping experience. They contribute to consumer expectations about a retail category and also differentiate one brand of store from another within the same category. For example, the proscenium organization of fast food restaurants communicates rigidity and distance. The proscenium wall and service counter form a barrier between consumers and the spaces in back and focus consumer attention along the logic of linear perspective.

The circus model is more flexible. It moves the service area into the space of consumers and deconstructs the linear perspective of the proscenium by moving consumer attention to various points around a circular counter or kiosk structure. Carnival is not so much a store design as it is a social strategy within the store. Carnivalesque strategies deconstruct the spatial and exist-ential differences between consumers and service staff altogether by relaxing the boundaries between commercial and non-commercial functions of the store. Brands like Whole Foods, for example, engage customers in social causes and offer classes and services that contribute to consumers' well-being and experience of community.

Most service sites include a blend of design schemes. Although superstores, such as K-Mart, are positioned to low price rather than shopping entertainment, they also include branded cosmetic displays with mirrors and samples that engage consumer trial and brand identification.

E-scapes. In recent years, the introduction of mobile applications has added another dimension to servicescapes defined by the movement of consumer attention between the physical site and the firm's e-scapes online (Koernig 2003). Confronted with flight delays, consumers may be waiting to board one flight while checking other, more convenient flights. Facing long lines at the cinema, consumers may purchase tickets using the theater's mobile app. Some mobile apps offer additional service options, such as concierge services and videos, to entertain consumers while they wait in line, or highlight promotions and new products in the store.

Inasmuch as mobile applications offer consumers an opportunity to be in two places at one time, they represent a form of *heterotopia*. Foucault (1986 [1967]) coined this term to highlight the movement in human consciousness between the presence of the physical environment to the senses and the representation of (absent) reality to the imagination, as in a human looking at his or her reflection in the mirror. To the extent that service heterotopias divide consumer focus between the branded servicescape and virtual spaces on their mobile phones, they disrupt consumer identification and closure with the retail spectacle and promise greater consumer agency and control than the traditional, one-dimensional servicescape.

IMPLICATIONS FOR SEMIOTIC RESEARCH DESIGN

The material, conventional, contextual, and performative dimensions of servicescape semiotics contribute to the distinct design and research objectives of servicescape research. They influence the scope of the data set, the format of data collection and fieldwork, and the analysis of the data.

Data Set

To decode a service category, researchers identify patterns of meaning over a large sampling of stores, including competitors and peripheral service categories. The data set includes multiple stores for the same brand and competitive stores in the same category in order to differentiate category codes from the various iterations of the code for different franchises and different brands. It may include new service types such as yogurt and cupcake stores, as well as institutional service sites such as post offices or churches.

To gain insights from emergent trends in architectural design and social organization, the data set includes external service categories such as entertainment venues, institutions, and even home design. If the objectives include assessing the relevance of a design scheme for the local culture, the data set will include sites that provide insights into traditional uses of space in the local market, such as indigenous markets and celebrations.

Data Collection and Field Guide

The field guide must include a specific list of the material dimensions that must be examined in all sites in the data set. Furthermore, it should include directions for assessing the overall integration of the semiotic system across all material dimensions of the site, including service technologies such as video screens, self-service online catalogues, and mobile apps.

Data Analysis

The binary analysis forms the initial sorting function of a semiotic analysis. It classifies design elements into a paradigmatic set of binaries related to the structural, social, and cultural dimensions of the servicescape. In the fast food example above, the service counter generates a series of binary oppositions, including service/consumers, active/passive, control/controlled.

A New Service Paradigm for Pizza Pick-Up

In response to the growing demand for pick-up service at Domino's Pizza stores, management took steps to improve the in-store experience by redesigning their service sites. They commissioned semiotics research in 2011 to assess the strengths and weaknesses of the current design scheme, compare and contrast their retail strategy with those of their competitors, and identify a distinctive design strategy for Domino's that would engage consumers in the brand experience at the point of purchase.

Semiotics-based research identified an opportunity for Domino's to claim ownership of a hybrid form of service site that would combine the "lean" (Bitner 1992: 59) service of the pick-up station with the esthetic appeal of a pizza kitchen. The Marketing Semiotics company also recommended opportunities for extending the service experience into cyberspace by expanding services on the brand's mobile app.

STUDY DESIGN

In order to develop a new design strategy for Domino's, the Marketing Semiotics company designed a research protocol that would expose not only the *dominant* codes structuring the category, such as the proscenium structure, but also the *recessive* codes that were fading from use and *emergent* codes that would provide direction for design innovation.

The field sites included Chicago, a city known for its many ethnic food stands and restaurants, and Los Angeles, a city famous for the variety and creativity of its fast and quick food service outlets.

Site Selection

A quick visit to Domino's and two competitors suggested that the retail sites for the pizza take-out category itself would offer little insight into emergent trends in food service. The layout and design of the stores were fundamentally identical. They were functional way-stations for picking up and preparing orders for delivery, not destinations. This observation provided the rationale for extending the scope of the research to include a broad range of service sites that related in some way to pizza pick-up service.

The data set included three Domino's sites each in Chicago and Los Angeles in varied locations, and two sites each for Domino's two main competitors in Chicago and Los Angeles. The data set also included at least two sites each from peripheral food service categories such as fast food, and external pick-up service categories such as post offices and dry cleaners (Figure 4.7). The peripheral food service sites offered both in-store and take-out service and included fast food, pizza restaurant franchises, independent pizza restaurants, and yogurt, cupcake, and coffee franchises in Chicago and Los Angeles. The

The Competitive Set			
Pizza Hut, Papa John's, Little Caesars			
Peripheral Categories—Food Service			
Fast food	Pizza franchises	Independent pizza shops	Other quick-service
Take out and in-store	Take out and in-store service	Take out and in-store service	Yogurt, cupcakes, coffee franchises
External Categories—Pick-up Service			
Post offices	Dry cleaners	Delivery services	Pharmacies

Figure 4.7. Data Set

external pick-up service sites included two post offices, two dry cleaners, and pick-up stations for UPS and Federal Express.

Data Collection

The guide for this study evolved over the first few days of data collection, giving researchers an opportunity to tailor the research scope to the most important dimensions of each service category. In the early stages of the fieldwork a standard blueprint emerged that reflects the dominant design codes for the category (Figure 4.8). The blueprint served as a framework for comparing and contrasting pizza franchise service with similar servicescapes in the data set.

The proscenium framing the service counter justifies comparisons between the disposition of consumers before the counter and the disposition of spectators before a proscenium stage. The service counter forms a surface for the commercial transaction and structures a binary opposition between the consumer spaces in front, where management has an opportunity to stage consumers in the store spectacle, and the service spaces behind the counter. The food is baked and boxed in the back stage area and the back wall spaces

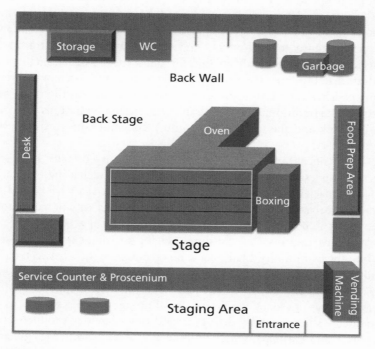

Figure 4.8. The Pizza Pick-up Floor Plan

expose operational functions of the store, such as the staff washroom and the garbage bins.

FINDINGS

The purpose of the findings summary below is to illustrate how the research protocol delivered key insights for innovation in pick-up site design. It does not aim to provide an exhaustive account of the quick-serve food retail sector. The findings illustrate the importance of broadening the scope of data collection beyond the competitive set itself, because they show the influence of design trends in peripheral service categories on pizza pick-up stores.

Lessons from External Service Categories

Ironically, at the time of the study, pizza pick-up sites had more in common with service stations in categories external to food service, such as post offices. Traditionally, service stations are not destinations but quick service stops for transferring goods or services from producer to consumer across a service counter. In most cases, like the post office, little attention has been paid to the design, décor, or consumer experience in these sites because consumers are not meant to spend much time in them. Walls and partitions block business operations from view, and the unadorned, even uncomfortable design of traditional post offices, dry cleaners, and passport offices reflects management's indifference to customers. The consumer experience traditionally consists of standing patiently in line for one's turn. Pizza franchises have the additional burden of exposing the backstage and back wall areas to consumers. This open layout places increased demands on the retail design to integrate the traditionally off-stage spaces of theater operations, such as the manager's desk and the garbage bins, into a coherent consumer experience and brand story.

Improvements at non-food service pick-up and drop-off sites such as post offices provide lessons for pizza pick-up design. The increasing competitiveness of pharmacies and mail delivery services over the years has forced management to evolve their service design in response to emergent trends toward greater transparency, consumer engagement, and social accountability. As a result, they have improved the consumer staging area and extended the service reach into the community. Pharmacies are opening the walls between customers and service operations and have added furnishings and wellness literature to the waiting area. They also participate in community medicine by offering services such as seasonal vaccines. Dry-cleaning franchises such as Tide sell branded t-shirts, laundry detergent, and other laundry products at their service sites, and participate in environmental causes by offering "green" dry cleaning. Even the post office has added convenience shopping for stamps, cards, and gift-wrapping to the waiting area.

Lessons from Pizza Franchises

The design of pizza pick-up franchises references old-fashioned codes such as squared-off forms, the proscenium layout, and an impassible divide between the service and consumer areas of the store. The staging area is sterile and uncomfortable, and the staff ignore customers except to take their payments. Although the space includes multiple surfaces for communicating the brand message, including the walls, flooring, seating, ceiling, and other furnishings, the franchises observed for the study failed to take advantage of these branding opportunities (Figure 4.9). Since the staging area in front of the counter is the customer's entrée into the brand, the bare and uncomfortable design scheme actually degrades the brand experience and sets the tone for consumer dissatisfaction with the food.

As a waiting room, the staging area offers management a captive audience and an opportunity to build and strengthen the brand relationship. However, at the time of the study, pizza pick-up sites neglected this opportunity. Apart

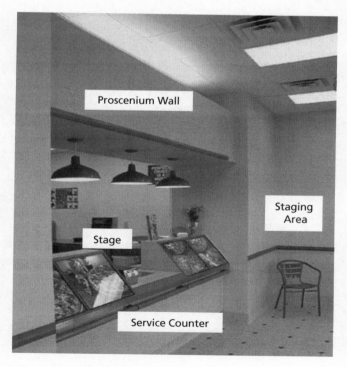

Figure 4.9. The Service Counter Proscenium

from the color scheme, logos, and merchandising cues, the staging area offers nothing to engage consumers, such as impulse purchases or video entertainment. The staff look back toward the food preparation area, rather than engaging consumers in eye contact.

Furthermore, according to convention, consumers expect the proscenium wall to frame some kind of scene, if only a scene of food preparation. In pizza franchises, however, the proscenium opens onto shelving and empty boxes rather than food (Figure 4.10). The pizza spectacle takes place off-stage, because the ovens open toward the backstage areas of the site, where staff box the food before handing it over to consumers. This design scheme downgrades the potential appeal of the service experience because it conceals the visual and olfactory rewards of fresh food coming out of the oven. The experience is further downgraded by the exposed, unadorned "back wall" spaces where the operational functions of the store are located. Consumers see a manager's desk, a computer and phones for taking orders, the staff washroom and coat rack, the garbage bin, discarded cartons, and other detritus from the day's work.

Figure 4.10. The Pizza Franchise "Spectacle"

Lessons from Fast Food Service Design

The fast food business model calls for standardized menu choices, restaurant designs, and service protocols that preclude consumer spontaneity and control. Like pizza franchises, fast food franchises consist of a single continuous layout divided by a service counter. Although fast food restaurants also include seating, service kiosks, and customer washrooms in the consumer areas, like pizza service franchises, they traditionally offer nothing in the way of consumer entertainment or impulse shopping in the staging area in front of the counter.

The fast food paradigm has been evolving, however, in response to the growing popularity of quick service categories such as branded cafés, juice bars, and cupcake shops that provide comfortable "third space" environments where consumers want to spend time. Brands such as McDonald's and Taco Bell, for example, have developed design protocols at select sites that introduce flexibility, creativity, and consumer pleasure into the fast food service equation. The new designs bring more transparency to the customer relationship. By lowering the service counter and eliminating the proscenium frame, they expose kitchen operations and bring service staff closer to consumers. The designs call for movable furnishings that allow customers more control and spontaneity in their seating arrangements, television screens, wireless Internet access, and mood lighting to encourage longer stays. Table 4.2 summarizes the binary oppositions between old and emergent codes in fast food service and provides a blueprint for a new service paradigm for pizza pick-up.

Table 4.2. A New Fast Food Service Paradigm

Fast Food Codes	Design Innovations
Product-centered	Consumer-centered
Closed counter	Open counter
Hidden kitchen	Transparent operations
Hard surfaces	Malleable surfaces
Immovable furnishings	Movable furnishings
Static social groupings	Dynamic groupings
No entertainment	TV, Internet
Squared shapes	Rounded shapes
Plastic	Wood, chrome
Florescent lighting	Accent lighting
Promotional signage	Visual pleasure
Primary colors	Designer colors

©2013 marketing semiotics

Lessons from Full-Service Pizza Restaurants

Although fast food brands have enhanced the visual esthetics, entertainment opportunities, and comfort of their servicescapes, they fall short of changing the dynamic of the service relationship itself. The service counter still forms an impassible barrier between consumers and the pleasures of food and food preparation behind the counter. Although consumers may take for granted this design convention in the fast food sector, pizzaria service is rooted in the informality and transparency of the pizza kitchen that joins chefs and consumers in a single space. The independent pizzerias observed in Chicago and Los Angeles illustrate this tradition. They all locate food preparation within view of diners and encourage dialogue between the kitchen staff and customers. Most of them offer seating at the service counter right in front of the ovens. The photos and personal memorabilia of the owners on the walls highlight the informal, intimate nature of the customer relationship. Furthermore, pizzerias engage with their communities by posting local events on message boards, adding local ingredients to their pizza toppings, and decorating interiors with local themes and colors. Pizza restaurant franchises such as the California Pizza Kitchen have followed suit by moving the ovens forward, lowering the service counter, and engaging consumers in the warmth and informality of pizza culture.

IMPLICATIONS FOR PICK-UP SERVICE INNOVATION

Findings at non-food service stations, fast food restaurants, peripheral food sites, and pizza restaurants provided insights for transforming pizza pick-up from a functional service stop to an engaging consumer experience. They apply to all four areas of the store and involve the material, conventional, cultural, and performative dimensions of servicescape design.

The Material Layout

Findings from McDonald's flagship store in Chicago highlight the importance of integrating the front and back areas of the site into a single design strategy and communicating the brand message on all material surfaces of the store, not just the service counter and staging area but in the back stage and back wall, office space, garbage bins, and doors into the overall design scheme. To highlight pleasure over function, the design should emphasize curves and rounded forms rather than angles and squares. Furthermore, the addition of video screens to the waiting area would entertain customers and provide an additional surface for engaging them in the brand story. The staging area could also include shopping opportunities in the form of branded merchandise and dessert items, in addition to self-service soft drink machines.

Domino's has already developed a mobile app that includes a video of a pizza going through the production process that is timed to the wait time for the order. However the moving image cannot substitute for a direct look into the pizza kitchen. To transform pizza pick-up from a way station to a destination, a new design strategy would engage consumers in the sensual delights of pizza making, from molding dough to watching and smelling freshly baked pizza coming out of the oven.

Conventions

Insights about the conventions associated with pizza culture illustrate the distinctive service codes that consumers associate with pizza service as opposed to fast food, including informality, transparency, and sociality. Drawing on the pizza kitchen metaphor, management should lower barriers between consumers and the pleasures of pizza. This means reducing or removing the proscenium wall around the service counter, moving food preparation and even the ovens from the back stage toward the stage behind the counter, and training staff to engage actively with consumers across the service counter in the process.

Emerging Cultural Trends

A design strategy that emphasizes informality, transparency, and consumer choice would also align pizza pick-up with emergent codes in food service generally. The growing popularity of new forms of quick food service, including coffee kiosks, cupcake franchises, and juice bars, reflects broader changes in service design that emphasize open plans, self-service options, and social interaction.

Customer Performance

Although all brands in the category had made cosmetic improvements to their stores over the years, the basic layout of pizza pick-up limited consumer attention to the small waiting area in front of the service counter and the row of boxes behind it. There was very low interaction between the service staff and customers across the counter, and nothing to entertain or engage consumers while they waited. By aligning the layout and design strategy of pizza pick-up sites with both pizza culture and emergent codes in quick service design, pizza pick-up could improve the dynamic of the consumer experience. A more open, free-flowing design scheme would activate consumer agency and shift consumer attention from the transaction process to the pleasure of food.

Furthermore, the addition of service technologies, such as video and stationary smart pads, offers an opportunity to engage consumer attention and identification more powerfully than brochures and signage. There is an opportunity to grow brand presence on consumers' mobile apps by linking pizza to entertainment, travel, and shopping opportunities near the store.

Conclusions

Although pick-up food service has been around since the 1940s, in recent years the pick-up experience has evolved into a short-term destination due to the growing emphasis on entertainment in retailing in general and emergent trends in the quick-service category in particular. The cupcake and yogurt franchises, juice bars, and coffee kiosks mentioned above are testimony to a set of emergent codes associated with "recreational" food stops. They are designed to satisfy not only the taste buds but also the visual and olfactory senses. Recreational food codes have raised consumer expectations of pick-up sites generally, forming a stark contrast with the sterile, uncomfortable, and unappealing designs of pizza pick-up sites. The "retailtainment" trend extends even to the design of functional service stations, such as government offices and hospitals. This trend reflects perhaps a broader cultural phenomenon in which commercial spaces, including websites, have replaced domestic space for generating consumer sociality, pleasure, and even identity formation.

Rather than speculate with social scientists (Debord 1994 [1967]) about the origins of this cultural phenomenon, the present discussion emphasizes the importance of the cultural context for servicescape design, inasmuch as it accounts for changes in the very purpose and goal of the quick service pick-up site. It also underscores the importance of semiotics-based methodologies—from the study design to the theory of codes—for innovation in servicescape design.

By extending the data set beyond a given site or competitive set to the broader contexts of the service category and the general culture, semiotics-based research anchors the analysis of any given site or set of sites in the cultural codes structuring the meaning, experience, and sociality of public space. The semiotic concepts and methodologies presented here account for the collective meanings and experiences structured by service design and also provide tools for developing design innovations that are rooted in cultural reality.

5 Cultural Branding

Brands are sign systems that consumers associate with the brand name, logo, and other proprietary assets. Brands, like consumers, are products of their environments. They draw meaning from their positioning in the competitive set, from the perception of value in the product category, and from trends in popular culture. Brands also contribute to the cultural system because the relationship between culture and brands is dialectical. Through repeated contact with marketing messages, consumers come to associate certain symbols with specific product categories, and incorporate these codes in turn into their repertoire of cultural codes. They learn to read instantly the design cues associated with organic, natural, and processed foods, for instance, without reading the ingredient panel.

Cultural branding defines the practice of managing this dialectic in order to build brand equity. In this chapter I present a semiotic approach to cultural branding and demonstrate how to apply theory to practice by means of examples and case studies.

Brands enter the social consciousness by means of the ubiquitous, multi-surfaced touch points connecting consumers and marketing signs in the public sphere, from ads and merchandising to mobile messaging and sponsored events (Thompson and Arsel 2004). Consumers, in turn, actively contribute to brand meaning when they weave marketing signs into their narratives (Holt 2002), rituals (Ritson and Elliott 1999; Peñaloza 2001), and self-generated advertising (Muñiz and Schau 2007). Consumer-generated meanings then move within popular culture via word of mouth and digital media channels including Facebook, Twitter, and YouTube, where they build, support, or deconstruct brand meaning.

Cultural brand management consists of managing the semiotic interface between the brand system and the culture system throughout the strategic planning process—from developing creative strategy and new product innovation to designing sponsored events and social media campaigns. Cultural branding strategy relies entirely on the give and take between the meaning of marketing signs and reference to the context, reiterating a theme that runs throughout this book. Furthermore, cultural branding practice places the brand, not the isolated advertisement, interview, or retail site, at the center of the research process. It demands a research methodology that decodes the semiotics of a generous sampling of data, not a single text.

The issue of cultural branding has importance not only for brand management, but for marketing scholarship as well. It raises important philosophical questions that are central to the semiotic enterprise. At the risk of sounding tedious, the first part of the chapter debates questions such as the nature of culture, the relation of signs to phenomena, and the symbolic function that is responsible for merging culture and signs in discourse. By defining culture as a semiotic *construction* rather than a transcendent origin of meaning, semiotic theory places in question current theories of cultural branding, which rely on the assumption that culture transcends its inscription in representations such as advertising.

The semiotics of cultural branding is consistent with the structural tradition in anthropology and linguistics,[1] inasmuch as it treats culture and brands as sign systems structured by codes, rather than disparate epistemological systems. It also draws upon post-structural theories that emphasize the dialectical relation between signs, meaning, and consumer agency in the production of cultural meaning. In the theoretical discussion that follows, I compare and contrast the semiotics of cultural branding with key theories of how brands acquire cultural meaning. To frame the theoretical discussion in marketing practice, I begin by introducing a business problem that was resolved by means of a cultural branding research process.

CASE PREVIEW: FINDING A CULTURAL POSITIONING FOR MY TEA

A few years ago, a North American client decided to bring back a bottled tea brand that the company had sold to a global conglomerate twenty years prior to the study. I will refer to the brand with a pseudonym, My Tea, rather than use the actual trademark.[2] The client had already developed creative strategy for the launch and commissioned semiotic research to develop what they called "compelling words and icons" for advertising copy. The case study illustrates the importance of semiotic research in the early stages of new product development, not just at creative execution. It also illustrates how strategic semiotic research saved a brand from oblivion by clarifying a clear and strong cultural positioning in relation to competitors and extending the brand's reach in the ready-to-drink (RTD) category.

The project posed research challenges because the client lacked critical information about the brand's performance over the past twenty years when My Tea was under prior management. Researchers lacked information on the brand's target segment, advertising, and positioning strategy for the past twenty years—data that is critical to developing creative strategy. Recent advertising had been pulled from YouTube, and there were very few samples

---

[1] For example, Lévi-Strauss 1967; Geertz 1973; Douglas and Isherwood 2002 [1979]; Eco 1979; Saussure 2011.

[2] At the time of publication there were no other tea brands called "My Tea," and the author disclaims any unintended association between this invented name and an actual brand on the market.

of the product on display at the supermarket. Although the tea's brand name was still widely recognized, the brand lacked a clear identity and positioning and had fallen behind category trends for healthier, natural alternatives to sugary soft drinks. Even if management revived key brand associations from the past, the cultural positioning of earlier campaigns was out of step with the popular culture of the current target, Millennials.

Researchers encouraged management to postpone creative execution until they had defined a distinctive and current cultural positioning that would distinguish My Tea from competitors, align the brand with emergent category trends, and inspire relevant, targeted advertising. The case illustrates how the semiotic approach to cultural branding exposed a new cultural space for My Tea that served to revitalize and differentiate the brand and extend its market reach.

The Cultural Perspective on Marketing

The cultural perspective on marketing has evolved since Douglas and Isherwood (2002 [1979]) introduced structural anthropology to the realm of consumer behavior in the 1970s. From McCracken's (1986) account of advertising's role in symbolic consumption to Holt's (2004) theory of iconic brands and consumer culture theory, marketing scholars agree that brands have symbolic value, but give various accounts of how brands acquire cultural meaning. These debates warrant discussion here because they clarify the theoretical framework for the present, semiotics-based approach.

THE THEORY OF MEANING TRANSFER

Grant McCracken (1986) stimulated important debates on meaning in the marketplace by proposing a theory of meaning transfer to account for the cultural meaning of goods.[3] However, meaning transfer theory oversimplifies the nature of culture, the process of meaning production, and distinctions between the symbolic function of goods in general and brand meaning.

McCracken (1986) proposes a phenomenological account of symbolic consumption that is based upon the assumption that culture transcends its representation in marketing signs (Figure 5.1). He states: "The original location of the cultural meaning that ultimately resides in consumer goods is the culturally constituted world" (p. 72). He reiterates: "Meaning first resides in

---

[3] For instance, Aaker 1997; Fournier 1998; Hirschman et al. 1998; Aaker et al. 2001; Kozinets 2001.

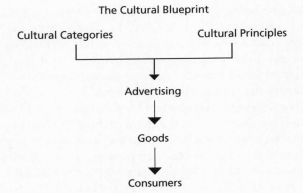

Figure 5.1. The Meaning Transfer Hierarchy

the culturally constituted world" (p. 72). Consumer goods "make manifest" or "substantiate" cultural categories as the result of "meaning transfers" that move from culture, to goods, to the minds of consumers (p. 74). McCracken claims that advertising is the "conduit" through which "meaning constantly pours from the culturally constituted world to consumer goods" (p. 73). McCracken does not explain where culture originated, how it became segmented into categories, or how goods took on meanings in the days before advertising. In terms of Geertz (1973), McCracken has reified culture as a self-contained origin from which representations, from ritual to advertising, draw meaning.

McCracken's meaning transfer hierarchy also moves in one direction, from the cultural blueprint to goods to consumers, through the medium of advertising and other media, rather than taking into account the effects of consumer actions on culture. The model also conflates epistemological distinctions between phenomenal reality, i.e. "culture" and symbolic representation i.e. advertising, raising unresolved philosophical questions about the relationship of signs to reality.

Furthermore, the notion of "meaning transfer" does not sufficiently account for the complexity of symbol formation, which includes primary and secondary symbolic functions. The primary symbolic function relies upon innate mental processes that enable humans to project meanings into material signs, including possessions, and organize them into discourses.[4] Even Saussure (2011 [1916]), whose structural approach to linguistics eschewed mentalist accounts of language, built the theory of the sign on the dialectical relationship between a mental concept and a material signifier, such as a phoneme. This general symbolic function, not metaphysics, accounts for the

---

[4] See, for instance, Freud 1955 [1909]; Klein 1975 [1930]; Lacan 1977 [1953].

cultural meaning of goods, such as the prestige associated with ostentatious display. This insight leads Douglas and Isherwood (2002 [1979]: 40) to conclude, "We shall assume that the essential function of consumption is its capacity to make sense."

This general symbolic function is the *condition of possibility* of the secondary symbolic function that is responsible for forming brand discourses in advertising and other media. The secondary symbolic function does not transfer meaning directly from culture to things, but transfers meaning from one sign system to another in marketing communication. For example, the advertisement for Coke that associates an open Coke bottle with the tagline "Open Happiness" transfers meaning from the sign for "bottle" to the sign for "happiness" in order to communicate the brand's equities in happy feelings.

CONSUMER CULTURE THEORY

The influence of structural semiotics on consumer culture theory is reflected in an important stream of consumer research that explores the dialectical relationships between the culture system, including codes, myths, and consumer rituals, and symbolic representations, from ostentatious consumption to fashion and servicescape design (Figure 5.2). Earlier lines of research account for the ways advertising reflects cultural tensions (Sherry and Camargo 1987) and influences consumer behavior (Ritson and Elliott 1999). More recently, Thompson, Rindfleisch, and Arsel (2006) examine the influence of consumer-generated brand myths and stories on the meaning and value of brands, Thompson and Arsel (2004) explore the effects of global brand strategies on local culture, and Thompson and Tian (2008) clarify how brands construct popular memory by means of commercial myths. Cayla and Eckhardt (2008)

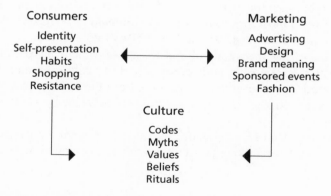

Figure 5.2. The Dialectic of Consumers, Culture, and Marketing

study how global brands expand the repertoire of national identities available to consumers and form the basis for transnational brand communities. There are countless other examples of culture-sensitive scholarship that cannot all be summarized here.

Another line of research[5] examines the phenomenological relationship between brands and consumer experiences in branded retail settings and emphasizes the complex and even contradictory intersections of the culture system and the brand system in the marketplace.

In a study of consumer resistance, Holt (2002) presents an approach that challenges McCracken's "culture as blueprint" model. Holt emphasizes that brands enter consumer culture as discourses that produce as well as reflect culture. Holt goes so far as to say that in a free market there exists "a symbiotic relationship between market prerogatives and the cultural frameworks that orient how people understand and interact with the market's offerings" (p. 71). By emphasizing the vital and dynamic relationship between brands and consumers, Holt provides insights into ways consumers push back, critique, and even reinvent iconic brands in their own quest for personal and social identity. "Brands have become the preeminent site through which people experience and express the social world, even as the worlds that move through brands are less orchestrated by managers than before" (p. 83).

HOLT'S MODEL OF CULTURAL BRANDING

Holt (2004) takes a somewhat different tack in a book devoted to iconic brands. He proposes a practical model of cultural branding to account for the force and sustainability of iconic brands such as Mountain Dew or Marlboro (Figure 5.3). Iconic brands confront "acute cultural contradictions" by identifying with cultural myths that resolve, in the symbolic realm, unmet consumer needs for an aspirational lifestyle. For example, Philip Morris leveraged the tensions between the myth of the endless American frontier and the actual fenced-in lives of most Americans when the company developed the Marlboro cowboy campaign between 1954 and 1999 (Papatoto 2012).

Unlike his earlier theory of cultural resistance, which engages consumers in a dialectical relationship with the brand, Holt's cultural branding model proposes a one-way movement of meaning from the brand to consumers. It emphasizes how marketers influence consumer behavior by means of iconic advertising.

Furthermore, Holt's model is not so much a protocol for *building* brand strategy as an interpretation of the cultural resources of individual advertising

---

[5] For example, Holt 2002; Kozinets 2002; Kozinets et al. 2002; Kozinets et al. 2004; Diamond et al. 2009.

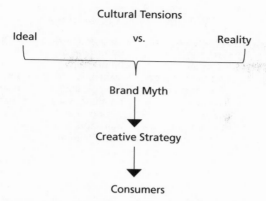

Figure 5.3. Holt's Cultural Branding Model

campaigns. He limits analysis to the relationships between brands and consumer culture, leaving out consideration of the competitive tensions structuring relations between brands in the marketplace, or semiotic tensions between the brand, the category, and peripheral categories.

THE SEMIOTICS OF CULTURAL BRANDING

The semiotics of cultural branding extends Lévi-Strauss's (1967 [1958]) application of structural linguistics to anthropology and is based upon the assumption that culture, like language, is a sign system, not a transcendent origin of meaning (Geertz 1973; MacCannell 1979). Structural anthropology models the structure of non-linguistic sign systems such as culture after the dialectic relation between signifier and signified in the linguistic sign. Structuralism extends the theory of codes to non-linguistic systems in order to account for the binary logic organizing the cultural world.

SYMBOLIC CONSUMPTION

In Lévi-Strauss (1967 [1958]), Geertz (1973), and Douglas and Isherwood (2002 [1979]), symbolic consumption involves the two-way *exchange* of meaning between the culture system and consumer behavior. Geertz (1973) clarifies that the culture system is inseparable from its representation in signs and symbols. In other words, culture is itself a semiotic system, always and already implicated in and dependent upon its inscription in concrete symbols, such as consumer goods or rituals. Eco (1979) adds another twist to this dialectic, emphasizing the cultural nature of sign systems. Eco builds upon Saussure's (1993 [1910]) insight that the code (*la langue*) is a "social product" and signs are "units of culture."

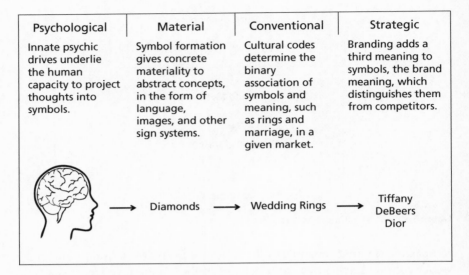

Psychological	Material	Conventional	Strategic
Innate psychic drives underlie the human capacity to project thoughts into symbols.	Symbol formation gives concrete materiality to abstract concepts, in the form of language, images, and other sign systems.	Cultural codes determine the binary association of symbols and meaning, such as rings and marriage, in a given market.	Branding adds a third meaning to symbols, the brand meaning, which distinguishes them from competitors.

Figure 5.4. Symbolic Consumption

Symbolic consumption depends upon the interplay between psychological, material, and conventional dimensions of meaning production (Figure 5.4). Social groups project meanings into material symbols such as possessions in special rituals and social relationships in order to mark them with value. Inasmuch as the group shares these meanings, they are "codified" within a given culture. For example, diamonds communicate a promise to wed in the West, a meaning that is not traditionally shared by Chinese consumers. However, as Peñaloza (2001) reflects, "Consumers and marketers negotiate cultural meanings in relation to each other in the marketplace" (p. 381). In the process, they twist cultural codes in response to trends and foster cultural change. For example, the J. Walter Thompson agency introduced DeBeers diamonds into the China market as the modern girl's best friend.

THE BRAND SYSTEM

The semiotic approach to cultural branding adds a strategic dimension to symbolic consumption because it focuses on the meanings that consumers associate with the brand name and logo, not the goods themselves. In contrast with McCracken's cultural blueprint or Holt's cultural branding model, strategic semiotic research locates the brand, not culture, at the center of cultural brand strategy. As demonstrated in Figure 5.5, the brand identity, values, target, and symbolic equities form a kind of filter or moderator for incorporating cultural meanings into the brand system. For example, to align the brand with consumers' lifestyles and values, management gains insights about the brand's target segment, rather than trying to reach a broad, undifferentiated target.

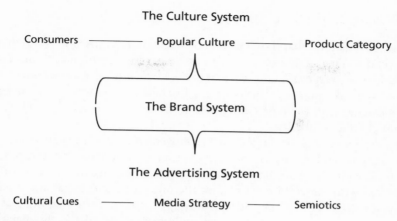

Figure 5.5. The Semiotics of Cultural Branding

The brand system also orients creative strategy and motivates the form and content of advertising campaigns. In this way, advertising forms a "synthesis of a culture's worldview and ethos" (Sherry 1987: 448), not the origin of the brand's cultural meaning, as McCracken claims. Advertising communicates the brand's cultural positioning in discourses associated with the brand name and logo. Thus, advertising and other mass media both mirror and contribute to cultural production, and they both reflect and influence consumer behavior.

Lastly, in order to account for the movement of meaning between the culture, brand, and representation systems, semiotics draws upon theory from the psychology of language. Cognitive linguists explain the relationship between signs and culture and other sign systems in terms of rhetorical operations such as metaphor and metonymy (Danesi 2013). By comparing, contrasting, and extending meanings from one sign system to the other, rhetorical operations forge synergies between brands, culture, and marketing.

A Cultural Strategy at Coca-Cola

A case in point is the integrated media campaign, "Move to the Beat of London," developed by Coca-Cola to promote its participation in the 2012 London Olympics. The campaign website explains that Coke aimed to actively engage the interest of teenagers in the Olympic Games and to encourage them to participate in a healthy, active lifestyle. The campaign demonstrates how Coke created cultural, social, and media connections between the brand, consumers, and popular culture to penetrate the youth market.

A BRAND-CENTERED CULTURE

Figure 5.6 illustrates that the Coke brand system, not culture, motivates these connections. First of all, the campaign confronts the common criticism that soft drinks are responsible for the obesity epidemic, by motivating youth to "move"—to take an interest in sports and live healthy lifestyles. The campaign also resonates with the First Lady Michelle Obama's "Let's Move" campaign against childhood obesity.

To actively engage consumers in the movement, the campaign leverages both cultural and media connections between consumers and the brand system. Rhetorical associations compare, contrast, and extend the meanings associated with the culture system, on the one hand, and social and media systems, on the other. They form pathways between Coke's equities as a socially responsible, connected, global, and youthful brand and the digitally connected, altruistic, and multicultural youth culture of young Millennials.

Furthermore, the "Move to the Beat" campaign appeals to two key interests of consumers in the youth cohort—music and sports, and also responds to a strong identification of young consumers with group membership.

The campaign not only leverages cultural correspondences between consumers and the Coke brand but also reaches consumers at their most active points of media participation. The campaign synthesizes sponsored music and sporting events, a social media project, consumer-generated content, traditional media, and community outreach into a complex, multimedia hypertext.

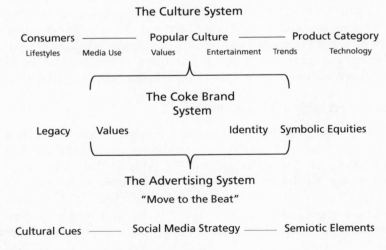

Figure 5.6. A Cultural Brand Strategy for Coke

The social media project invites consumers to participate in a music video production by signing into the digital application, "Create my beat," through Facebook. The agency MRY developed an algorithm that synthesizes the Coke Olympic anthem with the social activities and musical preferences participants post on their Facebook pages. According to MRY, "Your social activity has been mixed with the track, producing a dynamic music video with concert footage, athletes, and your Facebook photos. Over 3.5 million custom tracks were created, that were then combined into a single global beat that the whole world could move to." (Please see: http://vimeo.com/61095042.)

THE ROLE OF RHETORIC

In summary, Coke's "Move to the Beat" campaign both *resembles* and *creates* a *contiguous* connection between brand semiotics and the culture, interests, and media behaviors of young Millennials. According to cognitive linguistic theory, rhetorical operations actually form cognitive paths in the brain between disparate systems of meaning, such as culture and brands (Lakoff and Johnson 1980; Jakobson 1990 [1956]). By taking a closer look at the "Move" hypertext, the following figure illustrates how rhetorical operations compare, contrast, and extend the meanings associated with consumer culture and the Coke brand. These connections motivate in turn the content and media strategy of the advertising campaign (Figure 5.7). For the purposes of this illustration, I focus on four paths of association—happiness, community,

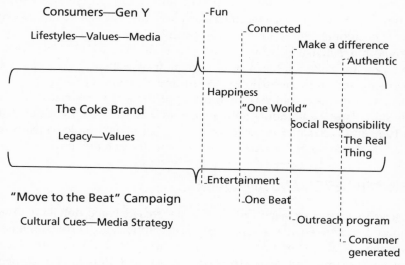

Figure 5.7. Rhetorical Pathways

social responsibility, and authenticity—that link the culture system and the "Move" campaign to the Coke brand.

Coke's historical association with happiness links to the needs of young consumers for fun and leads to the entertainment value of the campaign. Coke's "One World" global perspective matches the media connectedness of young Millennials and motivates the use of social media to reach this target. Coke's commitment to social causes has a long history and responds to the desire of young Millennials to make a difference in their communities. And Coke's historical association with "The Real Thing" aligns with consumer needs for authenticity, because the campaign draws directly from authentic, consumer-generated content.

Finding a Cultural Strategy for My Tea

The brand-centered cultural strategy that Coke used to structure the "Move" campaign was built upon Coke's strong and deep equities in social responsibility, personal relationships, and happiness. Creative strategy would have focused on leveraging connections between these equities and contemporary consumer culture. The research process for this kind of study would be fairly straightforward. Researchers would begin with a semiotic analysis of historical advertising for the brand and match findings with the current needs and behaviors of the target market.

In contrast, the case study for My Tea involved a brand of bottled tea that had lost equity over a twenty-year period when a third party took over its distribution. By the time management took back the brand, it not only lacked a clear positioning in relation to competitive brands such as Lipton and Arizona, but had fallen behind category trends that favored unprocessed beverages. To make matters worse, current management lacked access to advertising and consumer data developed under previous management. All that remained was an old campaign from the 1970s that associated My Tea with silly, slapstick humor. Although the ad was still being circulated on YouTube, it was a matter for speculation whether many people remembered the ad or if it could be leveraged in the current strategic process.

RESEARCH DESIGN AND APPROACH

To develop a new campaign for My Tea, researchers could not simply trace connections between the brand's historical equities and current trends in consumer culture. They first had to clarify ways to distinguish the brand from competitors. But who are their competitors? Bottled teas compete with a wide range of ready-to-drink beverages for consumer choice, so researchers broadened the data scope to include advertising for Sodas, Waters, bottled Teas, and Sports and Energy drinks. The data set was also expanded beyond the Tea category to include all tea formats, such as loose and bags, and included both mainstream and specialty markets for tea.

Furthermore, all beverage types claimed to offer "refreshment," so it was necessary to identify how "tea refreshment" was different from the refreshment of Soda drinks, bottled Water, Energy drinks, and Sports drinks. Researchers identified five cultural spaces based upon the distinct messages, emotions, and visuals each beverage type associates with refreshment. They then mapped the five spaces on a visual brandscape (Figure 5.8) that showed very clearly how tea related to other beverage types. The brandscape tool is vital for making new product and promotion decisions because it provides a road map for steering brands clear of cultural associations with declining categories, such as sweetened Soda drinks. It also shows how brands such as Lipton extend their product lines into more than one cultural space, thus expanding their markets.

To clarify My Tea's distinct personality and identity within the bottled Tea category, researchers investigated the possibility of leveraging the brand's historical equities in silly humor. Researchers conducted focus groups to assess the memorability of the old slapstick campaign from the 1970s. They conducted media and secondary research into popular comedy styles in contemporary

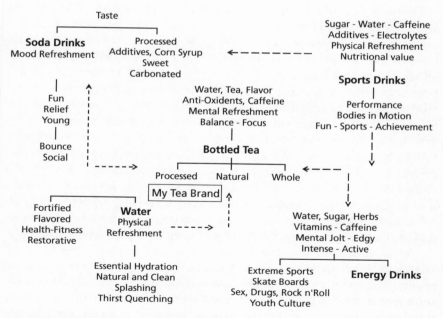

Figure 5.8. The Ready-to-Drink Brandscape

entertainment and popular culture. Researchers watched dozens of programs and ads on YouTube and read current theater reviews and newspaper articles related to Generation Y culture.

CULTURAL BRANDING RESEARCH

The case illustrates the basic principle of the semiotics of cultural branding, namely that brands align with culture along the lines of symbolic associations. It also highlights the cultural dimension of product categories, which conform to very specific codes and conventions structuring the meaning of products within the category. Category codes shape consumer expectations of a product or service. They also influence brand strategy because they define the parameters within which a brand can innovate without confusing consumers or devaluing the brand. For example, the pastels and playful décor of ice cream shops signal the category's association with sweet indulgence and play. The same design scheme would be out of place in the legal profession, where formal interiors and bland color schemes communicate the category's association with sober, rational professionalism. The décor is the most obvious element of a code system that includes staff behavior, transaction rituals, and the customer relationship for the category. Consumers learn these codes the same way they learn language, through consistent, long-term exposure in their day-to-day encounters with the market.

The study focused on cultural discourses found in popular culture, such as films, books, and Internet sites for the segment. This approach reflects the influence of Lévi-Strauss (1967 [1958]: 80–96) on marketing semiotics research. Lévi-Strauss discovered the myths structuring meaning in a research setting by uncovering patterns in the disposition and treatment of goods, rituals, signage, and sacred artifacts. He claimed that such symbols communicated "significant knowledge of the unconscious attitudes of the society or societies under consideration" (p. 86). Lévi-Strauss actually spent very little time in the field with informants, relying instead on cultural texts and artifacts, such as restaurant menus. By comparing and contrasting the preparation and presentation of food in Chinese and French contexts, for example, Lévi-Strauss (1966 [1965]) made inferences about the values, myths, and social organization of each culture. Following Lévi-Strauss, marketing semiotics research collects data from popular media and marketing texts, from advertising to package design. Such "artifacts" contribute to cultural production as surely as the rituals, traditions, and ethnic identities studied by anthropologists.

Although the study of cultural discourses does not preclude the use of primary consumer research in any given project, it has the advantage over consumer research of providing access to the broad cultural myths structuring meaning in a product category or consumer segment on a mass scale. In this case, primary research with consumers was conducted in a second phase to confirm and refine findings from phase one, the study of popular culture.

THE READY-TO-DRINK CATEGORY

Research began with an audit of the marketing communications, packaging, labeling, and point-of-purchase signage in the broad competitive environment, consisting of the RTD category as a whole, including Soda, Tea, Water, and Energy and Sports drinks. Bottled coffee was not included because its share of market was not on a par with other categories. Each subcategory associated refreshment with different consumer benefits, different areas of the body, different mood states, and distinct cultural discourses. As the map of the RTD category shows (Figure 5.8), these subcategories overlap along the lines of their symbolic associations, i.e. the clear benefits of water are shared by tea; the energizing effects of sports drinks are shared with Energy drink space, and so on. The terms associated with each beverage category on the map were drawn from advertising, packaging, retail displays, and websites for leading brands of RTD beverages.

Soda and Energy Drinks

Sweet, carbonated soda drinks and energy drinks represent opposite poles of the RTD category. Soda drinks refresh the mood and tickle the tongue. Unlike newer categories, soda drinks do not claim any nutritional value, but emphasize pleasure, play, "bounce," and sociality. The Soda category has been declining in recent years due to changing attitudes toward processed foods, corn syrup, and obesity. Soda companies such as Coke and Pepsi have counteracted these trends by increasing their involvement in social causes and community outreach and developing new products in the other beverage categories.

In contrast, Energy drinks form a growth category associated with purpose and substance. Energy drinks refresh the mind and stimulate the body to work harder. They claim a nutritional value because they contain electrolytes, herbs, and vitamins. The Energy drink culture was originally associated with extreme street sports like skateboarding and an edgy, even Goth lifestyle. As brands from other categories develop and extend into the Energy space, Energy drink culture has expanded into a lifestyle preference associated with edgy humor, intense intellectual pursuits, Olympic sports, and cutting-edge rock music.

Standing at opposite ends of the RTD spectrum, the Soda and Energy spaces define the paradigmatic dimensions of the RTD category along the lines of two cultural binaries, body/mind and play/purpose. This initial binary analysis provided a roadmap for mapping the cultural positionings of the other beverage types in the RTD category (Figure 5.9).

Sports Drinks

Sports drinks have held their ground over the years. They overlap with Soda drinks because of their emphasis on play and ingredients including chemical additives, intense sweetness, and, in the case of Coke's Powerade, carbonation.

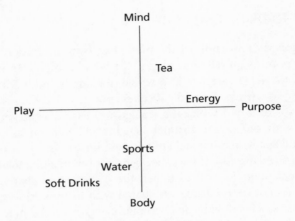

Figure 5.9. The Strategic Dimensions of the RTD category

Sports drinks sidestep the culture wars against sweet, processed drinks because they are fortified with "vital nutrients" such as salts and electrolytes to refuel and refresh after physical activity. The Sports category also overlaps with the Energy space because of its emphasis on performance, personal achievement, and in some brands, the use of caffeine. The combination of physical activity, fun, and performance positions Sports drinks between play, body, and purpose.

Water

Water refreshes the body by providing hydration and quenching thirst. It provides a clear and natural alternative to processed beverages. The pleasure of water is associated with splashing and cleansing the body. In the face of fierce competition from other beverage categories, water brands such as Evian have moved into health and beauty discourses, promising clear skin, youthful energy, and other esthetic benefits. As the category trends toward flavored, enhanced, and fortified waters, brands such as Vitamin Water and Smart Water edge into the Sports and Energy spaces on the one hand and the Tea space on the other. Flavored waters share equities with soda drinks. Water fits within the play/body and body/purpose spaces on the grid.

Bottled Tea

Tea refreshes the mind by providing the natural stimulation of tea extract. Processed sweetened teas such as My Tea are positioned as an alternative to sodas. The Tea category cannot be fixed in a single quadrant due to the wide range of products on the market, including Processed teas that share equities with Soda, Natural teas that balance body and mind, and Whole teas that communicate social activism and global awareness. Brands such as Lipton have extended beyond the Processed beverage space into the Natural and Whole Tea and Energy drink spaces.

THE BROADER TEA CATEGORY

This cursory analysis of the RTD category provides insights into the effects of broader category trends on the perception and performance of any given brand. These trends are in constant flux as brands respond to market trends and extend into new categories to grow market share. In other words, a brand's relevance and value depend not only upon the immediate competitive environment, but upon the ever-shifting relationships between the brand, the product category, and other categories in a market sector such as RTD beverages. To account for the breadth of these influences on the brand, the Marketing Semiotics company expanded the scope of research beyond the mass market of processed bottled teas and focused on tea and tea culture as represented in advertising and packaging for a wide range of teas. Researchers included all tea formats and smaller specialty brands available online or at upscale stores such as Whole Foods Market.

THE MAINSTREAM MARKET

In-store research into My Tea's competitors in the Processed bottled tea category yielded very narrow insights about broader trends related to Tea. To achieve economy of scale, supermarkets trim down their offerings to mass brands that appeal to the largest common denominator of customers. Within the Processed bottled Tea category, competitors such as Arizona, Lipton, and Rock Star differ in terms of flavorings, packaging formats, and brand personalities, but they do not reflect the intense cultural tensions within food culture that have doomed Processed teas and sodas to irrelevance.

In the past fifteen years or so, changes in consumer knowledge and expectations about health and wellness have prompted a revolution in the production and marketing of food and beverage. The codes associated with Processed beverages, such as the use of additives, corn syrup, mysterious chemicals, and complex ingredient panels, have given way to emergent codes related to Natural and Whole food discourses. Natural products communicate clarity and simplicity, and transparency, and they are accessible to the average customer. In the Natural tea space, brewed tea, natural sugar, and simple, recognizable ingredients have replaced the tea extracts, corn syrup, and chemical additives used in processed teas. Whole tea brands promise product authenticity and integrity, as well as the cultural equities associated with ethical food production, Fair Trade policies, and sustainable agriculture.

Within the supermarket space, RTD brands such as Lipton and Snapple have extended new products into the Natural and Whole tea categories, along with newer brands such as Starbucks' Tazo. However, these kinds of brands occupy a relatively narrow shelf space in the supermarket and underrepresent the growing strength of Tea in the food and beverage sector, the range of cultural associations that Tea represents, and the potential strategic opportunities it suggests for My Tea across the RTD category.

THE SPECIALTY MARKET

In contrast with the on-site research in the supermarket research, three days of research at a Whole Foods mega-store in Chicago exposed the broad scope and depth of the contemporary cultural discourses related to tea in all formats, as illustrated in Figure 5.9. The aisle devoted to tea includes every imaginable ingredient, flavor, and food-sourcing alternative in the marketplace, from natural and traditional teas to raw, whole, and exotic teas from Africa and the Amazon.

The point of purchase display also reflects the strategic uses of package design and labeling to communicate each brand's cultural positioning. Whereas the mainstream tea market uses labeling and package design to communicate brand ownership and basic nutritional benefits, the specialty tea market uses package design and messaging to communicate the brand's cultural positioning as related to ingredient sourcing, safety, sustainable agriculture, environmental protection, and alternative, New Age spirituality.

Furthermore, in contrast to European tea culture, which homogenizes tea's ethnic origins and represents Britain's colonial reach into India and China, contemporary tea discourses celebrate the cultural integrity of their sources in Asia, Africa, and the Amazon. In place of European blends of black and green teas, contemporary brands boast the use of whole, exotic plants such as rooibus, yerba maté, and white tea, emphasizing the multicultural, one-world perspective of the new food culture.

EMERGING ISSUES IN FOOD CULTURE

On-site observations of the cultural discourses on packaging for tea at Whole Foods confirmed findings from secondary research in sources such as the popular press, specialty magazines, and food websites. The bifurcation of food production into Processed, Natural, and Whole categories represents the distinct ideological and ethical discourses related to food sourcing, safety, and social responsibility in contemporary culture. These kinds of discourses define the cultural positioning of food and beverage brands in terms of

Figure 5.10. Cultural Dimensions of Tea

their relation to one of these ideological discourses. These discourses play out with particular force in the growing tea market. The grid in Figure 5.10 represents the complex implications between Processed, Natural, and Whole tea categories and the brand's ideology, integrity, and modernity.

The Semiotics of Tea

The cultural positioning of each brand of tea is communicated by distinctive semiotic codes. New Age brands such as Enlighten employ inspiring language, bright colors, flowery fonts, and exotic patterns suggestive of India and the Near East. Social activist brands employ straightforward designs and use the label to display stories and images from the social causes they support, such as Rishi's sponsorship of Jane Goodall's Roots and Shoots foundation. Bottled tea brands such as Honest and Ito En communicate their commitment to product integrity and clarity in clear bottles and clean-cut designs, and very simple ingredient panels. Even when a brand such as Republic of Tea develops product lines in several cultural spaces, they differentiate packaging for each product line according to the design codes appropriate for their cultural positioning.

In addition to package design semiotics, certification badges adorn packaging as testimony to the brand's commitment to one or more of the following causes, including Fair Trade, wind power, the Rainforest Alliance, and organic, non-GMO, and Kosher food production. In other words, the meaning of food consumption has transcended its traditional association with nutrition, flavor, and sociality and become a vehicle for social activism and cultural resistance.

Tea in the RTD Category

Looking closely at the meanings associated with Processed, Natural, and Whole teas (Figure 5.10), from mob dancing on the one hand to ethical marketing on the other, researchers found that the Tea category is structured by the same body/mind and play/purpose binaries that structure the RTD category generally (Figure 5.9). This insight prompted an analysis of the semiotic dimensions of the Tea category on a double vector grid defined by the opposition of Processed teas and Whole teas (Figure 5.11).

Processed teas occupy the lower left body/play quadrant due to the ingredients and benefits they share with sodas. Whole teas belong in the mind/purpose quadrant due to their association with social causes, global consumer culture, and spiritual development. Natural teas balance mind and body, play and purpose, and straddle several quadrants.

Furthermore, these cultural binaries correlate with the rhetorical styles of Processed and Energy teas. In the lower left quadrant, My Tea is associated with slapstick, a light style of comedy associated with bodies in moving, slipping, falling, and splashing. In the upper right quadrant are energy drinks such as Red Bull, characterized by irony and satire, which are more intellectual forms of comedy associated with political and social criticism. Findings from the media research confirmed that My Tea's association with slapstick comedy was as out of date as its use of processed ingredients.

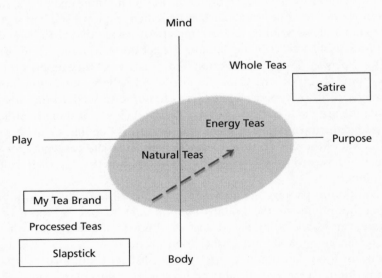

Figure 5.11. A New Cultural Space for My Tea

My Tea in Contemporary Culture

A recent Nielson survey found that humor is the lens through which Gen Ys view the world, themselves, and others (Carter 2012). Research into the entertainment and media preferences of Gen Ys revealed a very distinctive trend toward weird humor. It ranges from the intellectual and satirical styles of Jon Stewart, Steven Colbert, and *Saturday Night Live* to the dark humor of films such as *Hunger Games* and the lowbrow humor of Comedy Central and *Family Guy*. Contemporary comedy builds upon duplicity, absurdity, and role-play to take aim at political and cultural targets. It also characterizes a popular trend in advertising, movies, and stage shows such as the *Book of Mormon*. The irreverent sting of satire spares nothing, even the sacred spaces of religion, big business, and racial politics.

A CULTURAL STRATEGY FOR MY TEA

The research suggested several options for My Tea management. They could develop new advertising for the current brand, develop new products in the Natural and Whole tea categories, enter peripheral categories such as Energy drinks, or all three of the above. In any case, given the importance of humor for the Gen Y segment, researchers encouraged management to leverage their historical equities in humor, however weak they may be. They would have to align the slapstick style from the 1970s with contemporary styles of comedy. Furthermore, if they were to extend the brand into Natural and Whole teas and Energy drinks, they would also need to adapt the brand's comedic style to the tone of each beverage category, including the down-to-earth tone of the Natural space, the loftier tone of the Whole space, and the edgy, satirical tone of the Energy drink space.

Conclusion

The My Tea case illustrates how semiotic research has direct and material impact on the market value of brands by leveraging the brand's strategic relationship to competitors, category trends, and consumer culture. This approach clarifies the brand's cultural positioning by matching its historical identity with a specific cultural space on the map. By taking the broad view of brands in relation to the cultural dimensions of the category, semiotics also identifies a strong and innovative strategy for updating the brand and extending it into new products and consumer segments. Furthermore, by comparing and contrasting the brand's traditional image with trends in popular media and entertainment, the semiotics of cultural branding aligns creative strategy with the current mood and tastes of the target market.

6   Semiotic Ethnography

Consumer ethnography has gained in popularity over the past decade because of its promise to account for the rich cultural factors influencing consumer behavior. In contrast with focus groups and in-depth interviews, conducted in the artificial environments of research facilities, ethnography stages encounters with consumers in their lived environments. Semiotic ethnography in particular is a form of qualitative research that aims for a "thick description" (Geertz 1973) of the field site. It is "thick" because it accounts for the complex and dynamic character of meaning production and the tentative nature of any particular interpretation of consumer behavior. This chapter reviews the theory and practice of semiotic ethnography and its application to marketing research.

In this chapter I extend the recent literature on commercial ethnography[1] by rigorously analyzing the theoretical foundations of semiotic ethnography in structural semiotics, the evolution of semiotic theory over the past century, and its implications for value creation in the marketplace. I draw insights from examples and a case study that challenge and advance current theories and I illustrate concepts by means of figures and illustrations.

I also guide readers through the design and practice of semiotic ethnography with reference to cases from actual business projects. Case studies and examples illustrate how to translate ethnographic findings into actionable business solutions for marketers. The discussion covers a range of management applications, from advertising research to new product positioning and public policy marketing. I preview the case study below in order to ground the theoretical discussion which follows in marketing research practice.

Case Preview—Creating Value in the Luxury Sector

The case presented later in the chapter focuses on the luxury semiotics and the behavior of affluent consumers in Paris, France. It forms part of a global research study that aimed to identify historical, cultural, and marketing factors that influence the perception of value in the luxury sector across three markets: China, Europe, and North America. Research led to actionable

---

[1] See Sunderland and Denny 2007; Cefkin 2010; Jordan 2012; Denny and Sunderland 2014.

recommendation for developing a global merchandising strategy for an international distributor of luxury brands. The case also advances knowledge about the cultural basis of value creation in cross-cultural contexts. Findings shed light on the complex and even contradictory nature of consumers' interpretations of value in this sector. They highlight the role of context on value creation. What defines value for consumers in one setting may not define value in another. It focuses on a theory of semiotic performance that accounts for the ways consumers shift perspectives between two or more cultural frames and value systems in their quest for distinction, pleasure, and rare experiences.

The Semiotic Paradigm in Ethnographic Research

Herzfeld (1983b) coined the term "semiotic ethnography" to describe an interpretive practice that brings structural semiotics to bear on the design and interpretation ethnographic practice. He claims that semiotic ethnography is distinct because it reflects upon the ethnographic disposition itself: "A truly semiotic ethnographic focus must be reflexive to the point of recognizing both the contingent nature of such interpretive devices, and the contextual nature of all cultural phenomena" (p. 100). Semiotic ethnography accounts for the multiple discourses, cultural perspectives, and sign systems at play in the interpretive process (Winner 1983). It exposes tensions and synergies between consumers' statements and their ritual behaviors, social interactions, and the disposition of their possessions in domestic space. It reflects upon the ethnographic disposition itself, including the intersubjective joining ethnographer, informant, and the informant's narrative.

A distinctive feature of semiotic ethnography is the implication of theory and practice at every stage of research, including design, data collection, and analysis. When Herzfeld (1983b) claims that semiotic ethnography is the "pragmatic embodiment of theory," he refers to the dialectical tension between the spontaneous unfolding of events in the lived environment and the theoretical toolkit ethnographers bring to the field to make sense of these events. Unlike hypothesis testing, which uses research to prove a theory, semiotic ethnography employs theory to decode the field site and also uses field operations to advance theories about the traditions, social organization, and perception of value in a given setting.

Semiotics invites the ethnographer to reflect upon the role of cultural codes in the perceived meaning and value of cultural signs (Joseph 1983). For example, when studying wedding rituals in Shanghai, the ethnographer may reflect upon the meaning of "bride," "marriage," and white dresses for young Chinese consumers. Modern Chinese weddings consist of a pastiche of cultural codes drawn from local legend and one hundred years of colonization, foreign occupation, the Cultural Revolution, and global capitalism.

Semiotic ethnographers are trained to identify emerging patterns in the data and use this information to refocus the study, adjust the research protocol, or improvise in order to gain deeper insights into the early stage findings. They know when to digress from the structured protocol to follow up on a lead suggested by an informant or organize a spontaneous focus group with the informant's friends. They also accept the inherent instability of meaning and consumer identity in the ethnographic encounter, recognizing, rather than trying to rationalize, the inevitable shifts and contradictions within the consumer narrative. Far from undermining the validity of findings, these kinds of digressions increase the range of potential meanings associated with a brand or category. They also lead to more nuanced and spontaneous insights about the research topic.

FROM STRUCTURALISM TO SEMIOTIC ETHNOGRAPHY

Semiotics-based ethnography builds upon the dual legacies of structural linguistics and the structural tradition in French sociology leading from Durkheim (1997 [1893]), Mauss (2000 [1925]), and Lévi-Strauss (1974 [1963]) and Bourdieu (1977 [1972]). For example, Lévi-Strauss proposed that the ethnographic field site is a textual system organized by binary codes.

Codes structure the consistency and universality of cultural norms and meanings for social groups over time. The binary analysis reflects the dialect-ical structure of the cultural categories organizing these norms and meanings. For instance, the good/evil binary structures morality; the male/female binary structures gender; the dominant/dominated binary structures power, and so on. Lévi-Strauss drew inferences from the organization of cultural binaries, such as masculine/feminine, into paradigmatic systems that define a culture's myths and beliefs. He found, for instance, that the binary raw/cooked leads to inferences about a culture's belief system, social organization, and myths.

Lévi-Strauss applied Saussure's theory of signs to the study of culture and found parallels between language and cultural systems. He dismissed the notion that culture is a transcendent essence originating in Nature, because culture, like language, consists of a system of codes and conventions that social groups deploy in order to make sense of their world. This principle led to the concept of cultural relativism, which levels the traditional hierarchies dividing society's insiders from its "others." Cultural relativism places in question the notion that some cultures are more "primitive" than others and takes stock of the distinct codes structuring meaning and value in each cultural system.

The structural tradition influenced Bourdieu's (1984 [1979]) cultural ana-lysis of status distinction in elite French society. In the notion of the *habitus*, Bourdieu explained class distinction in terms of one's access to cultural capital or special knowledge, as opposed to the intrinsic superiority of one over the other. Though Bourdieu criticized structuralism for its overemphasis on universal laws, he nonetheless acknowledged the influence of Lévi-Strauss when he compared the cultural system or *habitus* to a kind of "language" (1998 [1994]).[2]

Structuralism found a home in French scientific circles because it conforms to the Cartesian tradition in French culture and thought. The emphasis on abstract principles over pragmatism is evident in all areas of French life, from the legal system to urban planning. Furthermore, since Durkheim and Mauss, like Lévi-Strauss and Bourdieu, spent little to no time in the field, they tended toward abstract reasoning and theory development, basing their findings on the analysis of data from surveys and secondary sources.

Semiotic ethnography evolved out of the debates of American anthropologists such as Sahlins (2004 [1965]), Geertz (1973), and Herzfeld (1983a and 1989) with structural semiotics. Drawing upon their experiences in the field, they challenged structuralism's emphasis on the formal organization of the textual system and brought attention to the effects of the ethnographic disposition on meaning production. Semiotic ethnographers do not so much reject the theory of codes as clarify the equally important role of consumer performance and agency in the deployment of codes in daily practice. As Joseph (1983) declares, "Semiotics insists that at least certain aspects of behavior are coded and that its task is to unravel how a people constitutes its codes of signification" (p. 211). The ethnographic disposition stages the intersection of context, reference, and the complex inter-subjective relationship between ethnographer and informants in the active production of meaning.

The focus of American anthropologists on the ethnographic disposition reflects developments in post-structural semiotics itself, which, by the 1950s, was already moving away from the focus on signs and codes to issues of reference and subjectivity in discourse (Benveniste 1971[1958]). I discuss these developments further on in the chapter.

SEMIOTICS AND VALUE CREATION

The notion that signs create value runs through the semiotic literature and originates in Saussure's (2011 [1916]) comparison of signs to coins, whose value is dependent upon their relationship to other factors in the monetary system. In sign systems, these other factors consist of variables in the cultural context. The cultural relativism of value has important implications for cultures in contact, because it implies that the value attached to a term in

---

[2] "But the essential point is that, when perceived through these social categories of perception, these principles of vision and division, the differences in practices, in the goods possessed, or in the opinions expressed become symbolic differences and constitute a veritable *language*" (Bourdieu 1998 [1994]: 8).

one language may not be transferable to the same term in translation. Saussure cites the example of the French word "*mouton*," which translates into English as both the animal "sheep" and the meat "mutton." Since the French lexicon does not differentiate between mutton and sheep, this example suggests something of the complexity of translating signs and meaning from one culture to another. It also warrants further discussion.

Sahlins (1976) interprets this example as evidence of a cultural limitation of the French, who "have not yet been able to participate in the higher distinction between the raw and the cooked" (p. 63). However, Whorf (1956) reminds us that linguistic differences do not reflect the superiority of one culture over another, but the different value systems that cultures bring to bear on meaning production.

Whorf's Hypothesis

In comparative linguistic studies, Whorf found that the importance of a concept in a culture determines the scope and function of its lexicon. This idea sheds light on the role of cultural value in the sheep/mutton example. The frugality of the French lexicon for sheep may not reflect France's lack of "higher distinction between raw and cooked," as Sahlins claims, but the different values assigned to sheep in French and British cultures. The French lack a special word for cooked sheep because their gastronomical traditions assign greater value to lamb, "*agneau*"—a milder, tenderer meat—than mutton, at the table. As a result, the French language includes a larger lexicon for lamb, "*agneau*," associated with the raising and preparation of lamb for the table.

While the English order lamb or mutton in a restaurant, French usage emphasizes the cut and preparation of the meat. One orders a *gigot*, the leg of lamb, or some other cut, such as *côtelette*, *selle*, or *filet*. Furthermore, the importance of the lamb lexicon in France reflects the relative importance of gastronomical arts and industry in French culture over wool and textiles. In English, by comparison, the sheep/mutton distinction reflects the relative importance of the wool and textile industries in the United Kingdom as compared to gastronomy (Figure 6.1).

The point of this example is to explain how cultural codes structure the perceived value of goods and product categories and determine the way these goods are represented in signs, symbols, and ritual behavior. This insight has important implications for the case study on luxury, because it accounts for differences in the perceived value of luxury goods from one market to another on the basis of cultural difference.

Lévi-Strauss (1966 [1965]) extends the principle of semiotic value from language to cultural symbols, whose worth is not defined strictly by their exchange value in a supply and demand economy, but by the intangible

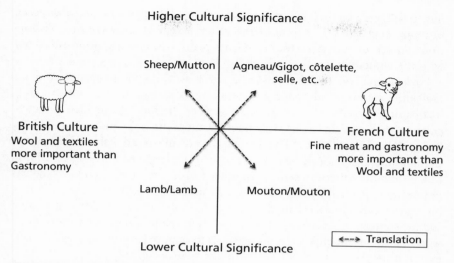

Figure 6.1. Two Cultures, Two Value Systems

benefits they bring to consumers' social strategies for gaining security, status, and power. This principle applies to all kinds of cultural phenomena, from gestures to product rituals, and is entirely dependent on the context and the social situation in which the communication is framed.

For example, there is no special word for "hug" in the French language, which reflects the different values French and Americans give to physical intimacy as a sign of greeting. While it is not uncommon for informal acquaintances in the United States to wrap their arms around each other in a physical embrace, the French greet acquaintances with the famous kiss on each cheek, while keeping bodily contact at a minimum. For intimate relations they add a third kiss on the cheek and maybe a squeeze on the arms. They acquiesce stiffly to taking hugs from Americans. This cultural difference is reinforced by the contrasting meanings of the English word "embrace" and its French homonym "*embrasser.*" In English "to embrace" involves some form of hug. By contrast, the French term "*embrasser*" refers primarily to kissing, reflecting once again the different values each culture assigns to public signs of intimacy.

Code Switching

Cultural codes play a role in the shared rituals and meanings of consumers in groups, but are guidelines, not laws. Consumers may "switch codes" in a given situation to navigate the social world and achieve personal goals. Sahlins (2004 [1965]) highlights a tension within semiotics between the code and the living, breathing actions of consumers as they put codes into action. To hug or not to hug may be dictated by a social strategy that gains for the individual prestige or influence, in spite of the value system of their culture. Visitors from France may borrow the American custom to communicate solidarity with the United States.

For example, on a recent trip to San Francisco, French President François Hollande was observed hugging a compatriot during a tour of a technology incubator. A reporter for *Le Monde* described "le hug" as an "act of reconciliation" between President Hollande and the technology industry in Silicon Valley (Coutausse 2014). The French President found value in hugging, though hugging is not valued in France, because it served a strategic semiotic function in the American setting. In other words, the value of cultural signs is not entirely dictated by the code—i.e. Americans hug, the French do not—but by the individual's calculations about the value of the sign or gesture in a specific context. What is really at stake here is the issue of semiotic performance, when consumers manipulate cultural codes to achieve personal and social goals, even if it means acting out of step with their native culture.

The Semiotics of Performance

The semiotics of performance is a theory of the ongoing implication of consumer decisions and semiotic codes in meaning production (Oswald 1989a, b). It includes but is not limited to the strategies consumers employ to present a certain image to society (Goffman 1959). The semiotics of performance also accounts for the moment-to-moment strategies consumers employ to implement codes to their advantage. It has important implications for ethnographic research because it accounts for the dynamic of inter-subject-ivity and reference joining ethnographer, informant, the informant narrative, and the cultural context in the field setting.

Though the theory of semiotic performance has evolved significantly over the past century, it is actually not a new idea, but is embedded in code theory itself. In Saussure (2011 [1916]), it takes the form of the ongoing dialectic between linguistic codes [*la langue*] and active speech [*la parole*] that enable speakers to adapt the code to the needs of a given communication event. The dialectic of code and performance has parallels in non-linguistic systems. For instance, the *Rules of the Road* define ideal norms that drivers execute with more or less precision.

In the 1920s and 1930s, the Prague Structuralists extended the notion of performance to include linguistic functions that could not be explained by code theory alone because they mark the effects of extra-linguistic events on meaning, such as the speaker's intentions, their interactions with the receiver of the message, and reference to the context (see Garvin 1964; Veltrusky 1981; Jakobson 1990a, b [1983]). They drew special attention to the inter-personal dynamic structuring relationships between the actors involved in the semiotic event, including ethnographic fieldwork (Hymes 1982).

The Prague Structuralists anticipated developments in speech act theory in the 1950s, which exposes the potential ambiguity and "untruth" of statements taken out of context (Austin 1955). For example, ironic statements imply a kind of complicity between speaker and receiver of a message, whose shared perception of the context determines the meaning and intention of the statement. To grasp the irony of a statement such as "That's just great!" the listener would have to know that the speaker is referring to something that is *not* that great, such as a financial loss.

The work of the Prague School linguists, which was obscured by political events in Europe in the 1930s and 1940s, also anticipated by about thirty years the burning issues of post-structural semiotics in post-war France, from Benveniste's (1971 [1958]) theory of discourse to Derrida's (1983 [1972]) deconstruction of the linguistic sign, where he exposed the theatricality of sign-play in action.

The semiotics of performance presented here builds upon the work of Benveniste (1971 [1958]), a French linguist who shifted attention from the structure of signs to the organization of signs into discourses. Since discourse is a statement produced by someone for someone else, whether in conversation, in narrative, or some other form of representation, discourse theory expands the focus of semiotics from the sign to the dynamic of reference and intersubjectivity in semiotic performance. Performative functions include "shifters" (Jakobson 1990 [1958]), adverbs of time and place, and rhetorical figures. Shifters are indexical signs that mark relations of subjectivity, spatiality, and time in discourse. They include the personal pronouns [I/you/he/she/it], the demonstrative pronouns [this/that], and adverbial pronouns [here/there]. Discourse theory also accounts for the inscription of narrative voice and point of view in representation by means of rhetorical figures and tone, such as irony.

Deixis is a performative function that stages the implication of actors, utterances, and reference to the context in all kinds of semiotic systems, from theater and cinema to the servicescapes which structure consumers' participation in the retail spectacle. Deixis also structures the interpersonal, spatial, and temporal dynamic of the ethnographic disposition itself.

Implications of Deixis for Marketing Research

Since the deictic function structures relations of identity and reference in discourse, it has more than academic interest for the research practitioner because it sheds light on the complexity of cultural identity and its impact on brand choice. For instance, the Ford Motor Company commissioned semiotic ethnographic research in the Mexican American market in California for use in new product development and advertising strategy for the F-150 truck. Working with an Mexican American researcher, ethnographers highlighted the tensions at play in the lives of ethnic consumers, who try to maintain ties to their home

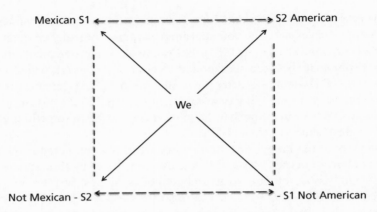

Figure 6.2. The Immigrant's Dilemma

culture and also establish a home in the United States. These tensions were reflected in their ambiguous use of the pronoun "we." Sometimes "we" referred to their memories of Mexico, at others their life in the United States. These reference points turned out to be cultural ideals rather than realities. Mexico represented a legendary homeland; the United States represented the American Dream. As Mexican Americans living in California, respondents felt like outsiders in their home country and marginalized in the new one. The grid below illustrates the deictic dimensions of the immigrant's dilemma. They are positioned culturally as neither "here" nor "there" (Figure 6.2).

Respondents did not surrender to the alienation of their outsider status, however, but employed consumption strategies to manage their relationships to various contexts. Food preparation, dress, brand choice, and even accents were adapted according to the social situation. With extended family, these experiences leaned toward Mexican traditions; with colleagues and neighbors they leaned toward mainstream American traditions. Ethnic consumers may also show off their cultural difference with behaviors that contrast with their milieus. These insights into ethnic consumer behavior support Peñaloza's (1994) findings about symbolic "border crossings" and reiterate my own findings from research with Haitian Americans (Oswald 1999). I found that ethnic consumers "culture swap" when they shift perspectives between multiple cultural contexts and value systems by means of symbolic consumption.

First generation immigrants also form perceptions of brands in the automotive category based upon their relative degree of identification with either home or host culture. In an ethnic market dominated by Ford and Chevy, Ford loyal buyers said they chose Ford because they identified with the brand's association with the American Dream of upward mobility, self-determination, and material success. Chevy-loyal buyers chose Chevrolet because they identified with the brand's association with tradition, pride of place, and family heritage.

The semiotics of performance has important implications for consumer ethnography because it exposes the multiple, overlapping factors at play in the ethnographic disposition itself, including the ethnographer's own cultural perspective. The semiotic ethnographer's task involves deconstructing the multiple intersecting contexts consumers navigate to adapt to their environments.

The case below illustrates that the value consumers associate with luxury goods is not static, but changes in relation to the optics of a given context. These optics are structured in binary pairs that structure the perception of higher and lower value in a cultural context. They include the old money/new money binary that distinguishes "authentic" social status from imitations; the insider/outsider binary that marks France's pretentions to superiority in the realm of taste; and the personal/social binary that distinguishes consumers' existential goals, such as pleasure, from their social goals, such as status. Consumers employ a web of stratagems to leverage value in a given setting, even if it means acting or speaking in a manner contrary to their stated identities and intentions.

Case Study: Creating Value in the Luxury Sector

An ethnographic study of the French luxury culture examines the maneuvers consumers employ to adapt cultural codes to the social, financial, and existential demands of the moment. It sheds light on the changing face of luxury consumption since Veblen's (2009 [1899]) study of the Victorian leisure class and also supports his claims about the semiotic complexity of luxury consumption. Consumers use irony, paradox, and duplicity to leverage the value of luxury goods for personal and social gain.

RESEARCH OVERVIEW

The Paris ethnography formed part of a comparative study of luxury consumer behavior in France, China, and North America. Findings from the China study are discussed in my previous book, *Marketing Semiotics* (2012). The research was designed to identify the range of values and experiences wealthy consumers associate with luxury goods in order to develop retail and merchandising strategy for point of purchase displays worldwide.

Data Set and Design

The data set included secondary research into the global luxury sector, an advertising audit of major luxury brands, and in-depth ethnographic

interviews with eight very affluent consumers. Research also included informal conversations with family or friends of respondents at social gatherings.
Informants were recruited from a convenience sample drawn from the client's
social network in Paris, though they were not informed of the client's role in
the study or the research objectives. Informants included two socialites with
long-established wealth, the CEO of a pharmaceutical supply company, an
attorney, the owner of a beauty salon chain, a physician, an international
distributor of luxury brands, and one professional from the duty-free industry. Each informant was interviewed in French unless they chose to speak in
English. Interviews lasted at least two-and-a-half hours, either at home or a site
of their choice. Some informants were visited on multiple occasions and at
multiple sites, including home, work, and weekend retreats. The study identified historical, cultural, and marketing factors that contribute to the perceived
value that French consumers attach to luxury goods and brands.

The design included a structured questionnaire, unstructured discussions
related to informants' lifestyles, and, in some cases, participant observations
where the researcher was a guest at a social gathering. The interviews were
videotaped and each setting was photographed throughout to record details
of the informants' lived environment for ethnographic analysis and report
production.

Findings Summary

The case does not present a full account of the research, but summarizes key
findings that illustrate the concepts presented in the chapter. It presents in
depth the cultural performances of a key informant, Martin, a French businessman and heir to a family fortune.

Findings confirm Bourdieu's (1998 [1994]) insight that cultural codes, not
nature, define distinction and value in a given population. The ethnography
also highlights the intrinsic instability of cultural codes and value systems in
the practice of daily life. Informants switched between one code system and
another to adjust to new social situations and cultural settings, giving new
meaning to the adage "When in Rome, do as the Romans do." French
affluents may show off their fashion taste with their inner circle, but hide
their wealth from the public at large. To justify a purchase, they may rework a
foreign product or ritual to conform to their own cultural perspective. They
also tend to adapt their behavior to the cultural framework that the ethnographer unwittingly brings to the interview itself.

Findings also reflect the influence of mass marketing and global consumer
culture on French luxury culture. Though luxury goods still signify good taste
and mark class distinctions, the semiotics of taste and distinction shift and
change as French consumers come into contact with American consumer
values through advertising, the social media, and international travel. They

may criticize American materialism on the one hand and also collect vintage American luxury goods on the other.

THE DIALECTIC OF PERCEIVED VALUE IN THE FRENCH LUXURY SECTOR

The ambiguous relation of French consumers to luxury consumption is not a new phenomenon. It reflects tensions within the cultural politics of luxury over the history of modern France. Colbert, the finance minister under Louis XIV, shaped France's historical dominance of the luxury industry in the seventeenth century by means of strict sumptuary laws regulating the production, distribution, and consumption of luxury goods (Shovlin 2000). The laws restricted luxury imports and prevented craftsmen from working abroad. They also mitigated the emerging influence of the bourgeoisie by forbidding anyone but the ruling nobility to display the trappings of wealth. Colbert's contributions to the French luxury industry are commemorated in the name given to the present-day consortium of luxury manufacturers, the Comité Colbert.

Ostentatious consumption and waste both legitimized the authority of the old ruling class and eventually spelled its downfall (Schama 1989: 203–247). The French Revolution ended the *ancien régime*, but did not put an end to the demand for luxury goods (Auslander 2005). It did, however, change the cultural politics of luxury and its influence on luxury codes of behavior. The Revolution cast a pall over the culture of excess and ostentatious display and replaced it with a bourgeois value system that privileges hidden and timeless attributes of luxury over novelty and show.

The Semiotics of Luxury

Respondents identified three main codes structuring the meaning and value of luxury in French culture, including *la discrétion*, memory value, and deprivation. These codes represent intrinsic, transcendent, and priceless aspects of value that do not depend on the appreciation or judgments of others. They also signify a kind of insider knowledge shared not only by the French upper classes, but also by French consumers of luxury in general. Even shop girls who save up to buy a designer bag know these codes.

In contrast, ostentation, novelty, and excess represent materialistic aspects of luxury that measure value in terms of social acceptance and fashion. They mark the consumer as an outsider—a tourist or immigrant—whose values reflect new wealth and a lack of education in luxury culture. For many informants, these binaries represent clear cultural distinctions between France—with its emphasis on tradition and class distinction—and their perceptions of American culture—with its modernism and upward mobility

Table 6.1. The Dialectic of Perceived Luxury Value

Categories	Higher Value/Lower Value
Representation	Discretion/Ostentation
Perception	Time/Space
Substance	Deprivation/Excess

(Table 6.1). The two luxury market experts recruited for the study confirmed these findings.

The ethnography exposed nuances and ambiguities in the ways consumers actually perform luxury codes. Though informants universally recognized the importance of these codes in French luxury culture, in everyday practice they played with these binaries to suit the situation, sometimes following the code, at others twisting the code to meet personal and social goals. These cultural "performances" are motivated by several factors, including consumers' reticence to reveal their net worth, the encroachment of global consumer culture into the French luxury industry and culture, and the natural propensity of consumers in this sector to show off, follow fashion, and pamper themselves.

Representation: discretion versus ostentation. All informants agreed that attention to *la discrétion*—the art of "less is more"—is a hallmark of good taste in France. In contrast to status markers that reflect the owner's material wealth, discretion reflects the privileged knowledge of consumers who appreciate the intrinsic beauty and quality of things, rather than quantity. One brings a single rose, not a bouquet, to a dinner party, speaks in hushed tones in the boutique, prefers hidden brand logos to prominent ones and small delicacies over big servings at the table. Furthermore, this knowledge does not mark class distinctions within France because it is not reserved for France's elite, but is inscribed in France's national identity as the dominant luxury producer and arbiter of taste. Ordinary consumers that were encountered in the field understood the value of discretion. The French can spot a foreigner immediately by their ostentatious display of luxury logos, flashy new clothes, and excessive spending.

Discretion has existential as well as social dimensions. It is closely related to the philosophical concept of *immanence*, the elusive and temporary experience of being *in* the world but not *for* the world. Zaoui (2013) explains that *la discrétion* is not a form of disguise or dissimulation, but an attitude of quiet contemplation that momentarily eludes the gaze of the other. Discretion is also a personal strategy for guarding personal integrity and self-possession in the spectacle of the marketplace.

Perception: time versus space. Consumers attach "memory value" to goods that they have owned for a long time. Memory value is related to discretion since it endows goods with an intangible aura or *immanence* that has value only in the owner's eyes. It becomes inalienable wealth if it is passed down from one generation to the next (Weiner 1992). Since memory value is entirely based upon one's personal experiences with possessions, it cannot be exchanged for status, prestige, or money, and transcends the effects of fashion and style. When memory value is externalized as a status marker, it stands for the *patina*—the signs of wear and tear on antiques and family heirlooms which mark the owner's claims to gentrification and old wealth (McCracken 1988: 37).

Luxury goods have a greater potential to acquire memory value than cheap products because their materials and styling are designed to last. Rather than depreciate, luxury brands acquire memory value over the years that only the owner would recognize as valuable. Whether a moneyed elite or affluent professional, all informants reported that the Rolex inherited from a parent, the soft leather of an old pair of Gucci slippers, or one's first Chanel bag gains added luxury value because of its priceless role in the consumer's personal journey.

Jean-Marc, a lawyer with degrees from an elite Grande École, observed that in contrast to Americans, who buy new garments and discard them quickly, the French buy high quality garments meant to last. For the interview he wore his old Armani dressing gown over his slacks and shirt to show me how a typical French man of his class dressed for home. The dressing gown was priceless because it had "grown with him" over the years. Though he would not pass it down to the next generation, the garment had intrinsic personal value because it was inscribed with the memories of the past ten years of his life. Marie-Claire, a physician, buys very expensive designer brands for work, but wears the same outfit frequently and over a long period of time rather than changing her wardrobe with every season.

Consumption: deprivation versus excess. Deprivation consumption is the third characteristic of French luxury culture. It displaces the perception of value from the realm of the material consumption to the realm of rare and transcendent experiences. It is best exemplified in spartan vacations and difficult quests. Like discretion and memory value, deprivation consumption's value is based upon its intrinsic, spiritual benefits rather than material comforts or show.

Deprivation is perhaps the most elite form of luxury consumption because it is designed to stimulate the passions of wealthy consumers who have unlimited access to material satisfactions. This logic is reflected in the custom of using anorexic models in luxury advertising, prompting women to starve themselves to be fit consumers of luxury fashion. Deprivation consumption is reminiscent of the non-productive work of Veblen's leisure class, because it offers wealthy consumers the luxury of playing with scarcity and physical discomfort as an exotic pastime.

Deprivation consumption is a study in the complex semiotic structure of perceived value in the luxury sector, characterized by paradox, irony, and duplicity. The very association of deprivation with luxury is paradoxical because luxury is traditionally equated with opulence and comfort. Informants' accounts of deprivation vacations reflect the elaborate schemes they employ to manage these tensions in order to position themselves in elite consumer culture and/or discover extraordinary, transformative experiences.

For example, one informant was a middle-aged Countess who had family ties to European nobility. She reported that she endured a three-day camel trek across the Sahara to a remote nature retreat for a vacation. The resort lacked electricity and central heating and served simple, raw cuisine. She was not interested in the return to nature and simplicity advertised in the brochure, nor was she a fitness enthusiast or adventurer. The Countess chose the resort to emulate Prince Charles and Camilla who go there on vacation.

In the end, she cheated the system by sneaking creature comforts into the resort. She prepared for her deprivation vacation with a shopping spree at the Bon Marché, where she bought candles, duvets, and gourmet snacks to mitigate the discomforts she anticipated at the resort. Like Marie-Antoinette "playing peasant" at Versailles, the Countess played at deprivation, knowing full well that her status and wealth obviated any real experience of privation. Though the luxury of deprivation falls under the radar of ostentatious display, it does not escape the market because it endows consumers with experiences and cultural capital available to the privileged few. For example, Martin, whose story is summarized below, associated deprivation vacations with luxury because they put him in touch with rare, sacred experiences.

Globalization and the Deconstruction of Value Hierarchies

The globalization of the luxury sector and consumers' easy access to foreign travel also influence this ambivalence. For centuries, tensions between patina and novelty, discretion and ostentation, and deprivation and indulgence have marked distinctions between "legitimate" and false claims to gentrified status (see McCracken 1988). However, the conglomeration and mass marketing of luxury brands such as Gucci and Dior have effectively deconstructed the traditional hierarchies of value by making luxury—once the realm of old family businesses, exclusive clients, and rare goods—available to anyone who can pay.[3]

---

[3] For more information on the globalization of French luxury, see Hoffmann and Coste-Manière (2013).

For instance, the LVMH conglomerate manages a delicate balance between the risks associated with mass-marketing luxury brands, on the one hand, and losing market share, on the other. To meet the demands of an increasingly competitive global market, Louis Vuitton recently opened a megastore on the Champs Élysées that draws crowds of tourists and local shoppers seeking everything from costly couture to affordable accessories. The large scale of the building dwarfs the discrete, historical boutiques on the Place Vendôme and the Avenue Montaigne. Showy marketing tactics betray the influence of Disney World on the retail design and strategy (see Oswald 2012: 171), such as wrapping the large building in bows for the holidays. The interior design stages the shopper's experience as a Disney fantasy, moving them from one department to the next along shimmering, highly directive pathways.

Though these strategies contribute to France's competitiveness in the global marketplace, they also erode France's authority as the arbiter of good taste by adapting brand meaning to the tastes of the uninitiated masses. Globalization and social media have put cultures in contact with each other as never before, placing in question the idea of a national culture of luxury, and creating tensions within French luxury culture between old and new systems of luxury value.

The semiotic square in Figure 6.3 maps these tensions. The quadrant on top represents Traditional Luxury Culture; the quadrant on the bottom represents Global Consumer Culture. The grid illustrates how globalization has neutralized the strict binaries separating these two perspectives.

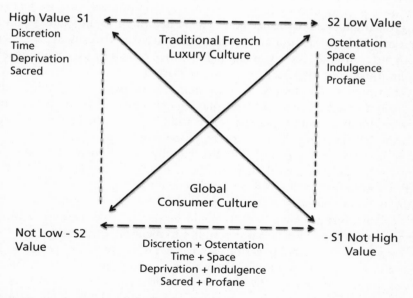

Figure 6.3. The Deconstruction of Value Hierarchies

Codes and Cultural Performance

Affluent French consumers may prefer *la discrétion* but they adjust their cultural lens to participate in global consumer culture, a culture shaped by America's taste for show, comfort, and novelty. The ethnography forms a narrative of the strategies that consumers employ to manage these encounters. It also draws attention to the semiotic specificity of the ethnographic disposition, which joins ethnographer, informant, and the informant's story in a narrative performance.

Informants rework foreign brands and rituals to conform to French values. They switch codes to adapt to new settings and new consumption experiences. To adapt to life in the United States, for example, French consumers learn to incorporate ostentatious consumption and self-indulgent spa treatments into their lifestyles in order to succeed in business, participate in society, or simply to share in the fun. Like Hollande's "le hug," these behaviors are not signs of cultural assimilation, but cultural strategies for meeting practical or spiritual goals.

In a group of peers, French affluents show off the latest fashions and also leverage their connections to succeed in business or gain admission to elite schools. With the general public, French affluents tone down their demeanor to blend in and hide from the tax collector. For example, when researchers, both Americans, phoned the Countess to set up our first interview, she was being fitted for an evening gown at Valentino in preparation for a gala. We imagined her in a world of inaccessible luxury and distinction set aside from our own. As a result, we had trouble spotting the Countess when we met her at a restaurant because she had adjusted her demeanor to the value system of her surroundings. Her jeans and t-shirt belied her status because it blended in with the crowd. She also assumed that the dress code for the occasion would be informal since the researchers were Americans.

The Countess also understates her public presentation to avoid thieves and tax collectors alike. She forbade videotaping in her apartment for fear that her opulent lifestyle might expose her to an audit by *le fisc*, the French Treasury. Martin, heir to a large family fortune, reflects on the popular maxim "*Pour vivre heureux, vivons cachés*" (To live happily, live hidden). He said, "In France, if you own a castle that has been in the family for four hundred years, you do not invite people over... unlike the United States, where you show off your mansion because you earned it." In France's rigid class system, the ostentatious display of wealth would be socially risky because it would invite hostility and even social unrest, not to mention a tax audit.

French affluents employ various stratagems to enjoy luxury goods under the radar of public scrutiny. Martin's Uncle Henri picked me up in an inauspicious Peugeot to drive to the family's eighteenth-century estate south of Paris. The spacious residence and grounds bespeak the family's wealth and the tattered antique furnishings and décor reflect the patina of

Figure 6.4. Memories of Ostrich Husbandry

gentrification. A large display of stuffed game marks the family's prolific hunting career. A stuffed ostrich is all that remains of their attempt to raise the birds on the property a few years ago (Figure 6.4). In contrast to these elite signifiers, Henri said he drove a Peugeot rather than a luxury car to tone down his public image.

MARTIN: A STUDY IN SEMIOTIC PERFORMANCE

The machinations consumers go through to make sense of luxury expose the essential instability of meaning and consumer identity in semiotic performance. Furthermore, semiotic performance is not simply a matter of role-play, which Goffman (1959) associates with image management, nor is it limited to back stage and front stage personas. Semiotic performance refers the movement of consumer attention and meaning between multiple frames of reference, including cultural, interpersonal, and existential dimensions of discourse.

Martin's story illustrates the shifting value systems of consumers who blend their French family traditions with their aspirations to modernity and global-ization, as represented in American consumer culture. It also highlights the part played by the ethnographer's cultural identity in drawing out these contra-dictions. Martin is the forty-year-old son of a French industrialist with ancestral ties to old money. He was recruited through his stepmother who has social connections to the client. Raised in France, Martin took a business degree in the United States and worked for several years in Los Angeles. He integrates his American experience into his personal and social identity by speaking English, collecting American antiques, and cultivating the attributes French consumers associate with American culture, such as modernism, boldness, and competi-tiveness. Martin's home, a penthouse in a modern building near the Champs Élysées, contains a blend of old and new, including modern décor and appli-ances, rare antiques collected from abroad, stuffed trophies from his hunting trips, and an Apple digital entertainment system.

The importance of Martin's narrative for semiotic ethnography resides as much in his manner of telling the story as in the events he describes, because it draws attention to the semiotic strategies consumers employ to manage their relationship to the ethnographer. Martin was affable and helpful when I entered his Paris home. He seemed keen on ingratiating himself with the researcher by speaking English and using irony and self-deprecation to talk about his wealth and status. During the interview, he clearly played to his "audience," a French-speaking American ethnographer, by alternating between French and American English and even apologizing for being French.

The French/American cultural contrast defined the early focus of the interview and became less important as the interview unfolded. He began the interview with the statement, "Sorry, but I am French," a kind of rhet-orical nod to the ethnographer's American identity. His use of irony suggests that he tailored his narrative to insinuate the ethnographer in his viewpoint, since the meaning and intention of an ironic statement presumes a certain degree of complicity between the speaker and receiver of a message. The irony was lost on me, however, since I do not share in his assumptions about Americans' dislike of the French. Martin also communicated ambivalence toward his elite French status, which at times seemed like a tactic for gaining the ethnographer's sympathy.

Martin went on to compare and contrast the French and American systems of luxury value. He extolled the French values that structured his worldview, contrasting the European elite taste for quality, discretion, and time-worn goods with Americans' taste for novelty and show. At the same time he identified with the American values of hard work, upward mobility, and personal initiative, and criticized the socialist leanings of French politics. His narrative folded these two worlds together, reflecting his own personal style and taste.

Between Two Cultures and Two Value Systems

To integrate these competing cultural resources into his French life, Martin filters American consumer culture through the lens of French luxury codes. For example, he collects high-end memorabilia from American popular culture. He adapts the American style of luxury, which he associates with flashy, ostentatious display and novelty, to his French propensity for discretion. He buys vintage goods rather than new products from the United States because they represent the French values of enduring quality and timeless styling and also reference an iconic moment in American consumer culture, the 1950s. He then reworks them in various ways in line with French cultural tradition.

For example, he bought a vintage Bentley automobile that once belonged to the Hollywood star Jane Mansfield in the 1960s. Since the shiny blue exterior and white leather interior were "more suited to Rodeo Drive than to Paris," he had it painted a "mouse grey" and changed the white leather to beige. Not only was the Bentley a subtler brand choice than a flashy Lamborghini, but the age and muted colors of the vintage car also concealed its price tag from all but the initiated.

Martin also filters his taste for American wooden boats through the lens of French luxury values. A few years ago he purchased a Cris-Craft runabout, circa 1951, complete with an American flag on the stern. He chose the Cris-Craft because the mahogany, polished brass, and classic styling used in construction represented enduring quality. The brand had the added value for Martin of referencing a golden age in America when Cris-Craft was a status symbol for the stars. He bought the boat in Chicago through a French dealer and had it refurbished and shipped to France. At the risk of bringing bad luck on his boat, he changed the boat's masculine name "because boats are feminine in France."

The boat purchase points to the rewards of deprivation and hard work in Martin's perception of luxury. Though Martin inherited great wealth, he believes he must work to steward the wealth to the next generation. Luxury is not therefore an entitlement of his rank, but a reward for hard work. Work also goes into the planning, shopping, and purchase of luxury goods as well as refitting the purchase to suit his lifestyle. Work may also take the form of the rigors associated with what I call deprivation vacations.

Martin gifted himself the boat as a reward for the successful completion of a project. He also prepared for the purchase through a long period of research and shopping. He planned to purchase a wooden boat for many years, researching brands and styles in trade magazines and boat shows. When it came time to purchase the Cris-Craft, he knew exactly the model and year he would buy. It took the dealer about six months to find it, and another three months to move it from Chicago to Paris. Buying the boat was a quest that enhanced the boat's value and pleasure in relation to the time and effort that went into the purchase. Martin gave a similar account of a deprivation vacation he took in the Siberian wilderness.

The Photo Narrative

When asked about some photos on the desktop of his computer, Martin walked me through a photo narrative of a recent hunting trip in the Siberian tundra, hundreds of miles from civilization. He displayed the photos on a wide format television monitor connected to his computer. Martin and his father, experienced hunters, arranged a hunting expedition through a French company. A Russian guide and local hunters guided the trek, set up camp, and prepared food. Unlike the Countess's deprivation vacation, Martin sought the rigors of the hunt. His special knowledge of hunting and the wilderness shaped his interpretation of the trip as a luxury experience. "We were looking for this—the outside, the wild, Nature." They lived off the land in tents without bathrooms, walking up to nine hours a day across frozen terrain in search of bears. Martin and his father relied on their guides to survive because "you couldn't last two days out here on you own."

The ethnographic disposition. The photo-narrative is a technique used in ethnographic research to elicit consumers' reflections upon a life event they recorded in photos. It stages the ethnographic disposition around at least three narrative positions defined by the ethnographer, the informant, and the informant's story in word and image (Figure 6.5). Each position represents a different perspective on the subjectivity and space-time of the ethnographic performance, including:

- the informant's inner experience [I/me], in the present and presence of self-perception;
- the informant's inter-subjective relationship with the ethnographer [I/you] in the "here and now" of the interview; and
- the informant's objectification in the photos [I = he] in the "there and then" of the story.

The cultural perspectives of the French informant and American ethnographer add another layer of complicity between ethnographer and informant, since both were fluent in the other's language.

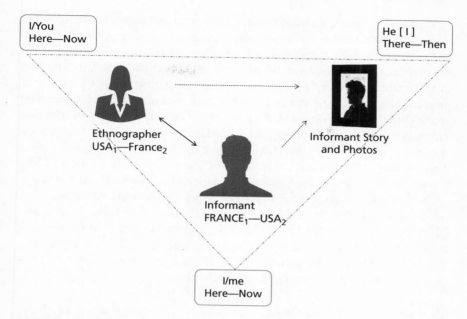

Figure 6.5. Ethnography as Performance

The ethnographic disposition puts in motion the dynamic of deixis mentioned earlier, the performative dimension that structures relationships between the actors in the space-time of discourse. Silverstein (1976) adapted deixis to the ethnographic disposition, where it accounts for the shifting interpersonal positions of first and second person in the interview [I/you] and between "I" and "he" in the informant's story about himself. Deixis also structures shifts in the space-time of the informant's story between the "here and now" of the ethnographic encounter and the "there and then" of the informant's story and photo journal. Informants also conflate these dualities together in the present of the narrative. In statements such as "You couldn't last two days out here," i.e. in the tundra, Martin relives the events in photos in the present moment of the interview. He refers to his image as "I" and "me."

Benveniste (1971 [1958]) refers to such doublings as transgressions of the unity of time, space, and person in discourse. He cites Rimbaud's poetic verse, "*Je est un autre*" [I is an other] as an example of poetic distance and psychic alienation. However, our analysis of the ethnographic disposition suggests an alternative interpretation of these doublings. The movement of reference and subjectivity in ethnographic performance exposes what Derrida (1973 [1967]) found to be the essential division of the self and the instability of meaning in the movement between thought and representation or speech.

Though Benveniste extended structural semiotics to include questions of subjectivity and reference, Derrida altered the course of structuralism when he deconstructed the metaphysical assumptions on which it is founded. By drawing attention to the essential split between thought and its representation in material signs, Derrida placed in question phenomenology's ideal of the primordial unity of logic and being as the condition of possibility of meaning and identity. Derrida does not *deny* the role of logic and unity in meaning production, but denies their original, transcendental status. He redefines logic and unity as semiotic *constructions*, subject to the norms of culture, rather than "givens" that transcend culture. Discourse is a medium for melding tension and difference into transitory sensations that the world makes sense.

The critique of phenomenology has important implications for semiotic ethnography because it underscores the difficulty of arriving at a single, quantifiable interpretation of the field site and the identities of informants. It also directs attention to the ways consumers mitigate division, ambiguity, and cultural difference by means of symbolic consumption and the narratives they construct to give meaning to their experiences.

Rhetorical moves: from stranger to confidante. The ethnography also draws attention to the rhetorical strategies consumers employ to integrate division and ambiguity into a coherent and meaningful account of their experiences. As Martin's narrative unfolds, changes in his rhetorical style reflect a growing trust in the ethnographer and his immersion in the story on screen. Over the course of the photo narrative, shifts in his rhetorical style, from irony to sincerity, reflect an evolution in Martin's relationship to his story, on the one hand, and the ethnographer, on the other.

At the beginning of the narrative, Martin adopts an ironic point of view that highlights the contrasts between the traditional luxury vacation and the mean deprivations of the trek. Referring to the old Russian propeller plane that took them to the site, he says "That's our luxury aircraft," and our "first class seats." Referencing an unheated camping hut, he says "That's our luxury condominium." The small cot is "my luxury bed."

Irony structures distance and contrast between what Martin says and what he means. Irony keeps the ethnographer at bay while Martin eases into the narrative. As the interview progressed, Martin drops his defenses as well as the ironic tone, using direct discourse in its place. Showing the ethnographer a photo taken deep in the wilderness, he tries to put words to the awe and wonder he experienced in the natural environment. Referencing a photo with the fold-up shower stall they set up next to the mountain, Martin invited the ethnographer to look at the scenery, rather than joking about contrasts between camping life and five-star hotels. "Look at the view around the shower." He essentially let the image communicate the ineffable power of the natural environment on his psyche.

As Martin moved closer to the story on the screen, he finally found words to explain why deprivation vacations are luxurious. He said these adventures expose consumers to sacred, ineffable experiences of nature, from the awe-inspiring views to the adrenaline rush of the hunt. The rigors of the trip were a small price to pay for the freedom, beauty, and connection to the sacred they put within reach. "You walk ten to fifteen miles and you come upon little treasures, wild flowers, mountain views, pristine lakes." By shedding material comforts and leaving social rank behind, he shared a deep connection to his local guides, even though he could not speak their language.

Martin described the rigors of survival that put him in touch with primitive human instincts, such as killing for food. After nine days of trekking the frozen tundra, he brought down a bear, saying that the thrill of the kill grows in proportion to the effort it took to get there. Commenting on a photo of himself holding the heart of the bear, he said that hunting brought out the barbarian within, "the barbarian that we have been for 500,000 years." From one photo to the next, his beard grows longer, his skin is more sunburned in the mountain air, and his demeanor more peaceful and happy.

Martin practiced a ritual familiar with hikers of marking the journey with tokens found on the land. Martin built a shrine from the horns of mountain sheep whose skeletons are scattered along the route, "killed by wolves or starvation." He made the shrine to honor the dead wildlife and leave his own mark on the landscape. The story culminates with a photo of Martin seated in a meditative position next to his work, carried away by the vast blue skies and towering mountains (Figure 6.6).

Border crossing. The journey ends and the tourist returns home. As the conversation returned to Paris and the interview, Martin made a point of saying that within forty-eight hours of leaving Siberia he was walking down Fifth Avenue in New York, headed to a business meeting. His experience sheds light on a form of luxury intrinsic to the border crossing itself.

In fact, time, money, social capital, and private jets contribute to the enhanced mobility of the very rich and their easy access to authentic cultural experiences. In Paris, Martin enjoys the timeless value of vintage boats and cars that only old money would buy. In Siberia he takes in the transcendence and authenticity of the austere natural environment. In New York he is exhilarated by the competitive energy of a city on the edge of global consumer culture. At each border crossing consumers tilt their perspectives to the values of the local culture, all the while remaining anchored in their own. These findings suggest that the perceived value of luxury goods may depend not only upon the immediate context of consumption, but also upon the *frisson* evoked when stepping into a different culture, either literally or by means of symbolic consumption.

Implications for Luxury Brand Strategy. The ethnography of French luxury culture sheds light on the competing cultural influences on brand meaning

Figure 6.6. Martin's Shrine

and perceived value in contemporary markets. It also draws attention to the value inherent in the cultural encounter itself, whose excitement and romance draw from the intrinsic dissonance of cultures in contact. Findings suggest that global luxury brand strategy should leverage rather than mitigate these tensions. Rather than blending brand meaning with the local culture, it means anchoring French brands in the heritage and values of French luxury, while drawing upon local language and iconography to translate these qualities into local messaging and merchandising *tactics*. By providing access to the semiotic sensibilities of local markets, semiotic ethnography enables marketers to leverage the "Frenchness" of French luxury brands in marketing strategy targeted to consumers in local markets worldwide.

Ethnography in the Marketing Semiotics Paradigm

This brief excursion into the luxury market draws attention to the practical aspects of semiotic ethnography for decoding consumer behavior, building a cultural brand positioning, and leveraging cultural meanings to create value. Furthermore, the theoretical discussion of the chapter highlights the importance of ethnography for marketing semiotics, a research practice rooted in the "pragmatic embodiment of theory" (Herzfeld 1983b: 99). In the section below I present practical guidelines for designing semiotic ethnography and review the implications of this chapter for brand rhetoric, cultural branding, and retail design.

THE SCOPE AND LIMITS OF COMMERCIAL ETHNOGRAPHY

In the marketing context, the scope and design of semiotic ethnography are determined by the business objectives of the project. Commercial ethnographers must balance deep insights with the practical demands of time, cost, and deliverables. An exploratory research protocol was employed for the Paris ethnography because of the broad exploratory nature of the objectives. In other cases, the design may be focused on a narrow marketing goal. I review below a range of ethnographic protocols for market research, ranging from very structured to emergent design, in conformity with the marketing objectives and scope of each project.

Narrow Objectives, Structured Protocol

The first protocol follows a very structured design that focuses on a narrow range of consumer experiences—women's personal care rituals. Findings would be used to meet a very precise marketing objective—to understand how to develop merchandising strategy for the launch of a new make-up line at K-Mart stores in North America. An agency recruited respondents from a database and screened them on the basis of general demographic factors including age, gender, and product use. The design included a one-hour observation of consumers performing their daily make-up routines and another hour with them in the store discussing the current merchandising strategy. Though the study focused primarily on product use and point of purchase behavior, it met the very narrow objectives of the project and led to actionable recommendations for new product merchandising.

Semi-Structured Exploratory Research

The next protocol follows a semi-structured research design that includes direct questioning, projective tasks such as story telling, and observations at consumers' homes and in their vehicles.

The Ford Motor Company commissioned an exploratory study in the consumer truck market to prepare for the launch of the new F-150. An agency recruited respondents from a Polk list of drivers in three markets and screened them through a segmentation algorithm developed by Ford in a large survey prior to the study. The protocol also called for informal observations of drivers in their homes and driving their trucks.

Recruiting to a segmentation algorithm has the disadvantage of limiting the exploratory function of ethnography because it selects only respondents who already conform to the values and lifestyles profile identified in prior studies. Over several years and many projects with Ford, researchers had gained the client's trust and persuaded them to eliminate the segmentation algorithm in recruitment for exploratory research. By eliminating the algorithm from the screener, recruiters could select respondents who broke from the mold and provided insights about Ford and competitors that were overlooked in Ford's prior studies in this market.

Researchers also obtained permission to digress from the observational research schedule in order to follow up on a line of investigation with an informant who promised deeper, more nuanced insights into consumer behavior in the truck category. For example, researchers arranged an ad hoc focus group at the workplace of the informant with four of his partners, all undercover detectives with the L.A.P.D. The interactions among the men shed light on the complex role of the truck as an accessory to their job, a complement to their identity, and a facilitator in their social performance. This additional flexibility led to innovative recommendations for brand strategy, new product development, and promotional advertising.

Emergent Design

At the opposite end of the spectrum, emergent design is a loosely structured protocol that allows the design and informant network to develop in the fieldwork process. For example, this protocol was employed for a study of consumers on Chicago's West Side, commissioned by the Garfield Park Conservatory Alliance. The objective was to understand why local residents failed to participate in enrichment programs offered at the Conservatory, a world-class horticultural institution located in what had become one of Chicago's most crime-ridden disadvantaged neighborhoods. Lacking a formal database of local residents, ethnographers developed an informant network over three months, beginning with community leaders and teachers who led the ethnographers to informants in halfway houses, churches, and at home.

The research approach paid off. By observing residents in their neighborhoods, researchers discovered contradictions between the community gardening traditions of local residents and the institutional practices of formal horticulture at the Conservatory. They found that these contradictions doomed to failure the Conservatory's programming strategies. Findings led to recommendations for developing a culturally sensitive marketing strategy for the Conservatory, which included installing an outdoor community garden into the Conservatory campus, holding farmers' markets on Conservatory grounds, and offering classes in public horticulture to local residents.

Conclusion

Semiotic ethnography is a fitting end to this book, because it illustrates the scope and depth of semiotic research for marketing, its application to business problems, and its rich theoretical heritage in linguistics, semiotic theory, the social sciences, and marketing strategy. Semiotic ethnography also forms a link between primary research with consumers and the other research areas presented in the book, including advertising research, brand rhetoric, cultural brand strategy, and servicescape design. In all areas of semiotics-based research, ethnography can be used to confirm findings obtained from the analysis of advertising, explore consumer perceptions and experiences of retail designs and merchandising, or clarify and enrich cultural brand strategy with complex, nuanced insights about consumers and their brands.

The chapter also supports the overarching argument advanced in the book, that semiotics-based research provides a fuller account of consumer behavior and culture by bringing theory to bear on the intrinsic ambivalence and complexity of signs, meaning, and subject-address in the field site. It proposes methods for analyzing the performative dynamic of the ethnographic disposition and the rhetorical devices consumers employ to manage these kinds of performances.

The chapter acknowledges the contributions of American anthropologists who introduced continental semiotics to ethnographic fieldwork and laid the foundation for the interpretive tradition in consumer research. As practicing ethnographers, writers such as Sahlins, Geertz, and Herzfeld also pushed the boundaries of semiotic theory for ethnography with insights drawn from the messy, unpredictable flow of meaning and behavior in the field site.

Following upon their example, *Creating Value: The Theory and Practice of Marketing Semiotics Research* builds a foundation for the study and practice of semiotic research for marketing. It also advances knowledge in marketing science and semiotics in turn, by teasing out tensions as well as synergies between theory and its applications to all areas of marketing research, from advertising and servicescape design to consumer behavior.

■ REFERENCES

Aaker, David A. (1991). *Managing Brand Equity: Capitalizing on the Value of a Brand Name.* New York: Free Press.

Aaker, David A., and Erich Joachimsthaler (1999). "The Lure of Global Branding." *Harvard Business Review* 77(6) (November–December): 137–144, 217.

Aaker, Jennifer L. (1997). "Dimensions of Brand Personality." *Journal of Marketing Research* 34 (August): 347–356.

Aaker, Jennifer L., Susan Fournier, and S. Adam Brasel (2004). "When Good Brands Do Bad." *Journal of Consumer Research* 31 (June): 1–16.

Aaker, Jennifer Lynn, Verónica Benet-Martínez, and Jordi Garolera (2001). "Consumption Symbols as Carriers of Culture: A Study of Japanese and Spanish Brand Personality Constructs." *Journal of Personality and Social Psychology* 81(3) (September): 492–508.

Aristotle (1982). *The Poetics*, trans. James Hutton. New York: Norton.

Aristotle (2004). *The Rhetoric*, trans. W. Rhys Roberts. Mineola, NY: Dover Press.

Arnould, Eric J., and Craig J. Thompson (2005). "Consumer Culture Theory (CCT): Twenty Years of Research." *Journal of Consumer Research* 31(4): 868–882.

Arsel, Zeynep, and Craig J. Thompson (2011). "Demythologizing Consumption Practices: How Consumers Protect Their Field-Dependent Identity Investments from Devaluing Marketplace Myths." *Journal of Consumer Research* 37(5) (February): 791–806.

Askegaard, Søren, Eric J. Arnould, and Dannie Kjeldgaard (2005). "Postassimilationist Ethnic Consumer Research: Qualifications and Extensions." *Journal of Consumer Research* 32(1) (June): 160–170.

Auslander, Leora (2005). "Regeneration Through the Everyday? Clothing, Architecture and Furniture in Revolutionary Paris." *Art History* 28(2) (April): 227–247.

Austin, John (1955). *How to Do Things with Words*, ed. J. O. Urmson. New York: Oxford University Press.

Bachelard, Gaston (1994 [1958]). *The Poetics of Space*, trans. Maria Jolas. Boston, MA: Beacon Press.

Baker, J., M. Levy, and D. Grewal (1992). "An Experiential Approach to Making Retail Store Environmental Decisions." *Journal of Retailing* 68: 445–460.

Baker, Julie, A. Parsuraman, Dhruv Grewal, and Glee Voss (2002). "The Influence of Multiple Store Environment Cues on Perceived Merchandise Value and Patronage Intentions." *Journal of Marketing* 22 (April): 120–141.

Bakhtin, Mikhail Mikhailovich (2009 [1965]). *Rabelais and His World*, trans. Helene Iswolski. Bloomington: Indiana University Press.

Barthes, Roland (1977a). "Introduction to the Structural Analysis of Narrative," in *Image, Music, Text*, trans. Stephen Heath. New York: Hill and Wang: 79–124.

Barthes, Roland (1977b [1964]). "Rhetoric of the Image," in *Image, Music, Text*, trans. Stephen Heath. New York: Hill and Wang: 32–51.

Barthes, Roland (1977c). "The Third Meaning: Notes on Some of Eisenstein's Stills," in *Image, Music, Text*, trans. Stephen Heath. New York: Hill and Wang: 52–68.

Baudrillard, Jean (1981 [1972]). *For a Critique of the Political Economy of the Sign*, trans. Charles Levin. St. Louis, MO: Telos Press, 1981.

Becker, Gary, and Kevin Murphy (2001). *Social Economics: Market Behavior in a Social Environment*. Cambridge, MA: Harvard University Press.

Belk, Russell (1975). "Situational Variables and Consumer Behavior." *Journal of Consumer Research* 2 (December): 157–164.

Belk, Russell (1988). "Possessions and the Extended Self." *Journal of Consumer Research* 15(2): 139–168.

Belk, Russell (ed.) (2006). *Handbook of Qualitative Research Methods in Marketing*. Northampton, MA: Edward Elgar Publishers.

Belk, Russell, Melanie Wallendorf, and John F. Sherry, Jr. (1989). "The Sacred and the Profane in Consumer Behavior: Theodicy on the Odyssey." *Journal of Consumer Research* 16(1) (June): 1–38.

Bellizzi, Joseph A., and Robert E. Hite (1992). "Environmental Color, Consumer Feelings, and Purchase Likelihood." *Psychology & Marketing* 9(5) (September/October): 347–363.

Bellizzi, Joseph A., Alyn E. Crowley, and Ronald W. Hasty (1983). "The Effects of Color in Store Design." *Journal of Retailing* 59: 21–45.

Benveniste, Émile (1967). "La forme et le sens dans le langage," in *Le Langage*, Société de philosophie de langue française, Actes du XIIIe Congrès, t. II, Neuchatel: La Baconnière: 29–47. Proceedings of the Thirteenth Congress of the French Language Philosophical Society, Vol. 2. Neuchatel: La Baconnière: 29–47.

Benveniste, Émile (1971 [1966]). "Man and Language," in Émile Benveniste, *Problems in General Linguistics*, trans. Mary Elizabeth Meek. Coral Gables, FL: Miami University Press: 195–248.

Berners-Lee, Tim, and Robert Cailliau (1990). *WorldWideWeb: A Proposal for a HyperText Project*. The World Wide Web consortium. <http://www.w3.org/>

Bitner, Mary Jo (1992). "Servicescapes: The Impact of Physical Surroundings on Customers and Employees." *Journal of Marketing* 56 (April): 57–71.

Blommaert, Jan (2013). "Semiotic and Spatial Scope: Towards a Materialist Semiotics," in Margit Böck and Norbert Pachler (eds), *Multimodality and Social Semiosis: Communication, Meaning-Making, and Learning in the Work of Gunther Kress*. Oxford/New York: Routledge: 29–38.

Bordwell, David, Janet Staiger, and Kristin Thompson (1985). *The Classical Hollywood Cinema: Film Style & Mode of Production to 1960*. New York: Columbia University Press.

Bourdieu, Pierre de (1977 [1972]). *Outline of a Theory of Practice*, trans. Richard Nice. Cambridge, UK: Cambridge University Press.

Bourdieu, Pierre de (1984 [1974]). *Distinction: A Social Critique of the Judgment of Taste*, trans. Richard Nice. Cambridge, MA: Harvard University Press.

Bourdieu, Pierre de (1998 [1994]). *Practical Reason: On the Theory of Action*, trans. Giesele Sapiro. Stanford, CA: Stanford University Press.

Bryman, Alan, and Emma Bell (2007). *Business Research Methods*, 2nd edn. New York: Oxford University Press.

Buhl, Claus (1991). "The Consumer's Ad: The Art of Making Sense of Advertising," in Hanne Hartvig Larsen, David Glen Mick, and Christian Alsted (eds), *Marketing and Semiotics*. Copenhagen: Handelshojskolens Forlag: 104–127.

Carlson, Marvin A. (1990). *Theater Semiotics: Signs of Life*. Bloomington: Indiana University Press.

Carter, Bill (2012). "In the Tastes of Young Men, Humor is Most Prized, a Survey Finds." *New York Times*, February 19. <http://www.nytimes.com/2012/02/20/business/media/com edy-central-survey-says-young-men-see-humor-as-essential.html?scp=1&sq=%20In%20the %20Tastes%20of%20Young%20Men,%20Humor%20is%20Most%20Prized%20&st=cse>

Castarède, Jean (1992). *Le Luxe*. Paris: Presses universitaires de France.

Cayla, Julien, and Giana M. Eckhardt (2008). "Asian Brands and the Shaping of a Transnational Imagined Community." *Journal of Consumer Research* 35 (August): 216–230.

Cefkin, Melissa (ed.) (2010). *Ethnography and the Corporate Encounter: Reflections on Research in and of Corporations*. New York: Berghahn Books.

Chandler, Daniel (2002). *Semiotics: The Basics*. New York: Routledge.

Coke (2012). <http://www.coca-cola.com/theolympics/en-US>

Coke Corporate Press Release (2011). "The Great Happyfication": Animated Short Reveals the Secrets to Happiness. September 28. <http://www.coca-colacompany.com/press-center/ press-releases/the-great-happyfication-animated-short-reveals-the-secrets-to-happiness#TCCC>

Coutausse, Jean-Claude (2014). L'offensive de charme de François Hollande dans la Silicon Valley. *Le Monde*. <http://www.lemonde.fr/politique/article/2014/02/12/hollande-un-presi dent-mefiant-d-internet-dans-la-silicon-valley_4365327_823448.html>

Danesi, Marcel (2013). "On the Metaphorical Connectivity of Cultural Sign Systems." *Signs and Society* 1(1) (Spring): 33–49.

Dano, Florence, Elyette Roux, and Simon Nyeck (2003). "Les hommes, leur apparence et les cosmétiques: Approach sociosémiotique," *DM Decisions Marketing*, 29 (January–March): 718.

Daymon, Christine, and Immy Holloway (2002). *Qualitative Research Methods in Public Relations and Marketing Communications*. New York: Routledge Press.

Debord, Guy (1994 [1967]). *The Society of the Spectacle*, trans. Donald Nicholson-Smith. Brooklyn, NY: Zone Books.

Deighton, John (1992). "The Consumption of Performance." *Journal of Consumer Research* 9(3) (December): 362–372.

Denny, Rita M., and Patricia L. Sunderland (2014). *Handbook of Anthropology in Business*. Walnut Creek, CA: Left Coast Press.

Denzin, Norman K., and Yvonna S. Lincoln (2005). *The SAGE Handbook of Qualitative Research*, 3rd edn. Thousand Oaks, CA: Sage Publications.

Derrida, Jacques (1973 [1967]). *Speech and Phenomena, and Other Essays on Husserl's Theory of Signs*, trans. David B. Allison. Evanston, IL: Northwestern University Press.

Derrida, Jacques (1983 [1972]). *Dissemination*, trans. Barbara Johnson. Chicago: University of Chicago Press.

Derrida, Jacques (1998 [1967]). *Of Grammatology*, trans. Gayatri Chakravorty Spivak, 3rd edn. Baltimore: The Johns Hopkins University Press.

Diamond, Nina, John F. Sherry, Jr., Albert M. Muñiz, Jr., Mary Ann McGrath, Robert V. Kozinets, and Stefania Borghini (2009). "American Girl and the Brand Gestalt: Closing the Loop on Sociocultural Branding Research." *Journal of Marketing* 73(3) (May): 118–134.

Donovan, Robert J., and John R. Rossiter (1982). "Store Atmosphere: An Environmental Psychology Approach." *Journal of Retailing* 58 (Spring): 34–57.

Douglas, Mary, and Baron Isherwood (2002 [1979]). *The World of Goods: Towards an Anthropology of Consumption.* New York: Routledge.

Dumont, Jean Paul, and Jean Monod (1970). *Le foetus astral: Essai d'analyse structurale d'un mythe cinématographique.* Paris: Christian Bourgeois.

Durkheim, Émile (1995 [1912]). *The Elementary Forms of Religious Life,* trans. Karen E. Fields. New York: The Free Press.

Durkheim, Emile (1997 [1893]). *The Division of Labor in Society,* trans. George Simpson. New York: The Free Press.

Eckhardt, Giana M., and Michael J. Houston (2002). "Cultural Paradoxes Reflected in Brand Meaning: McDonald's in Shanghai, China." *Journal of International Marketing* 10(2) (Summer): 68–82.

Eco, Umberto (1979). *Theory of Semiotics.* Bloomington: Indiana University Press.

Einstein, Albert (2009 [1931]). *Cosmic Religion, with Other Opinions and Aphorisms by Albert Einstein.* Mineola, NY: Dover Publications.

Eisenstein, Sergei M. (1969 [1942]). *The Film Sense,* trans. Jay Leyda. New York: Harcourt Brace & Co.

Eisenstein, Sergei M. (1969 [1949]). *Film Form: Essays in Film Theory,* trans. Jay Leyda. New York: Harcourt Brace & Co.

Eliade, Mircea (1987 [1957]). *The Sacred and the Profane: The Nature of Religion,* trans. Willard R. Trask. New York: Harvest/Harcourt Books.

Feldman, Martha S., Jeannine Bell, and Michele Berger (2003). *Gaining Access: A Practical and Theoretical Guide for Qualitative Researchers.* Lanham, MD: Alta Mira Press.

Fiore, Ann-Marie, Yan, Xinlu, and Yoh, Eunah (2000). "Effects of a Product Display and Environmental Fragrancing on Approach Responses and Pleasurable Experience." *Journal of Psychology and Marketing* 17: 27–54.

Firat, A. Fuat, and Alladi Venkatesh (1995). "Liberatory Postmodernism and the Reenchantment of Consumption." *Journal of Consumer Research* 22 (December): 239–267.

Floch, Jean-Marie (2001 [1990]). *Semiotics, Marketing and Communication: Beneath the Signs, the Strategies,* trans. Robin Orr Bodkin. New York: Palgrave Macmillan.

Fortini-Campbell, Lisa (2001 [1991]). *Hitting the Sweet Spot: How Consumer Insights Can Inspire Better Marketing and Advertising.* Chicago: The Copy Workshop.

Foucault, Michel (1986 [1967]). "Other Spaces: Utopias and Heterotopias," trans. Jay Miskowiec. *Diacritics* 16(1) (Spring): 22–27.

Foucault, Michel (2001 [1977]). "L'oeil du pouvoir," in *Dits et Ecrits II.* Paris: Gallimard: 190–207.

Fournier, Susan (1998). "Consumers and their Brands: Developing Relationship Theory in Consumer Research." *Journal of Consumer Research* 24 (March): 343–373.

Freud, Sigmund (1955 [1909]). "Analysis of a Phobia in a Five-Year-Old Boy," in "Two Case Histories," trans. James Strachey, from *The Standard Edition of the Complete Psychological Works of Sigmund Freud.* London: The Hogarth Press: Vol. 10: 1–149.

Freud, Sigmund (1965 [1899]). *The Interpretation of Dreams*, trans. and ed. James Strachey. New York: Avon.

Freud, Sigmund (1977 [1909]). "Lecture Three in Five Lectures on Psychoanalysis," trans. James Strachey. New York: Norton: 28–41.

Friedman, Thomas (2005). *The World is Flat: A Brief History of the Twenty-First Century.* New York: Farrar, Straus, and Giroux.

Gangadharbatla, Harsha (2008). "*Facebook* me: Collective Self-Esteem, Need to Belong, and Internet Self-Efficacy as Predictors of the I-generation's Attitudes toward Social Networking Sites." *Journal of Interactive Advertising* 8(2) (Spring).

Garvin, Paul L. (1964). *A Prague School Reader on Esthetics, Literary Structure and Style.* Washington, DC: Georgetown University Press.

Geertz, Clifford (1973). "Thick Description: Toward an Interpretive Theory of Culture," in *The Interpretation of Culture.* New York: Basic Books: 3–30.

Genette, Gérard (1972a). "Discours du récit," in *Figures III.* Paris: Le Seuil: 67–268.

Genette, Gérard (1972b). "Métonymie chez Proust," in *Figures III.* Paris: Editions du Seuil: 41–63. [The English translation, "Metonymy in Proust," reprinted in *Swann's Way* by Marcel Proust (2013). Norton Critical Edition, New York: W. W. Norton: 591–602.] (C. K. Scott Moncrieff, trans. Susanna Lee, editor of Proust's book.)

Genette, Gérard (1982 [1966]). "Proust Palimpsest," in *Figures of Literary Discourse*, trans. Alan Sheridan. Oxford: Blackwell: 203–228.

Genette, Gerard (1983). *Narrative Discourse: An Essay in Method*, trans. Jane E. Lewin. Ithaca, NY: Cornell University Press.

Genette, Gérard (1993 [1968]). "Introduction" to *Les Figures du Discours de Pierre Fontanier.* Paris: Flammarion: 1–15.

Giesler, Markus (2012). "How *Doppelgänger* Brand Images Influence the Market Creation Process: Longitudinal Insights from the Rise of Botox Cosmetic." *Journal of Marketing* 76 (November): 55–68.

Gobé, Marc (2010 [2001]). *Emotional Branding: A New Paradigm for Connecting Brands to People.* New York: Allworth Press.

Goffman, Irving (1959). *The Presentation of Self in Everyday Life.* New York: Anchor Books.

Goldschein, Eric (2011). "The Incredible Story of How DeBeers Created and Lost the Most Powerful Monopoly Ever." *Business Insider*, December 19. <http://www.businessinsider.com/history-of-de-beers-2011-12?op=1>

Goleman, Daniel (2005 [1995]). *Emotional Intelligence.* New York: Random House.

Greimas, Algirdas (1984 [1966]). *Structural Semantics: An Attempt at a Method*, trans. Daniele McDowell, Ronald Schleifer, and Alan Velie. Omaha: University of Nebraska Press.

Guyer, Peter (2009). "The Rapidly Growing Global Coffee and Tea Markets." Originally published in *The American Exporter*, October 2009. <http://www.athenaintl.com/news/articles/the-rapidly-growing-global-coffee-and-tea-markets.html>

Hall, Edward T. (1990). *The Hidden Dimension.* New York: Doubleday-Anchor.

Hall, Emma (2012). "Coke Uses Olympics as Link to Healthful Lifestyles: Global Campaign Includes U.S. Component Highlighting American Athletes." *Advertising Age*, July 3.

Halliday, M. A. K. (1978). *Language as Social Semiotic: The Social Interpretation of Language and Meaning.* London: Edward Arnold.

Heath, Stephen (1982). "On Screen, in Frame: Film and Ideology," in *Questions of Cinema*. Bloomington: Indiana University Press: 1–18.

Heilbrunn, Benoît (1997). "Representation and Legitimacy: A *Semiotic* Approach to the Logo," in Winifred Nöth (ed.), *Semiotics and the Media*. Berlin: Mouton de Gruyter: 175–190.

Herzfeld, Michael (1983a). "Looking Both Ways: The Ethnographer in the Text." *Semiotica* 46: 151–166.

Herzfeld, Michael (1983b). "Signs in the Field: Prospects and Issues for Semiotic Ethnography." *Semiotica* 46: 99–106.

Herzfeld, Michael (1989). *Anthropology: Theoretical Practice in Culture and Society*. Chicago: University of Chicago Press.

Hirschman, Elizabeth C., Linda M. Scott, and William D. Wells (1998). "A Model of Product Discourse: Linking Consumer Practice to Cultural Texts." *Journal of Advertising* 27 (Spring): 33–50.

Hodge, Robert, Ian Vere, and Gunther R. Kress (1988). *Social Semiotics*. Ithaca, NY: Cornell University Press.

Hoffmann, Jonas, and Ivan Coste-Manière (2013). *Global Luxury Trends: Innovative Strategies for Emerging Markets*. New York: Palgrave Macmillan.

Holstein, James A., and Jaber F. Gubrium (1995). *The Active Interview*. Thousand Oaks, CA: Sage.

Holt, Douglas B. (1995). "How Consumers Consume: A Typology of Consumption Practices." *Journal of Consumer Research* 22(1) (June): 1–16.

Holt, Douglas B. (2002). "Why Do Brands Cause Trouble? A Dialectical Theory of Consumer Culture and Branding." *Journal of Consumer Research* 29(1) (June): 70–90.

Holt, Douglas B. (2003). "What Becomes an Icon Most?" *Harvard Business Review* 81(3) (March): 43–49.

Holt, Douglas B. (2004). *How Brands Become Icons: The Principles of Cultural Branding*. Cambridge, MA: Harvard Business Review Press.

Houston, Mark B., Lance A. Bettencourt, and Sutha Wenger (1999). "The Relationship between Waiting in a Service Queue and Evaluations of Service Quality: A Field Theory Perspective." *Journal of Psychology and Marketing* 15(8) (December): 735–753.

Humphreys, Ashlee (2010). "Semiotic Structure and the Legitimation of Consumption Practices: The Case of Casino Gambling." *Journal of Consumer Research* 37 (October): 490–510.

Hymes, Dell (1982). "Prague Functionalism." *American Anthropologist* 84(2) (June): 398–399.

Jakobson, Roman (1960). "Closing Statement: Linguistics and Poetics," in Thomas Sebeok (ed.), *Style in Language*. New York: Wiley Press: 350–377.

Jakobson, Roman (1987 [1921]). "On Realism in Art," in Krystyna Pomorska and Stephen Rudy (eds), *Language in Literature*. Cambridge, MA: Harvard University Press: 19–27.

Jakobson, Roman (1990 [1956]). "Two Aspects of Language and Two Types of Aphasic Disturbances," in Linda R. Waugh and Monique Monville-Burston (eds), *On Language: Roman Jakobson*. Cambridge, MA: Harvard University Press: 115–133.

Jakobson, Roman (1990 [1958]). "Shifters and Verbal Categories," in Linda R. Waugh and Monique Monville-Burston (eds), *On Language: Roman Jakobson*. Cambridge, MA: Harvard University Press: 386–392.

Jakobson, Roman (with Krystinya Pomorska) (1990a [1983]). "The Space Factor in Language," in Linda R. Waugh and Monique Monville-Burston (eds), *On Language: Roman Jakobson*. Cambridge, MA: Harvard University Press: 176–183.

Jakobson, Roman (with Krystinya Pomorska) (1990b [1983]). "The Time Factor in Language," in Linda R. Waugh and Monique Monville-Burston (eds), *On Language: Roman Jakobson.* Cambridge, MA: Harvard University Press: 164–175.

Jeong, Se-Hoon (2008), "Visual Metaphor in Advertising: Is the Persuasive Effect Attributable to Visual Argumentation or Metaphorical Rhetoric?" *Journal of Marketing Communications,* 14(1) (February): 59–73.

Johnson, Lauren (2012). "Red Bull Records Builds Social Presence via Mobile Ad Campaign." <http://www.mobilemarketer.com/cms/news/advertising/13169.html>

Jordan, Ann (2012 [2002]). *Business Anthropology,* 2nd edn. Long Grove, IL: Waveland Press.

Jordan, Brigitte (ed.) (2012). *Advancing Ethnography in Corporate Environments: Challenges and Emerging Opportunities.* Walnut Creek, CA: Left Coast Press.

Joseph, Roger (1983). "The Semiotics of Reciprocity: A Moroccan Interpretation." *Semiotica* 46 (2/4): 211–231.

Kahle, Lynn R., Sharon E. Beatty, and Pamela M. Homer (1986). "Alternative Measurement Approaches to Consumer Values: The List of Values (LOV) and Values and Lifestyle Segmentation (VALS)." *Journal of Consumer Research* 13 (December): 405–409.

Katilius-Boydstun, Marvin (1990). "The Semiotics of A. J. Greimas: An Introduction." *Litanus: Lithuanian Quarterly Journal of Arts and Sciences* 36(3). <http://www.lituanus.org/1990_3/90_3_02.htm>

Keller, Kevin Lane (1993). "Conceptualizing, Measuring, and Managing Customer-Based Brand Equity." *Journal of Marketing* 57 (January): 1–22.

Keller, Kevin Lane (2001). "Building Customer-Based Brand Equity: A Blueprint for Creating Strong Brands." *Marketing Management* (July/August): 15–19.

Klein, Melanie (1975 [1930]). "The Importance of Symbol Formation on Development of the Ego," in *Love, Guilt, and Reparation (The Writings of Melanie Klein,* Vol. 1). London: Hogarth Press: 124–139.

Klein, Melanie (1984). "Envy and Gratitude," in *Envy and Gratitude and Other Works 1946–1963 (The Writings of Melanie Klein,* Vol. III). London: Hogarth Press: 141–175.

Klingman, Anna (2007). *Brandscapes: Architecture in the Experience Economy.* Cambridge, MA: MIT Press.

Koernig, Stephen K. (2003). "E-scapes: The Electronic Physical Environment and Service Tangibility." *Journal of Psychology and Marketing* 20(2) (February): 151–167.

Kozinets, Robert V. (2001). "Utopian Enterprise: Articulating the Meanings of Star Trek's Culture of Consumption." *Journal of Consumer Research* 28: 67–88.

Kozinets, Robert V. (2002). "Can Consumers Escape the Market? Emancipatory Illuminations from Burning Man." *Journal of Consumer Research* 29(1) (June): 20–38.

Kozinets, Robert V., John F. Sherry, Benet DeBerry-Spence, Adam Duhachek, Krittinee Nuttavuthisit, and Diana Storm (2002). "Themed Flagship Brand Stores in the New Millennium: Theory, Practice, Prospects." *Journal of Retailing* 78: 17–29.

Kozinets, Robert V., John F. Sherry Jr., Diana Storm, Adam Duhachek, Krittinee Nuttavuthisit, and Benet DeBerry-Spence (2004). "Ludic Agency and Retail Spectacle." *Journal of Consumer Research* 31(3) (December): 658–672.

Kwass, Michael (2003). "Ordering the World of Goods: Consumer Revolution and the Classification of Objects in Eighteenth-Century France." *Representations* 82 (Spring): 87–116.

Lacan, Jacques (1977 [1953]). "The Function and Field of Speech and Language in Psycho-analysis," in *Écrits: a Selection*, trans. Alan Sheridan. London: Tavistock: 30–113.

Lakoff, George, and Mark Johnson (1980). *Metaphors We Live By*. Chicago: University of Chicago Press.

Larsen, Hanne Hartvig, David Glen Mick, and Christian Alsted (eds) (1991). *Marketing and Semiotics: Selected Papers from the Copenhagen Symposium*. Copenhagen: Handelshøjskolens Forlag.

Lefebvre, Henri (1971). *Au-delà du structuralisme*. Paris: Anthropo.

Lefebvre, Henri (1991 [1974]). *The Production of Space*, trans. Donald Nicholson-Smith. Oxford: Basil Blackwell Publishing.

Lévi-Strauss, Claude (1966 [1962]). *The Savage Mind*, trans. anon. Chicago: University of Chicago Press.

Lévi-Strauss, Claude (1966 [1965]). "The Culinary Triangle," trans. Peter Brooks. *The Partisan Review* 33: 586–596.

Lévi-Strauss, Claude (1967a [1958]). "Language and Kinship," in *Structural Anthropology*, trans. Clair Jacobson and Brooke Grundfest Shoepf. New York: Basic Books: 1–238.

Lévi-Strauss, Claude (1967b [1958]). "The Structural Study of Myth," in *Structural Anthropology*, trans. Claire Jacobson and Brooke Grundfest Schoepf. New York: Basic Books: 206–231.

Lévi-Strauss, Claude (1969 [1964]). *The Raw and the Cooked*, trans. John and Doreen Weightman. New York: Harper Torch Books.

Lévi-Strauss, Claude (1974 [1963]). *Structural Anthropology*, trans. Claire Jacobson and Brooke Grundfest Schoepf. New York: Doubleday Anchor.

Lévi-Strauss, Claude (1987 [1950]). *Introduction to the Work of Marcel Mauss*, trans. Felicity Baker. London: Routledge and Kegan Paul: 1–23.

Levitt, Theodore (1986 [1983]). *The Marketing Imagination*. New York: Simon and Schuster.

MacCannell, Dean (1979). "Ethnosemiotics." *Semiotica* 27(1–3): 149–171.

Man, Paul de (1973). "Semiology and Rhetoric," *Diacritics* 3(3) (Fall): 27–23.

Manning, Peter (1987). *Semiotics and Fieldwork*. Thousand Oaks, CA: Sage Publications.

Marcus, George E., and Michael M. J. Fischer (1999). *Anthropology as Cultural Critique: An Experimental Moment in the Human Sciences*, 2nd edn. Chicago: University of Chicago Press.

Mariampolski, Hy (2006). *Ethnography for Marketers: A Guide to Consumer Immersion*. Thousand Oaks, CA: Sage Publications.

Marlowe, Christopher (2005 [1590]). *Doctor Faustus*, ed. David Wootton. Indianapolis, IN: Hackett Publishers.

Maurice, Charles, and Charles W. Smithson (1984). *The Doomsday Myth: 10,000 Years of Economic Crises*. Stanford, CA: The Hoover Institution Press, Stanford University.

Mauss, Marcel (2000 [1925]). *The Gift: The Form and Reason for Exchange in Archaic Societies*, trans. W. E. Halls. New York: W. W. Norton & Co.

McCracken, Grant (1986). "Culture and Consumption: A Theoretical Account of the Structure and Movement of the Cultural Meaning of Consumer Goods." *Journal of Consumer Research* 13 (June): 71–84.

McCracken, Grant (1988). *Culture and Consumption: New Approaches to the Symbolic Character of Consumer Goods and Activities*. Bloomington: Indiana University Press.

McMains, Andrew (2011). "An 'Unagency' for the 'Uncar'." *Adweek,* October 25, 2011. <http://www.adweek.com/news/advertising-branding/unagency-uncar-136041>

McQuarrie, Edward F., and David Glen Mick (1992). "On Resonance: A Critical Pluralistic Inquiry into Advertising Rhetoric." *Journal of Consumer Research* 19(2) (September): 180–197.

McQuarrie, Edward F., and David Glen Mick (1996). "Figures of Rhetoric in Advertising Language." *Journal of Consumer Research* 22(4) (March): 424–438.

McQuarrie, Edward F., and David Glen Mick (1999). "Visual Rhetoric in Advertising: Text-Interpretive, Experimental, and Reader Response Analyses." *Journal of Consumer Research* 26 (June): 37–54.

McQuarrie, Edward F., and David Glen Mick (2003a). "The Contribution of Semiotic and Rhetorical Perspectives to the Explanation of Visual Persuasion in Advertising," in Linda Scott and Rajeev Batra (eds), *Visual Persuasion: A Consumer Response Perspective.* London: Lawrence Erlbaum Associates: 191–221.

McQuarrie, Edward F., and David Glen Mick (2003b). "Visual and Verbal Figures under Directed Processing Versus Incidental Exposure to Advertising." *Journal of Consumer Research* 29 (March): 579–587.

McQuarrie, Edward F., and Barbara J. Phillips (2007) "Developing a Toolkit for Differentiating Advertising Style," in Edward F. McQuarrie and Barbara J. Phillips (eds), *Go Figure: New Directions in Advertising Rhetoric.* New York: M. E. Sharpe: 257–276.

Mehrabian, Albert, and James A. Russell (1974). *An Approach to Environmental Psychology.* Cambridge, MA: MIT Press.

Merriam, Sharan B. (2009). *Qualitative Research: A Guide to Design and Implementation.* San Francisco, CA: Jossey-Bass Publishers.

Metz, Christian (1981 [1977]). *The Imaginary Signifier,* trans. Ben Brewster, Annwyl Williams, and Celia Britton. Bloomington: Indiana University Press.

Metz, Christian (1991 [1971]). *Film Language,* trans. Michael Taylor. Chicago: University of Chicago Press.

Mick, David Glen, and Claus Buhl (1992). "A Meaning-Based Model of Advertising Experiences." *Journal of Consumer Research* 19 (December): 317–338.

Mick, David Glen, and Laura G. Politi (1989). "Consumers' Interpretations of Advertising Imagery: A Visit to the Hell of Connotation," in Elizabeth C. Hirschman (ed.), *Interpretive Consumer Research.* Provo, UT: Association for Consumer Research: 85–96.

Mick, David Glen, James E. Burroughs, Patrick Hetzel, and Mary Yoko Brannen (2004). "Pursuing the Meaning of Meaning in the Commercial World: An International Review of Marketing and Consumer Research Founded on Semiotics." *Semiotica* 152(1/4): 1–74.

Muñiz, Albert M., Jr., and Thomas C. O'Guinn (2001). "Brand Community." *Journal of Consumer Research* 27 (March): 412–432.

Muñiz, Albert M., Jr., and Hope Jensen Schau (2007). "Vigilante Marketing and Consumer Created Communications." *Journal of Advertising* 36(3): 35–50.

Nationwide Press Release (2013). "Nationwide Insurance Finds nearly One-fourth of Car Owners Name their Four-wheeled 'Baby'." The Nationwide website, September 30, 2013. <http://www .nationwide.com/about-us/093013-jtn-baby.jsp>

Neumüller, Moritz (2000). "Applying Computer Semiotics to Hypertext Theory and the World Wide Web," in *Open Hypermedia Systems and Structural Computing.* Springer: Berlin: 77–120.

Obermiller, Carl, and Mary Jo Bitner (1984). "Store Atmosphere: A Peripheral Cue for Product Evaluation," in American Psychological Association Annual Conference Proceedings, Consumer Psychology Division, ed. David C. Stewart, American Psychological Association: 52–53.

Ogilvy, David (2004 [1963]). *Confessions of an Advertising Man.* London: Southbank Publishers.

Oswald, Laura R. (1981). "Figure/Discourse: Configurations of Desire in *Un Chien Andalou.*" *Semiotica* 33: 105–122.

Oswald, Laura R. (1989a). *Jean Genet and the Semiotics of Performance.* Bloomington: Indiana University Press.

Oswald, Laura R. (1989b). "New Directions: The Semiotics of Spectacle." *Semiotica* 75(34–35): 327–334.

Oswald, Laura (1996). "The Place and Space of Consumption in a Material World." *Design Issues* 12(1): 48–62.

Oswald, Laura R. (1999). "Culture Swapping: The Ethnogenesis of Middle-Class Haitian-Americans." *Journal of Consumer Research* 25/4: 303–318.

Oswald, Laura R. (2012). *Marketing Semiotics, Signs, Strategies, and Brand Value.* Oxford: Oxford University Press.

Otnes, Cele, and Linda Scott (1996). "Something Old, Something New: Exploring the Interaction between Ritual and Advertising." *Journal of Advertising* 25(1) (Spring): 33–50.

Packard, Vance (1980 [1957]). *The Hidden Persuaders.* New York: Simon and Schuster.

Panofsky, Erwin (1991). *Perspective as Symbolic Form,* trans. Christopher S. Wood. New York: Zone Books.

Papatoto (2012). "What Made Marlboro the Biggest Brand Ever!!!" <http://papatoto.com/article/974258621691/What_made_marlboro_the_biggest_brand_ever!!!>

Parsons, Terence (2012). "The Traditional Square of Opposition," in Edward N. Zalta (ed.), *The Stanford Encyclopedia of Philosophy* (Fall Edition). <http://plato.stanford.edu/archives/fall2012/entries/square/>

Peirce, Charles Sanders (1988 [1955]). "Logic as Semiotic," in Justus Buchler (ed.), *The Philosophical Writings of Charles Sanders Peirce.* New York: Dover Press: 98–119.

Peñaloza, Lisa (1994). "Atravesando: Border Crossings: A Critical Ethnographic Exploration of the Consumer Acculturation of Mexican Consumers." *Journal of Consumer Research* 21/1 (June): 32–54.

Peñaloza, Lisa (1998). "Just Doing It: A Visual Ethnographic Study of Spectacular Consumption Behaviour at Nike Town." *Consumption, Markets and Culture* 2(4): 337–400.

Peñaloza, Lisa (2001). "Consuming the American West: Animating Cultural Meaning at a Stock Show and Rodeo." *Journal of Consumer Research* 28 (December): 369–398.

Perlut, Aaron (2013). "Domino's Global Growth Feeds Pizza Chain's Rising Success." <http://www.forbes.com/ . . . /dominos-global-growth-feeds-pizza-chains- . . . ;Mar%209>

Perron, Paul, and Frank Collins (eds) (1989a). *Paris School Semiotics I: Theory.* Philadelphia: John Benjamins Publishing Co.

Perron, Paul, and Frank Collins (eds) (1989b). *Paris School Semiotics II: Practice.* Philadelphia: John Benjamins Publishing Co.

Phillips, Barbara J. (1997). "Thinking into It: Consumer Interpretation of Complex Advertising Images." *Journal of Advertising* 26(2): 77–87.

Phillips, Barbara J. (2000). "The Impact of Verbal Anchoring on Consumer Response to Image Ads." *Journal of Advertising* 29(1): 15–24.

Phillips, Barbara J., and Edward F. McQuarrie (2002). "The Development, Change, and Transformation of Rhetorical Style in Magazine Advertisements 1954–1999." *Journal of Advertising* 31(4): 1–13.

Phillips, Barbara J., and Edward F. McQuarrie (2004). "Beyond Visual Metaphor: A New Typology of Visual Rhetoric in Advertising." *Marketing Theory* 4(1/2): 113–136.

Phillips, Barbara J., and Edward F. McQuarrie (2010). "Narrative Persuasion in Fashion Advertising." *Journal of Consumer Research* 37(3) (October): 368–392.

Pinson, Christian (1998). "Marketing Semiotics," in Jacob L. Mey (ed.), *Concise Encyclopedia of Pragmatics*. London: Pergamon Press, 1998: 538–544.

Polanyi, Michael, and Harry Prosch (1977). *Meaning*. Chicago: University of Chicago Press.

Rada, Roy (1991). *Hypertext*. New York: McGraw-Hill.

Reynolds, Thomas J., and Jonathan Gutman (1988). "Laddering Theory, Method, Analysis, and Interpretation." *Journal of Advertising Research* 28 (February–March): 11–31.

Richins, Marcia (1994). "The Public and Private Meanings of Possessions." *Journal of Consumer Research* 12(3) (December): 504–521.

Ricoeur, Paul (1976). *Interpretation Theory: Discourse and the Surplus of Meaning*. Fort Worth: Texas Christian University Press.

Ricoeur, Paul (2003 [1975]). *The Rule of Metaphor: The Creation of Meaning in Language*, trans. Robert Czerny with Kathleen McLaughlin and John Costello, S.J. New York: Routledge.

Ries, Al, and Jack Trout (2000 [1981]). *Positioning: The Battle for Your Mind*. New York: McGraw-Hill.

Ritson, Mark, and Richard Elliott (1999). "The Social Uses of Advertising: An Ethnographic Study of Advertising Audiences." *Journal of Consumer Research* 26 (December): 260–277.

Ritzer, George (2009). *Enchanting a Disenchanted World: Revolutionizing the Means of Consumption*, 2nd edn. Thousand Oaks, CA: Sage.

Sahlins, Marshall (1976). *Culture and Practical Reason*. Chicago: University of Chicago Press.

Sahlins, Marshall (2004 [1965]). "On the Sociology of Primitive Exchange," in Michael Banton (ed.), *Relevance of Models for Social Anthropology*. Oxford: Routledge: 139–236.

Sapolsky, Robert (2010). "This is Your Brain on Metaphors." *The New York Times*. <http://opinionator.blogs.nytimes.com/2010/11/14/this-is-your-brain-on-metaphors>

Saussure, Ferdinand de (2011 [1916]). *Course in General Linguistics*, ed. Perry Meisel and Haun Saussy, trans. Wade Baskin. New York: Columbia University Press.

Saussure, Ferdinand de (1993 [1910]). *The Third Course of Lectures on General Linguistics (1910–1911)*, trans. Eisuko Komatsu, ed. Roy Harris. Oxford: Pergamon Press.

Schama, Simon (1989). *Citizens: A Chronicle of the French Revolution*. New York: Random House.

Schmitt, Bernd H., and Shi Zhang (1998). "Language-Dependent Classification: The Mental Representation of Classifiers in Cognition, Memory, and Ad Evaluations." *Journal of Experimental Psychology: Applied* 4(4): 375–385.

Schmitt, Bernd H., Yigang Pan, and Nader T. Tavassoli (1994). "Language and Consumer Memory: The Impact of Linguistic Differences between Chinese and English." *Journal of Consumer Research* 21 (December): 419–431.

Schultz, Donald, and Heidi Schultz (1998). "Transitioning Marketing Communication into the Twenty-First Century." *Journal of Marketing Communication* 4: 9–26.

Scott, Linda M. (1994a). "The Bridge from Text to Mind." *Journal of Consumer Research* 21(4) (December): 461–480.

Scott, Linda M. (1994b). "Images in Advertising: The Need for a Theory of Visual Rhetoric." *Journal of Consumer Research* 21(3) (September): 252–273.

Scott, Linda M., and Rajeev Batra (eds) (2003). *Persuasive Imagery: A Consumer Response Perspective.* London: Lawrence Erlbaum Associates.

Scott, Linda M., and Patrick Vargas (2007). "Writing with Pictures: Toward a Unifying Theory of Consumer Response to Images." *Journal of Consumer Research* 34 (October): 341–356.

Sebeok, Thomas (1966). *Style in Language.* Cambridge, MA: MIT Press.

Sherry, John F., Jr. (1987). "Advertising as a Cultural System," in Jean Umiker-Sebeok (ed.), *Marketing and Semiotics: New Directions in the Study of Signs for Sale.* Berlin: Mouton de Gruyter: 441–459.

Sherry, John F., Jr. (ed.) (1990). "A Sociocultural Analysis of a Midwestern Fleamarket." *Journal of Consumer Research* 17(1) (June): 13–30.

Sherry, John F., Jr. (1991). "Postmodern Alternatives: The Interpretive Turn in Consumer Research," in Thomas S. Robertson and Harold H. Kassarjian (eds), *Handbook of Consumer Behavior.* Englewood Cliffs, NJ: Prentice-Hall, Inc.: 548–591.

Sherry, John F., Jr. (ed.) (1998). *Servicescapes: The Concept of Place in Contemporary Markets.* Lincolnwood, IL: NTC Business Books.

Sherry, John F., Jr., and Edwardo G. Camargo (1987). "'May Your Life be Marvelous': English Language Labeling and the Semiotics of Japanese Promotion." *Journal of Consumer Research* 14: 174–188.

Sherry, John F., Jr., Robert V. Kozinets, Diana Storm, Adam Duhachek, Krittomee Mittavitjosot, and Benet DeBerry-Spence (2001). "Being in the Zone: Staging Retail Theater at ESPN Zone Chicago." *Journal of Contemporary Ethnography* 30 (August): 465–510.

Shields, Rob (1991). *Lifestyle Shopping: The Subject of Consumption.* New York: Routledge.

Shovlin, John (2000). "The Cultural Politics of Luxury in Eighteenth-century France." *French Historical Studies* 3(4) (Fall): 577–606.

Silverstein, M. (1976). "Shifters, Linguistic Categories and Cultural Description," in K. Basso and H. Selby (eds), *Meaning in Anthropology.* Albuquerque: University of New Mexico Press: 11–55.

Simon, Herbert A. (1984). *Models of Bounded Rationality,* Vol. 1, *Economic Analysis and Public Policy.* Cambridge, MA: MIT Press.

Smith, Terry Donovan (1996). *Text and Performance: Semiotic Analysis for Dramaturgy and the Development of Production Concepts.* St Louis, MO: University of Washington.

Starobinski, Jean (1980). *Words upon Words: The Anagrams of Ferdinand De Saussure.* New Haven: Yale.

Stern, Barbara B. (1989). "Literary Criticism and Consumer Research: Overview and Illustrative Analysis." *Journal of Consumer Research* 16 (December): 322–334.

Stern, Barbara B. (1991). "Who Talks Advertising? Literary Theory and Narrative Point of View." *Journal of Advertising* 20 (September): 9–22.

Stern, Barbara B. (1993a). "A Revised Communication Model for Advertising: Multiple Dimensions of the Source, the Message, and the Recipient." *Journal of Advertising* 23: 25–36.

Stern, Barbara B. (1993b). "Feminist Literary Criticism and the Deconstruction of Advertisements: A Postmodern view of Advertising and Consumer Responses." *Journal of Consumer Research* 19 (March), 556–566.

Stern, Barbara B. (1995). "Consumer Myths: Frye's Taxonomy and the Structural Analysis of Consumption Text." *Journal of Consumer Research* 22 (September): 165–185.

Stern, Barbara B. (1996a). "Deconstructive Strategy and Consumer Research: Concepts and Illustrative Exemplar." *Journal of Consumer Research* 23(2) (September): 136–147.

Stern, Barbara B. (1996b). "Textual Analysis in Advertising Research: Construction and Deconstruction of Meanings." *Journal of Advertising* 25(3) (Fall): 61–73.

Strauss, William, and Neil Howe (2000). *Millennials Rising: The Next Great Generation.* New York: Vintage.

Sunderland, Patricia L., and Rita M. Denny (2007). *Doing Anthropology in Consumer Research.* Walnut Creek, CA: Left Coast Press.

Thompson, Craig J., and Zeynep Arsel (2004). "The Starbucks Brandscape and Consumers' (Anticorporate) Experiences of Glocalization." *Journal of Consumer Research* 31 (December): 630–642.

Thompson, Craig J., and Diana L. Haytko (1997). "Speaking of Fashion: Consumers' Uses of Fashion Discourses and the Appropriation of Countervailing Cultural Meanings." *Journal of Consumer Research* 24(1): 15–42.

Thompson, Craig J., and Kelly Tian (2008). "Reconstructing the South: How Commercial Myths Compete for Identity Value Through the Ideological Shaping of Popular Memories and Counter-memories." *Journal of Consumer Research* 34(5) (July): 595–613.

Thompson, Craig J., William B. Locander, and Howard R. Pollio (1989). "Putting Consumer Experience Back into Consumer Research: The Philosophy and Method of Existential-Phenomenology." *Journal of Consumer Research* 16 (September): 133–146.

Thompson, Craig J., Aric Rindfleisch, and Zeynep Arsel (2006). "Emotional Branding and the Strategic Value of the Doppelgänger Brand Image." *Journal of Marketing* 70(1): 50–64.

Tybout, Alice M., and Gregory Carpenter (2010). "Creating and Managing Brands," in Alice M. Tybout and Bobby J. Calder (eds), *Kellogg on Marketing*, 2nd edn. New York: John Wiley & Sons: 112–144.

Umiker-Sebeok, Jean (ed.) (1987). *Marketing and Semiotics: New Directions in the Study of Signs for Sale.* Berlin: Mouton de Gruyter.

Underhill, Paco (2009 [1999]). *Why We Buy: The Science of Shopping*, 3rd edn. New York: Simon and Schuster.

Üstüner, Tuba, and Douglas B. Holt (2007). "Dominated Consumer Acculturation: The Social Construction of Poor Migrant Women's Consumer Identity Projects in a Turkish Squatter." *Journal of Consumer Research*: 34(1) (June) 41–56.

Üstüner, Tuba, and Craig J. Thompson (2012). "How Marketplace Performances Produce Interdependent Status Games and Contested Forms of Symbolic Capital." *Journal of Consumer Research* 38(5): 796–814.

Van Maanen, John (2011 [1988]). *Tales from the Field: On Writing Ethnography*, 2nd edn. Chicago: University of Chicago Press.

Veblen, Thorstein (2009 [1899]). *The Theory of the Leisure Class*, ed. Martha Banta. Oxford: Oxford University Press.

Veltruský, Jiří (1981). "Jan Mukařovský's Structural Poetics and Esthetics." *Poetics Today* 2(1): 117–157.

Visconti, Luca M., John F. Sherry, Jr., Stefania Borghini, and Laurel Anderson (2010). "Street Art, Sweet Art? Reclaiming the 'Public' in Public Place." *Journal of Consumer Research* 37(3) (October): 511–529.

Wakefield, Kirk L., and Jeffrey G. Blodgett (1999). "Customer Response to Intangible and Tangible Service Factors." *Psychology & Marketing* 16(1) (January): 51–68.

Walker, Rob (2004). "The Way We Live Now: The Right-Hand Diamond Ring." *The New York Times Magazine*, January 4, 2004. <http://www.nytimes.com/2004/01/04/magazine/the-way-we-live-now-1-4-04-consumed-the-right-hand-diamond-ring.html>

Wang, Weigang, and Roy Rada (1998). "Structured Hypertext with Domain Semantics." *ACM Transactions on Information Systems* 16(4): 372–412.

Weiner, Annette B. (1992). *Inalienable Possessions: The Paradox of Keeping while Giving.* Berkeley: University of California Press.

Werder, Olaf (2007). "Brewing Romance," in Mary-Lou Galician, and Debra L. Merskin (eds), *Critical Thinking about Sex, Love, and Romance in the Mass Media: Media Literacy Applications.* Mahwah, NJ: Lawrence Erlbaum: 35–37.

Whorf, Benjamin Lee (1956). *Language, Thought, and Reality: Selected Writings of Benjamin Lee Whorf,* John B. Carroll (ed.). Cambridge, MA: MIT Press.

Willis, Susan (1991). *A Primer for Daily Life.* New York: Routledge.

Winner, Irene Portis (1983). "Some Comments on the Concept of the Human Sign: Visual and Verbal Components and Applications to Ethnic Research (a Wonderful Father)." *Semiotica* 46: 263–285.

Wollen, Peter (1972). "The Semiology of Cinema," in *Signs and Meaning in the Cinema.* Bloomington: Indiana University Press: 116–154.

Wunderli, Peter (2004). "Saussure's Anagrams," in *The Cambridge Companion to Saussure.* Cambridge, England: Cambridge University Press: 174–185. <http://dx.doi.org/10.1017/CCOL052180051X.012>

Yankelovich, Daniel (1964). "New Criteria for Segmentation." *Harvard Business Review* (March/April): 83–90.

Yankelovich, Daniel, and David Meer (2006). "Rediscovering Market Segmentation." *Harvard Business Review* 84(2) (February): 122–131.

York, Emily Bryson (2013). "Domino's Brings 'Pizza Theater' to Chicago: New Store Design Reflects Growing Carryout Business, Newfound Pride in Primary Product." *Chicago Tribune* online, April 24. <http://articles.chicagotribune.com/2013-04-24/business/ct-biz-0424-dominos-20130424_1_domino-second-largest-pizza-chain-carryout-business>

Zaher, L'Hédi, Jean-Pierre Cahier, and Claude Guittard (2008). "Cooperative Building of Multiple Points-of -View Topic Maps Using Hypertopic and Socio-Technical Approaches," in L. Maicher and L. M. Garshol (eds), *Scaling Topic Maps: Proceedings of the Third International Conference on Topic Maps Research and Applications.* New York: Springer, Vol. LNAI 4999: 154–159.

Zaltman, Gerald (1996). "Metaphorically Speaking." *Journal of Marketing Research* 8(2) (Summer): 13–20.

Zaltman, Gerald (1997). "Rethinking Market Research: Putting People Back In." *Journal of Marketing Research* 34(4) (November): 424–437.

Zaltman, Gerald, and R. Coulter (1995). "Seeing the Voice of the Customer: Metaphor-based Advertising Research." *Journal of Advertising Research* 35(4) (July–August): 35–51.

Zaltman, Gerald, and Lindsay A. Zaltman (2008). *Marketing Metaphoria*. Cambridge, MA: Harvard University Press.

Zaoui, Pierre (2013). *La discrétion, ou l'art de disparaître*. Paris: Editions Autrement.

Zhao, Xin, and Russell W. Belk (2008). "Politicizing Consumer Culture: Advertising's Appropriation of Political Ideology in China's Social Transition." *Journal of Consumer Research* 35(2): 231–245.

■ INDEX

Bold entries refer to figures, table or illustrations.

15185325R00123

Printed in Great Britain
by Amazon.co.uk, Ltd.,
Marston Gate.